Cinco de Mayo

Cinco de Mayo

◆

What Is Everybody Celebrating?

The Story behind Mexico's Battle of Puebla

Donald W. Miles

iUniverse, Inc.

New York Lincoln Shanghai

Cinco de Mayo
What Is Everybody Celebrating?

iUniverse books may be ordered through booksellers or by contacting:

iUniverse
2021 Pine Lake Road, Suite 100
Lincoln, NE 68512
www.iuniverse.com
1-800-Authors (1-800-288-4677)

ISBN-13: 978-0-595-39241-4 (pbk)
ISBN-13: 978-0-595-84448-7 (cloth)
ISBN-13: 978-0-595-83634-5 (ebk)
ISBN-10: 0-595-39241-5 (pbk)
ISBN-10: 0-595-84448-0 (cloth)
ISBN-10: 0-595-83634-8 (ebk)

Printed in the United States of America

In Memory of

Minerva González-Angulo Miles, PhD

Minerva grew up as a young señorita in Mexico City. She lived in a neighborhood near Chapultepec Hill, where the Emperor Maximilian's castle still stands. She would occasionally visit the castle and view the portrait of the emperor and empress whose story is a major part of this book. She taught elementary school in Mexico City, and then came to the United States on a scholarship as a foreign student.

Minerva married Don Miles in June of 1962, and then went on to become a United States citizen and to earn a bachelor's, a master's and a doctoral degree. She and Don raised a daughter who at this writing is a major in the Air Force Reserve and a son who works with the National Security Council at the White House. Minerva taught at public schools in Connecticut and Florida, and later at universities in Nebraska and Texas.

If it were not for Minerva's frequent visits and extensive travel throughout Mexico with her family, this volume would never have been written. She not only spent the time and effort helping with the research in libraries, museums, and bookstores throughout the United States and Mexico, but with Don she personally visited most of the historical locations mentioned in these pages. She gave the whole family an "insider's view" of a Mexico that most Americans would never get to see and enjoy.

Minerva died of lymphoma in May of 2006. She leaves a legacy of endearing friendships, fond memories, and the enrichment of many lives. She was the inspiration behind this book.

Minerva—from the entire family in both the U.S. and Mexico—this book is dedicated to you.

Contents

Part III   French Generals Are in Charge

May 30, 1863, through March 31, 1864

Part IV   The Emperor of Mexico

April 1, 1864, through July 15, 1867

Acknowledgments

As we stated in the dedication, this book probably would never have been written without the life journey of Minerva González-Angulo Miles. It was her decades of companionship, marrying this author, traveling with me and our two children throughout Mexico, and including us into the circle of her Mexican friends and relatives that sparked a general interest in topics relating to the country and its people.

I am also grateful for the ongoing support not only from our daughter, Juliette Ritzman and our son, Richard Miles, who both now enjoy a Mexican branch to the family, complete with an aunt, uncle, cousins, nieces, nephews, and a lot more. Juliette and Richard have identified sources for research and through their various transactions with family and friends have provided access to support that I would never have discovered. Richard's wife, Phoebe, accompanied us to the Library of Congress and helped us as we signed-up for researchers' cards and gained access to valuable documentation.

The family in Mexico provided a generous share of assistance, welcoming us into their homes and driving us to museums, libraries, and historical locations. They include Señor Arq. Gustavo González-Angulo and his wife, Enriqueta, as well as their sons and daughters: Bernardo, Teresina, Carolina, Xavier, and Gustavo. Teresina and her husband, Alonso Ortiz, gave us a tour of Fort Guadalupe in Puebla, the scene of the Cinco de Mayo battle itself, and Xavier sat with me atop the roof of a church in Medellín—just outside of Veracruz—as we chatted one evening about the history that surrounded us. Also, my thanks to Señorita Leticia Ramírez Adame, who hosted our family in her Mexico City office overlooking an Independence Day parade. None of us will ever forget that Mexican Independence Day is September 16, not May 5! It has all been a very rewarding and enriching experience. I hope this book provides some measure of satisfaction to all of those who played a role over many years in its development. ¡Muchísimas gracias!

Donald W. Miles

Introduction

It's easy to enjoy a Cinco de Mayo celebration. The festivities have become so popular in the United States that as many as half a million people show up for the annual event in Los Angeles alone. Latino communities throughout the country have used the fiesta as a way of showcasing their cultural traditions. Cheering and whistling to the music of *mariachi* bands, clapping to the steps of *folklórico* dancers, and savoring typical Mexican foods is attractive to almost anyone—Hispanic or not.

Ask around at one of these events about the historical significance of the fifth of May. A few of the participants may be able to tell you that the Mexicans defeated an invading French army at Puebla on that date in 1862. Beyond that, general knowledge of the circumstances becomes sketchy. Libraries have dozens of children's books about the day of the battle itself, but turn to the page just after the description of the battle, and you're likely to find paragraphs on "how to make a piñata" or "how to prepare for a Cinco de Mayo party at school." Left unanswered are questions like, "Why were the French there?" or, "What happened next? Did the French just go away?" and, "That was just one battle. Which war are we talking about?"

Add to that the misunderstanding among many people that May 5 is the Mexican Independence Day. That's not true. It's dead wrong, yet in some parts of Texas, for example, there are teachers who tell their students, "This is just like our Fourth of July, boys and girls." In fact, there was even a principal who said that to the whole school over the public address system a number of years ago. When this author challenged the assertion, the answer was, "Well, we've always taught it that way." End of discussion.

"*Surely*," I thought, "*there must be a book about this somewhere.*" Guess again. A search of libraries, bookstores, and online booksellers turned up little or nothing, other than children's books or titles that were out of print. Finally, I all but stumbled upon a gold mine of resources practically in my own back yard. "The Latin American Collection of the University of Texas at Austin," according to a book by Richard E. Greenleaf and Michael C. Meyer entitled *Research in Mexican History*, "is one of the best research libraries on Mexico." My wife was a faculty member at another university nearby, Texas State in San Marcos. Through a network of libraries, she had borrowing privileges at the University of Texas–Austin.

During many visits to the University of Texas–Austin's Benson Latin American Library, I found that they had more material on Mexico than anyone could read in a lifetime. There were more than a million pages of everything from books, journals, manuscripts, government documents, and beyond. There was just one problem: most of these books were also out of print. The vast majority were more than fifty years old. Some had been published as far back as 1868, and quite a few were so fragile that they could not be taken out of the library. There was no way the general public could have access to this information.

With Cinco de Mayo celebrations becoming more and more popular in recent years, there was clearly a need for a current book on the subject. That's why I decided to write one.

Besides living just across town from the Benson Library, I had another distinct advantage in undertaking this project. My wife was born and raised in Mexico City, and we travel to Mexico frequently to visit nieces, nephews, and in-laws, who have lived and worked in many of the cities described in this book. We've been to the fort at Puebla, where the famous battle took place, to Emperor Maximilian's castle at Chapultepec Park in Mexico City, to the Port of Veracruz, and to Orizaba, where the French army licked its wounds and awaited reinforcements after the defeat on May 5, 1862.

Over a number of years, we've also set foot in many lesser-known places, such as the Hill of the Bells in Querétaro, where Emperor Maximilian was executed; the small fishing village of Tlacotalpan, which was a haven for guerilla fighters and gun smugglers; and the fort at Goliad in what is now Texas, where Ignacio Zaragoza—the victorious general of Cinco de Mayo—was born. Just climbing Cerro del Borrego (Sheep's Hill) in Orizaba or standing at the sentry posts in a *baluarte* (bulwark) overlooking Veracruz Harbor brings the whole story to life, as opposed to simply getting it all from aging books deep in the stacks of libraries.

The story that evolved from all of these experiences has been organized into the four sections of this book.

Part One covers the reasons for the intervention not only by the French but also by the Spaniards and the British as well. At first, all three countries sent troops to collect foreign debts owed to them. Soon it became apparent that the French had a hidden agenda. Emperor Napoleon III wanted to block further expansion of the United States, first by conquering Mexico and then by using it as a base to help the Confederacy defeat the United States in the American Civil War. This part discusses how the United States under Abraham Lincoln responded to this situation, as well as the preparations among the Mexicans and the French—their armies and governments—leading up to and including the famous Battle of Puebla on May 5, 1862.

Part Two of *Cinco de Mayo* talks about the struggle that occurred after the French withdrew to Orizaba following their historic defeat at Puebla. A turnover in commanders on both sides took place when the victorious Mexican general, Ignacio Zaragoza, died and the French general who lost to him, the Count of Lorencez, was replaced. In addition, this part details the heroic legend of French foreign legionnaires, who fought to the death in the worst defeat in legion history, and the story of the second French attempt to capture Puebla. The French finally prevailed after a nine-week siege, only to find that world opinion was behind the Mexican defenders. At the time, there were fears in the United States that the French would use Mexico as a base to back the Confederacy, so President Lincoln and his secretary of state went out of their way to appear "neutral" in the Mexican situation. They didn't want to take on the French and the Confederates at the same time.

Part Three recounts Napoleon III's searches for a suitable candidate to appoint as emperor of Mexico, finally settling on Austrian archduke Ferdinand Maximilian. The French army had difficulty holding onto the country as this process unfolded, staying barricaded in Mexico City and holding military balls while the rest of Mexico was mostly controlled by guerillas and bandidos. As the American Civil War ended, various political and military figures from both the North and the South drifted into Mexico. Some of their adventures are quite colorful.

Part Four covers the reign of Emperor Maximilian and Empress Charlotte. These two rulers ran into all kinds of trouble, ranging from Maximilian's affair with a gardener's daughter and his total inability to handle finances, to the horrifying record of atrocities committed by an overzealous French colonel, and to various disputes between the emperor and the Catholic Church. American General Philip Sheridan also did some saber-rattling by holding maneuvers along the border with Mexico, setting off panics in both Mexico City and Paris. As a result of these events, Napoleon III decided to pull his troops out, leaving Maximilian in Querétaro with seven thousand of his Imperialista troops but surrounded by forty-one thousand Mexican troops in the hills overlooking the town. Within a few months, Maximilian was taken prisoner and executed. President Benito Juárez, who had never given up his office throughout the French intervention, returned to Mexico City.

By defeating the French at Puebla in 1862, Mexicans gained the confidence that they could eventually take their country back from the foreign invaders and regain their sovereignty. It took another five years, but they outlasted both the French army and Maximilian. Both Mexicans and Mexican Americans celebrate this victory every year on May 5—Cinco de Mayo. The full story can be found in the chapters that follow.

PART I

The French Army Arrives in Mexico

July 17, 1861, through May 5, 1862

1

Foreign Troops Prepare to Collect Mexican Debts

(March 1861 through January 1862)

Mexico's Gateway to the World

The seaport of Veracruz on the Gulf of Mexico is the oldest port city in the Americas. It was Mexico's gateway to the rest of the world for several centuries after Spanish explorer Hernán Cortés landed there in 1519. Whatever—and whoever—came and went from Mexico for about four hundred years traveled mostly through this port. In Spanish colonial times, Veracruz was for a time the only port allowed to handle trade with Spain. It has seen pirate raids, Spanish galleons hauling silver, the slave trade, new leaders coming in, exiled leaders going out, and numerous invasions—including some by Americans.

In peacetime, Veracruz wasn't all that bad. The locals didn't get the tropical diseases that plagued outsiders. Watching ships arrive from foreign ports was the favorite spectator activity. Vendors would gather dockside to sell souvenirs to arriving foreigners. Marimba bands and other wandering musicians provided entertainment in the main square near the cathedral, playing for customers seated in the shade of Los Portales—the arches—at cafés near the Hotel Imperial.

When commerce was functioning normally, merchants from Mexico City would either send freight wagons to the large *almacenes* (warehouses) in Veracruz or make arrangements with local *arrieros* (mule drivers) to have their imported goods hauled inland. By 1861, the stagecoach drivers, ranch hands, and others who worked with horses and mules were already wearing the new popular denim pants known as Levi's, which had been invented in California during the gold rush twelve years earlier.

Veracruz inhabitants who wanted to take a break from the sailors, the tourists, and the freight wagons knew they could escape inland by taking about an hour's ride on horseback to the hidden, tree-shaded village known as Medellín. There, even women could smoke cigars, gamble, or swim in the fresh water of the Río Jamapa, which they could not do in more conservative regions of Mexico.

After an eleven-year battle, Mexico had finally won independence from Spain in 1821. Forty years later, much of the trade coming through Veracruz was either from Europe or from Havana. Cigars and rum were the most popular items. There had been some commerce with the United States, but that was falling off as of 1861. U.S. ports around the Gulf of Mexico were falling into Confederate hands as the American Civil War got under way.

Mexico Had Just Finished a War

Mexican President Benito Juárez had been in the capital for only six months in July of 1861. He and his liberals had just won the three-year War of the Reform against the conservatives, which had lasted from 1858 through 1860. Juárez had been justice minister (a cabinet post similar to Attorney General in the United States) under liberal President Ignacio Comonfort in the mid-1850s, and during that time had written many of the laws that limited the powers and privileges of the Church in Mexico and took away most of its land. He had also introduced civil marriage—and divorce—and government responsibility for the education of women.

Conservatives had rebelled, and a junta of generals had forced President Comonfort to resign in December of 1857. Juárez knew that the Mexican Constitution called for the justice minister to succeed the president. When the conservatives tried to capture him, he fled aboard an American ship and eventually wound up in Veracruz. The War of the Reform that followed pitted rich conservatives and the Church against the *indígenas* (Indians), *mestizos* (mixed-race individuals), and other common people led by Juárez and his liberals. The liberals finally won, and the victorious Juárez entered Mexico City on January 11, 1861.

Treasury Was Empty

The fleeing conservatives had not only emptied the treasury but had seized foreigners' property, taken out loans, and even stolen a large sum from the British embassy. International law called for all new governments to pay off the debts of those they succeeded, no matter how they had come to power. The new government of Mexico, however, was all but bankrupt and simply could not pay.

On July 17, 1861, the Mexican Congress voted to suspend all payments on any foreign debt until Mexico could work something out with its creditors. Sir Charles Wyke, the British minister to Mexico, and Count Pierre Alphonse Dubois de Saligny, his French counterpart, broke off diplomatic relations. Wyke left the country. Saligny continued to live alone in the officially closed French Legation, trying to remain unnoticed while he awaited further developments. Spain's ambassador had already been expelled for backing the conservatives during the War of the Reform.

France, Britain, and Spain Prepare to Attack

Wyke called the Mexican move "bare-faced robbery."[1] Saligny had already written to Paris several months earlier, claiming that a "state of anarchy" prevailed in what he called "this wretched country." France's navy, he said, should be sent "to protect our interests."[2]

Both Wyke and Saligny immediately notified British and French naval bases in the Caribbean to be ready for an attack on Veracruz and possibly for one on Tampico, farther north along the Gulf Coast. Saligny wrote to Paris that the fort standing on an island just off Veracruz Harbor—Fort San Juan de Ulua—had been disarmed and that the Port of Veracruz itself was disorganized and vulnerable. He referred to Juárez as "an idiot and a rascal...who can find neither money nor ministers."[3] Why not strike them now, he urged, when no resistance will be offered?

Spain didn't have any representatives in Mexico but put its troops in Cuba on full alert, ready for a landing at Veracruz.

The United States Changes Its Mexican Policy

In the first few months after Abraham Lincoln was elected president of the United States in 1860, Lincoln and his secretary of state, William Seward, placed a high priority on replacing John B. Weller as ambassador to Mexico. Weller had continued the territorial expansionist policy of the previous administration under President James Buchanan. He pressed for settlement of alleged American claims and complaints of violated rights—anything that would give the United States an advantage in collecting debts or in forcing Mexico to give up even more territory.

Things came to a head as word reached Washington on March 11, 1861, that a force had entered Mexico from California, apparently intent on acquiring more territory. At the embassy, Weller replied to Mexican government reports of the raid that, first, he didn't believe it had happened, and, second, that Mexico ought to encourage colonization of its northern region by Americans who would invest money and effort in developing it.

In Washington, Lincoln and Seward saw it differently. They ordered an investigation and called Weller home, nominating Thomas Corwin as his replacement two days later. The sixty-seven-year-old Corwin was very popular with the Mexicans because of his Senate speeches in 1846 opposing the American invasion of Mexico at that time. At first he didn't want to give up his Senate seat, but within the week, he was confirmed and on his way to Mexico City.

Block the Confederates

Corwin's mission was to keep the Confederates from gaining any territory or recognition in a Mexico that had just been weakened by its War of the Reform, and also to do whatever it might take to keep the European powers from getting any sort of permanent foothold there. Within weeks, reports surfaced of a Confederate plan to seize the Mexican state of Baja California. Secretary of State Seward reaffirmed the United States' denial of any desire to acquire more territory and alerted the western U.S. army and navy forces to suppress any Confederate attempt to cross into Mexico.

Corwin had no trouble persuading his good friend, President Benito Juárez, to allow Union troops to sail from California and land at the Mexican port of Guaymas, just south of the Arizona border. They would then be in a position to march through Mexican territory to head off the Confederate forces in Arizona.

As the Mexican Congress suspended its foreign debt payments in July of 1861, Corwin's job to keep the European powers at bay took on a new urgency. He had already begun negotiating a postal treaty with Mexico to encourage communication and trade. The proposed pact would initiate steamship service between New York and Veracruz, effectively bypassing any territory held by the Confederates.

The owner of the steamship line was an Edward E. Dunbar from New York. Secretary of State Seward rejected a competing treaty being negotiated in Washington in favor of the one being put together in Mexico City by Corwin. There's no record of whether or not Seward knew that Corwin was one of Dunbar's partners in the steamship company.

Actually, Corwin had realized that Mexico was financially ruined and vulnerable to attack when he had arrived in the spring of 1861. The Mexicans had not yet suspended foreign payments when Corwin managed to convince the Lincoln administration that United States security and well-being would be threatened by a Mexican default. For the first time in its history, the United States was being asked to grant a loan to a friendly government to keep it afloat and ward off predators.[4]

The Spaniards, British, and French were just weeks away from landing at Veracruz when Corwin signed a bail-out loan treaty in November. He immediately sent it on its way to Washington for ratification.

Ambassador Corwin had no way of knowing it, but a similar treaty proposal was being drawn up in Washington, D.C., by Mexico's new chargé d'affaires. Twenty-five-year-old Matías Romero had already worked as a lawyer for Mexico's president, Benito Juárez, when Juárez was the governor of the state of Oaxaca. Romero had already had a number of conversations with Abraham Lincoln, and Lincoln had told him that if civil war broke out between the North and the South, the United States would hardly be in a position to back Mexico. He referred Romero to the new secretary of state, William H. Seward.

Seward did make one try at resolving the situation. He proposed that the United States pay Britain, France, and Spain on Mexico's behalf for the next five years, at an interest rate of 3 percent, and Mexico would then repay the U.S. at 6 percent after that. Certain mineral rights and public land in northern Mexico would be held as collateral for the U.S. loan. The three European countries rejected the proposal immediately, saying that the last thing they wanted was any kind of United States involvement.

Romero would not give up easily. He married an American woman from Philadelphia, Lucretia Allen, and began networking among politicians and business people in Washington and around the Northern states. He started raising funds, buying weapons, and recruiting soldiers for Juárez, clandestinely where necessary. He would be heard from again.

Napoleon III's Grand Design

Meanwhile in Paris, France's emperor, Napoleon III, had been looking for an opportunity to halt U.S. expansion and reestablish French influence in the Western Hemisphere. France had lost its last major stronghold by selling New Orleans and the entire Louisiana territory to the United States in 1803; then the Americans had gobbled up more than half of Mexico as a result of the independence of Texas from Mexico in 1836 and the Winfield Scott invasion of Mexico in 1848. When would they stop?

Napoleon III had hesitated to take on the United States directly, but now the news of the Civil War changed everything. It meant the Americans would be occupied with the conflict between North and South for some time. On hearing that the Spaniards and the British were planning to seize the Mexican customs house at Veracruz and begin collecting their duties, he decided that he'd not only send the French navy but would start looking for a European prince to install as an emperor in Mexico. Then, using Mexico as a base, he would help the Confederates win their war against the United States. This was an opportunity not to be missed.

Napoleon needed cover for his plan. He didn't want the Spaniards going into Mexico alone, for fear that the Mexicans might see it as their war for independence all over again. He wanted to use the moderate image of Britain to give the impression that all three nations were just in search of financial reconciliation—nothing more. The three powers signed the Convention of London on October 31, 1861, declaring that each would send troops to Veracruz. Spain would send seven thousand soldiers, France twenty-five hundred soldiers, and Britain just seven hundred marines. Each country would send appropriate naval forces for support and transportation.

Spanish Troops Land Prematurely

Apparently Pierre Saligny had not just been writing to Paris to get things stirred up. He had managed to incite the Spanish commander in Cuba into preparing for an attack, so Admiral Rubicalva cast off from Havana with six thousand troops on November 29, as soon as he heard that the Convention of London had authorized the three countries to intervene in Mexico. He never saw the official order telling him to wait until the other fleets got to Cuba so they could all go from there together.

The Spanish contingent from Havana dropped anchor in Veracruz Harbor on December 8 and formally took over the town six days later.

There wasn't much to take over. Mexican authorities had seen everything from pirate raids to foreign invasions come through Veracruz for several centuries, and they didn't want any bloodshed this time. They had quietly evacuated five thousand local inhabitants before the first troops landed, and various bands of guerillas and bandidos surrounded the inland periphery of the town in what amounted to a blockade. As Francisco Zarco, editor of the newspaper *El Siglo XIX*, put it, "Means of transportation were lacking, many families emigrating on foot, and if these events had not happened so swiftly it is likely that not a single Mexican would have remained in Veracruz."

Admiral Rubicalva's six thousand Spanish troops, finding themselves isolated, might just as well have stayed in Havana. All they managed to do was send a political shockwave through the whole country. After all, Mexico had defeated Spain after an eleven-year war for independence some forty years earlier. Were the Spaniards trying to come back? Rumors spread, and Mexican army recruiting offices were filled with applicants, far exceeding the fifty-two thousand volunteers that Juárez had called for. Whatever the Spaniards were up to, the Mexicans would be ready.

Even President Juárez misjudged the situation. He told some of his associates that the demands of France and England only pertained to money, and that negotiations would eventually work. On the other hand, he issued a proclamation urging Mexicans to prepare for a possible military confrontation with what he referred to as a "hereditary enemy," meaning Spain. That struck the nerve that brought him all the volunteers, but he had no idea that the Spaniards were the least likely to cause any harm. It would take a few months to discover that the French were the ones with the hidden—and dangerous—agenda.

The rest of the allied fleet that was supposed to meet Admiral Rubicalva off the western tip of Cuba finally arrived in Veracruz Harbor on January 7 and landed troops on January 8, 1862. General Prim, the Count of Reus, had 1,000 more troops with him and took command of the Spaniards, relieving Admiral Rubicalva. Admiral Jurien de la Gravière was in charge of the French contingent, and Commodore Dunlop headed the British marines.

General Prim had the advantage in that he was authorized as Spain's top diplomat as well as its military leader. He was a national hero in Spain, having performed brilliantly in the conquest of Morocco in 1859. His exploits had aroused feelings of nostalgia in the Spaniards, giving them a feeling of pride and unity. He was considered above all others as the most suitable for the task.

British Role Is Limited

Commodore Dunlop had to confer with the returning Sir Charles Wyke for any British diplomatic decisions. Militarily, Dunlop's instructions were simply to occupy Veracruz and go no further. Participation by the British in any advance on Mexico City was specifically prohibited.

Admiral Jurien was waiting for the irascible Pierre Saligny to make his way down to the coast from Mexico City before the French could speak with one voice. Jurien had been given three sets of instructions. One was public, the others confidential. The first was to follow the terms of the Convention of London and cooperate with the allies. The second was that the first was only a starting point. Knowing that the British would not leave Veracruz and that the Spaniards were not very popular in Mexico, the French believed they should lead the march inland to take Mexico City.

The admiral's third set of instructions was given to him verbally by Napoleon III himself. Upon arrival in Mexico City, Jurien was to convene an Assembly of Notables. The assembly would be made up of people who could be trusted to issue a call to one of Napoleon III's distant but royal relatives—Austrian Archduke Ferdinand Maximilian—to become Mexico's emperor. Then, the Spanish forces could be dismissed, leaving France a new foothold in the hemisphere.

Pierre Alphonse Dubois Saligny, the man who had so eagerly sought the foreign invasions, arrived in Veracruz later than the others, only to find that they had all agreed they'd rather resolve the problem by negotiating with the Mexicans than by using military force. He was not happy.

One thing they all agreed on was that they had ten thousand troops to feed and supplies were running short. They would have to push inland to nearby villages like Tejería and Medellín to buy food. On January 9, they advanced into the two towns, bought what they needed, and returned to Veracruz. Whatever Mexican forces that were in the area, guerillas or bandidos, did not attempt to stop them.

Filling Up the Hospitals

Health was the next problem they had to address. In the three weeks they had been there on their own, the Spaniards counted five hundred of their men who were suffering from yellow fever. Two weeks later, with the arrival of four thousand more troops from France and England, the Spaniards were forced to send four ships to Havana with eight hundred hospital patients. That freed-up three hundred hospital beds in Veracruz for the French, who had only been there for two weeks.

Not a single shot had been fired yet, but it was obvious that there would be more casualties from yellow fever than from anything else if the troops stayed in the port city. The military commanders decided they'd all have to set up encampments outside of town.

French and Spanish troops started to move inland on January 11. They were followed by a few dozen of Dunlop's British marines as a show of solidarity, but Dunlop preferred to keep the rest of his contingent aboard ships in the harbor.

The effort was so exhausting that it weakened even the Spanish veterans who had been with General Prim in Morocco a little over two years earlier, and the French veterans who had seen African desert duty in Algiers prior to that. The soldiers managed to travel for only a few hours before collapsing in the little village of La Tejería, about seven miles outside of Veracruz. There they set up camp—using ships' sails as tents—and waited in the stifling heat. The French and Spanish commanders knew they'd have to move farther inland just to stay healthy, but there were no animals or wagons available for transportation. The Mexicans had made sure of that when they evacuated Veracruz. Because of these conditions, Commodore Dunlop took his few marines back to their ships.

It wasn't just the climate that confounded the invaders. There were many small fishing villages up and down the Gulf coast not far from Veracruz, most of which had been hotbeds of Mexican liberal guerilla activity in the recent war against the conservatives. The locals were merchants by day, but guerilla fighters at night. Blacksmiths and wheelwrights secretly made weapons on the side at their carriage houses. Plantation owners grew bananas, coffee, avocados, and tropical fruits for their own people, and were always ready to ambush an enemy's supply lines as needed.

Who's in Charge?

At their meeting on January 13, the allied commissioners discovered that they each had a different set of conflicting orders. They were to negotiate, but each had a different list of demands. The British had been told just to seize the customs house and stay in Veracruz. The Spanish were hoping to recall past glory and reclaim their influence on the world stage just by sending Prim without any specific objective. And the French were secretly using the others to create an illusion of legitimacy until they got to Mexico City. They all decided to send home for further instructions.

Meanwhile, the morale of the troops was suffering from the tropical heat and humidity, coupled with poor sanitation. Soldiers were dropping from exhaustion and disease. Milling around with nothing to do, the soldiers considered Veracruz little more than a death camp. Those who ventured down the beach were all but eaten alive by sand fleas. Viewed from a distance, the whitewashed limestone houses of Veracruz looked like rows of tombstones. With many of the Mexicans gone, the preponderance of the remaining population appeared to be vultures. The large, ugly black birds sat quietly on the rooftops, waiting for something—or someone—to die.

2

The Gathering Confrontation

(March 1861 through April 1862)

Puebla: Bastion of Conservatism

Few Mexican cities could be considered as faithfully Catholic and as Spanish in their features as Puebla. In the 1860s, this most pious municipality had more than sixty churches, and as many as half of the young girls in town would rather enter one of the thirteen convents than get married. The magnificent cathedral had one of the tallest spires in all of Mexico, and the prosperous and highly polished citizenry were proud of their conservative way of life.

The Spaniards had built more than a thousand colonial-style buildings in the downtown area in the three centuries during which they had controlled Mexico. Puebla was still famous for the hand-painted tiles that adorned many of those structures. Situated in a broad valley with the Popocatépetl and Iztaccíhuatl volcanoes dominating the skyline to the west, Puebla stood astride the main road between Veracruz and Mexico City.

As General Ignacio Zaragoza stood on Cerro de Guadalupe, the peaceful hill overlooking the city, and peered out through his binoculars, "astride" was the operative word, both for the general and the town. No enemy approaching from the Gulf of Mexico could take the capital without taking Puebla first, and that's where the thirty-two-year-old Zaragoza decided the Mexicans would make their stand.

Zaragoza Was Born in a Texas That Still Belonged to Mexico

Zaragoza had been born March 24, 1829, in the Mexican state known as Coahuila y Tejas. Goliad, Zaragoza's birthplace, was in the part already called

Tejas. (In many names of Spanish origin, the letters "j" and "x" were often used interchangeably because they are pronounced the same way. "Tejas" and "Texas" in Spanish are both pronounced "TAY-hahss.")

Zaragoza's father had served as an army captain at the fort in Goliad under the Mexican dictator Santa Ana. When the Texans won their independence in 1836, the family moved to Matamoros and placed their son in an academy where most boys were expected to go on to the priesthood. After a subsequent move to Monterrey, the young Zaragoza joined the national guard and began working his way up through the military.

As a general, he had teamed up during the War of the Reform with his mentor, Jesús González-Ortega, and was named war minister by President Juárez when Ortega resigned to run for governor of the state of Zacatecas.

Now, just over two weeks before his thirty-third birthday, Zaragoza had stepped down as war minister and was on his way to the Mexican Eastern Army headquarters at San Andrés Chalchicomula (chal-chee-koh-MOO-lah), tucked in the Sierra Madre Oriental mountains. He and President Juárez agreed that General López Uraga should be replaced immediately. Uraga was not only accepting gifts of wine and cigars from France's Admiral Jurien, but had dined on several occasions with Minister Pierre Saligny and was corresponding almost every day with British diplomat Charles Wyke. The unidentified sources reporting those transactions also said that Uraga was sharply critical of Juárez and Zaragoza.

Uraga knew that Zaragoza was on his way to San Andrés, but he considered Zaragoza a "spy" for Juárez and, according to one report, was "determined to have (Zaragoza) shot at the slightest semblance of treason."[1]

Fifteen Hundred Killed in a Tragic Accident

What had put Uraga in direct touch with the French and British was a terrible accident, which had occurred on his watch at San Andrés Chalchicomula. It was customary for Mexican soldiers to be accompanied by their wives and the women who did all their cooking and cleaning. On March 6, local vendors were in the camp to sell tortillas, beans, and other vegetables while the women were lighting their cooking fires. The wind blew some sparks into a barn where twenty-three tons of gunpowder were stored, and seconds later there were corpses and severed heads and limbs falling everywhere.

More than a thousand soldiers were killed, along with almost five hundred women and several dozen vendors. It took several days just to count the casualties. More than two hundred others had lost limbs or eyesight, or had been wounded in other ways. Admiral Jurien, some forty miles away at Tehuacan, had sent French doctors as a goodwill gesture.

The admiral's viewpoint differed sharply from that of Pierre Saligny. Jurien was trying to show that the French were not there to persecute the Mexican people but to help them. Uraga sent "thank you" messages, and friendly, two-way communication was established. Saligny, seeing that General Uraga was responding positively, played along with dinner invitations.

With Zaragoza on the way, that was all about to change. Zaragoza would replace Uraga as commander in the field, and he would not be dining with the enemy.

France Seeks Mexican Collaborators

Uraga was not the only Mexican general the French wanted to capture as coconspirators. Juan Almonte had been among the top conservative generals during the War of the Reform, and was the Mexican minister in Paris while the conservatives were keeping Juárez at bay in Veracruz. Juárez had dismissed him as soon as the liberals regained Mexico City, but by then he had warmed up French contacts so well that he was sent to Maximilian's castle at Miramar by Napoleon III himself to recruit the Austrian archduke as emperor.

Almonte and Monsignor Labastida, bishop of Puebla, spent several days at Miramar with Maximilian. Among other things, they decided that Almonte and the bishop would form an interim government along with former dictator Santa Ana until Maximilian arrived.

Maximilian balked when Almonte passed along Napoleon III's request that he invest two hundred thousand dollars in the endeavor, to cover the costs of the interim government. He was even more skeptical when he learned that the British really didn't want to get involved. By April 1862, Maximilian was ready to back out of the deal, sensing that without British participation he would be little more than a puppet of Napoleon III, and that Napoleon "wishes to dominate Mexico without appearing to do so in the eyes of Europe."[2]

As Almonte returned to Mexico, a conservative general who had fought alongside him in the War of the Reform, Manuel Robles Pezuela, got in touch with him and offered to help. Juárez had pardoned Robles after the War of the Reform, on the condition that the general live quietly in Mexico City. Robles was caught writing to Almonte, and was forced to move to Sombrerete, a little town in the state of Zacatecas, and ordered not to leave. In spite of Robles' isolation, Almonte managed to invite Robles to meet with him at Córdoba. (In Mexico, it's still customary to put the mother's maiden name last, after the surname. Under this system, Robles Pezuela would normally be referred to as simply "Robles.")

The Juárez people became aware of Robles' trip beyond the boundaries of his parole and attempted to stop him at a roadblock. As he tried to gallop away, Robles was lassoed off his horse and brought before General Zaragoza at San Andrés Chalchicomula. He was sentenced to death by a court-martial.

News of Robles' death sentence reached Orizaba, where Mexican officials were negotiating with Britain's Charles Wyke and Spain's General Prim. Wyke and Prim immediately made it clear that the negotiations would be a lot easier if Robles were not executed. A messenger was sent from Orizaba that very evening, but he got lost in a thunderstorm. He arrived at San Andrés the next day at about 11:00 AM, only to find that Robles had been shot by a firing squad some five hours earlier.

The New American Ambassador

One man in a position to keep the United States government abreast of what was going on in Mexico was Ambassador Thomas Corwin. Telegraph lines had not yet been installed in Mexico, so the only way to get dispatches to Washington, D.C., was by courier. As early as November 1861, Corwin was using British couriers for the part of the journey within Mexico, saying it was the only safe way to get mail to the coast. By January 1862, however, he informed Washington that he would now be sending duplicate messages by separate couriers within Mexico, but he still could not be sure any of them could reach Veracruz safely. In February, he confirmed to Washington that the three European powers had landed troops, but that he wasn't sure whether or not they would wage war against Mexico.

Late in February, Corwin entrusted some of his dispatches to a young embassy employee named Ogden Yorke. Yorke was the son of expatriate Americans who mingled socially with the embassy staff in Mexico City. On March 4, 1862, Yorke left Mexico City at sunrise in a nine-passenger stagecoach, pulled by twelve mules that were exchanged every ten miles. The passengers had all agreed that, if they were attacked, they would all leap from the carriage and spread out so as to confuse the bandidos.

That's not what happened about ten miles east of Xalapa.

As fifteen or so bandidos came out of the underbrush, Ogden Yorke jumped from the coach and yelled to his fellow passengers to do the same. No one inside the coach moved. Yorke was the only target for the whole gang. He fired about eight shots and then fell dead as the gang swarmed over the carriage and robbed everyone, taking all their clothing and beating them almost to death.

Ambassador Corwin wouldn't give up. He sent one of his top diplomats, Edward L. Plumb, to carry the signed treaty proposal back to Washington that would give Mexico a bail-out loan from the United States. As Plumb rode along in the stagecoach, he noticed that much of the landscape between Puebla and Xalapa was hot and dry, at least until one passed Perote. At that point, deep, wooded ravines fell off to each side of the winding roadway. Forests of oak and pine appeared, and fresh, whitewater streams flowed down from snow-capped mountains to the north and northwest.

It was in this alpine terrain that the mule drivers made a detour to water the animals. As they came to a cold, clear stream, the *arrieros* (mule drivers) removed the bridles so that the animals could drink. All of the horses and mules in the convoy drank to their satisfaction and raised their heads as a signal that they were ready to resume the journey. All, that is, except for one mule.

The mule walked slowly toward the middle of the stream, heading toward a dark, deep pool. Suddenly, Edward Plumb began running up and down the bank of the stream, yelling frantically. That was his mule—the one carrying the treaty proposal which had been signed by the Juárez government. This was the treaty that guaranteed Britain, France, and Spain that they'd get their money if they would just cease their military operations in Mexico. It was the epitome of everything that Ambassador Thomas Corwin had been working on, and the mule carrying it gave every sign that it was about to roll over in the water.

Without hesitating, a quick-thinking *arriero* (mule driver) dashed into the water up to his neck, grabbed the mule by its muzzle, and directed it toward shore. The signed treaty proposal—and Plumb's reputation—were saved.

U.S. Civil War Begins

Back in the United States, the Civil War had started. The spring and summer of 1861 had gone badly for the North. In April, President Abraham Lincoln had called for seventy-five thousand troops. In May, he requested forty thousand more.

In spite of all the perils facing the nation, most Northerners did not really take the war seriously. In July 1861, many of them loaded their families into carriages with picnic baskets and headed from Washington, D.C., into nearby Virginia to watch the Battle of Bull Run as though it was a sporting event.

It wasn't.

The South won in a bloody confrontation, and a shocked U.S. Congress voted to raise an army of half a million men. There was no way the United States Senate could even begin to consider a treaty with Mexico.

The Union army began to hold massive recruiting parades in Washington, D.C., to enlist the soldiers that Congress had called for. Citizens came from hundreds of miles around to see all the artillery rolling by, the sword-carrying officers on horseback, and the long lines of men marching to the sounds of drums and bugles. After the parades, the public was invited to tour the army encampments just across the Potomac River.

A Circus Rider Meets Her Prince

Two very unusual people met at one of these encampments. Neither one could possibly have imagined that they would both play key roles in the story that was unfolding south of the border in Mexico. One was a European prince—Prince Felix Salm-Salm of Westphalia—who had fled Vienna to escape his heavy gambling debts. A veteran of both the Prussian and Austrian armies, he was serving as chief of staff for a German-speaking unit of the Union army. The other was a former Vermont farm girl who had run away from home to join a traveling circus at the age of fourteen. Agnes LeClerq Joy had been working as a bareback rider for the circus, but was visiting her sister in Washington to see one of the recruiting parades.

As Agnes and her sister toured the campsite, they were fascinated by the evergreen trees planted between the tents of the German-speaking troops from New York. Upon seeing Felix, she was charmed by his military bearing and somewhat in awe at the way he wore a monocle. He could not speak English, and she could not speak German, so they settled on Spanish. As he gave Agnes and her sister a tour of the camp, they discovered that Felix was a real prince and were totally enchanted. There was no doubt in Agnes's mind that she would pursue the relationship further.

Prim Heads New Commission

The first meeting of the Spanish, British, and French commissioners was held in Veracruz on January 9, 1862. Britain and France were each represented by two men, one of whom was in charge of diplomacy and the other of whom was there to handle military matters. For Spain, General Prim, the Count of Reus, wore both hats. He was named chairman of the allied commission.

Prim was no newcomer to these situations. He had been an expatriate in both England and France in order to escape a prison sentence when Spain had been under the conservative dictator, General Narváez, He had returned to perform both diplomatic and military duties when a more moderate government came into power. He had become a national hero during the conquest of Morocco in 1859, reviving a sense of nostalgia for the Spaniards, and it was this status that not only gave him the title Conde de Reus (Count of Reus) but made him the obvious choice for the current expedition.

Prim had a Mexican connection: his wife was the niece of Juárez's finance minister, Señor Gonzales Echeverría; however, at the age of forty-seven, Prim was a discreet professional who kept his political beliefs to himself. Still, his wife's nationality convinced Pierre Saligny—as well as Emperor Napoleon III and his wife Eugénie—that Prim was a spy for Juárez and would somehow try to thwart the British and French objectives.

At the first meeting, Admiral Jurien said that the allied powers desperately needed to replenish their food and supplies. He proposed that they defy the Mexican forces blockading Veracruz and venture out for about twenty miles to the towns of Medellín and Tejería to buy food.

The British delegates reluctantly agreed, even though they had been ordered not to go beyond Veracruz. The Mexican forces did not stop the troops as they undertook their food-buying mission, and they returned safely to Veracruz with their purchases.

About a week later, the commissioners met at the town of La Soledad, about twenty-five miles inland along the railroad from Veracruz, to talk about how much Mexico supposedly owed each nation.

The Mexicans owed the British more than the others put together—about US$69 million—and yet the British had the smallest military force there, with instructions to proceed no further than the Port of Veracruz. The Spaniards were owed about US$9 million and the French only US$2.86 million.

French Minister's Surprise

Then Pierre Saligny put in two more claims that left the others speechless. First, he wanted an additional $12 million to cover what he said were debts owed to French subjects and compensation for alleged injuries suffered by the French, without specifying how he had come up with that figure. Then he demanded another $15 million for a Swiss banker by the name of Jecker. Jecker had lent just $750,000 to conservative General Miguel Miramón to fight the War of the

Reform against Juárez, and now Saligny said the French were acting on behalf of Jecker in demanding $1 million a year at 30 percent interest for fifteen years.

It didn't seem to matter to Saligny that the Swiss government had asked the United States, not France, to represent its interests in Mexico. He claimed that Jecker had become a French citizen and was entitled to French backing in the matter. The truth—uncovered much later—was that Napoleon III's illegitimate half-brother, the Duke of Morny, was the holder of 30 percent of the Jecker bonds.

Saligny would not back down. The others sensed that they were being used, and that the French were just looking for an excuse to conquer Mexico. Britain's Sir Charles Wyke and Commodore Dunlop issued a statement saying that Saligny's claim "is inadmissible, the Mexican government will never accept it; before tolerating it, they will go to war, and the arms of England will never support such injustice." Wyke had privately attributed Saligny's intransigence to the French minister's personal hatred of Benito Juárez and to his obsession with overthrowing the liberal Mexican government, and he viewed Saligny's lust for money and power as "sick."[3]

Juárez Issues Death Decree

Enough details were leaking from these discussions that by now even President Juárez could sense that Saligny and the French had more than just a settlement of debts in mind. He issued a decree providing for the death penalty not just for anyone who was invading Mexico, but also for any Mexicans who were helping them. His proclamation was made on January 25 under the emergency powers that had just been granted to him by the Mexican Congress.

Pierre Saligny dismissed the Juárez decree. He said it only showed how barbaric Juárez and his administration were. Saligny knew full well that Napoleon III didn't want a settlement. He wrote to an acquaintance in France that "Mr. Juárez…is both an idiot and a rogue. This so-called Liberal Party is nothing but a collection of people with no respect for law or religion, with no intelligence, no honor, no patriotism, who have never had any political opinions but robbery."[4]

British diplomat Charles Wyke wrote home to his superiors in England that Saligny's demands were "perfectly outrageous" and served only as an excuse for the French to stay in Mexico.

3

Opposing Generals Get into Position

(February 12 to April 9, 1862)

Negotiation "*Sí*,"—Armed Force "*No*"

The allied representatives met with Juárez, but the president made it clear that while he was willing to negotiate a reasonable settlement, he would do whatever it might take to defend Mexico from any sort of military intervention. Juárez agreed to have his foreign minister, General Doblado, meet with the commissioners in La Soledad on February 19.

Doblado was a skillful negotiator, much to Saligny's dissatisfaction. He offered to let the three nations move their troops inland to the more healthful climate in the hills near Orizaba to escape from the heat and disease—if they would recognize the Juárez government and enter into good-faith negotiations about the debt. If the negotiations failed, the agreement would be that all of the troops would return to their previous positions in Veracruz before initiating any hostilities. This was not only a goodwill gesture to the allies to encourage negotiations, but it thwarted Pierre Saligny's demand that all troops be positioned in Mexico City before any talks could begin.

Saligny was furious, but he was overruled. Admiral Jurien agreed on behalf of France, and so did all three commissioners for England and Spain. Saligny immediately wrote to Paris, complaining not only about the Spanish and British commissioners but saying that Admiral Jurien was not carrying out the orders given to him by Napoleon III.

A Flare-up with Saligny

The situation boiled over when Wyke and Dunlop discovered that Saligny was pretending to reach agreement with the British and Spanish commissioners during their meetings at La Soledad but then told his French associates he had done no such thing. They complained to General Prim, and then Prim called in witnesses who confirmed the allegations.

This called for a direct confrontation with Pierre Saligny. Prim sent for Saligny and asked him point-blank, in front of Wyke and Dunlop, whether or not he had signed the agreements with Britain and Spain.

"No," replied Saligny.

Prim exploded. Shouting at the French minister as Wyke and Dunlop looked on, totally astounded, Prim asked him, "What? You're saying you did *not* sign them—right here—in this very place?"

Saligny still denied having done so.

Struggling to regain his composure, Prim calmly asked for an explanation.

Saligny replied with complete élan that while it was true that the commissioners had agreed to issue statements, and to print and publish them, none of them had actually picked up a pen and put his signature to any such document. Therefore, he considered all of the agreements null and void.

Prim couldn't believe what he was hearing. He ordered Saligny to leave immediately. Then, he wrote to Spain's ambassador in Paris and requested that he find some way of telling Napoleon III exactly what was going on.[1]

A Startling New French Buildup

Things became even more complicated on March 6, when French reinforcements suddenly arrived. Neither Saligny nor Jurien had requested them, but Napoleon III had sent them when he learned that the Spaniards had arrived from Cuba prematurely.

Along with the French reinforcements were two generals. One was Charles Latrille, the Count of Lorencez. He would be the new French commander, with Admiral Jurien now second in command. The other was General Juan Almonte, one of the leaders of the failed conservative rebellion against Juárez and the liberals during the War of the Reform. Almonte had been dictator Santa Anna's right-hand man in the massacre of the Texans at the Alamo in 1836. He had also been Mexico's minister to Paris while the conservatives held Mexico City and kept Juárez at bay. Juárez had dismissed Almonte as soon as the liberals took over, but now the general was returning with the French army, hoping to resurrect the defeated conservatives and establish a monarchy.

For Britain and Spain, that was the last straw.

Wyke had already written home to London that the French demands were "perfectly outrageous" and "so insulting" that the Mexican government would never accept them. Now both Wyke and Prim protested Almonte's presence among the French. Almonte, they said, was the recognized head of the party that had been at open warfare with the Juárez government, and that the general and some of those traveling with him were the very people whose names recalled "some of the worst scenes of a civil war which has proved a disgrace to the civilization of the present century."[2]

Since it was obvious that the French intended to meddle in the internal affairs of Mexico, said Prim and Wyke, Spain and Britain would withdraw. They sent a letter to Mexico's foreign minister Doblado stating they could not agree on any joint action. Instead, each nation would settle its accounts separately. Spain and Britain each did so, and began withdrawing their troops.

According to an agreement they had all signed with Doblado earlier, the French were also supposed to withdraw their troops to the Gulf area near Veracruz. When the others had left the country, the French would be able to make their next move regardless of anything they had signed.

Europeans in Culture Shock

The French, British, and Spanish soldiers were not the only Europeans in Veracruz. There were a number from various countries who were part of their governments' diplomatic entourages, some who were there on private business, and others who were simply tourists.

Those foreigners who did not come down with yellow fever or some other disease sought entertainment at events like bullfights. There, they could see firsthand what they may have already read about: bulls tortured, horses injured, and men wounded, as beautiful women applauded eagerly from the stands. As he left the bullring trembling and spattered with blood, with shouts of "*¡olé!*" still ringing in his ears, one such traveler wrote, "Surely people who need this sort of diversion are condemned by God."[3]

The women of Veracruz were certainly a diversion all by themselves. One of the best places for people-watching was Los Portales, the arched arcades next to the main plaza, with sidewalk cafés looking out at the seventeenth-century Palacio Municipal (city hall) and the eighteenth-century cathedral. One could watch women of all classes coming out of mass. Some were waving fans, others smoking cigars. The wealthier would wear satin *mantillas* (shawls), as black as their shining hair, while those who were up-to-date with the latest fashions wore imported shawls from India. Members of the lower class would have *rebozos* (coarse native shawls) wrapped around their heads and chests, covering just about everything above the waist other than their faces, but often barefoot or wearing homemade *huaraches* (sandals).

Another good place to view the locals was at the theater, where the lovely *jarochas* (peasant girls) from outlying villages would arrive in their provincial costumes. Nineteenth-century Mexican novelist Manuel Payno wrote that although they did not sit with the better families, they were clean and very gracious; they had lovely teeth and, of course, black expressive eyes, as well as fine facial features. There was something Andalusian about them, wrote Payno, who said that they were usually *morenas,* the ambiguously light brown-skinned girls who had always fascinated gentlemen of Spanish background.

Rather than being a public park or plaza, the Veracruz *alameda* (arboretum or grove) was a tree-shaded boulevard. It was very popular for evening strolls. Baron J. W. von Müeller, a traveling naturalist in the 1860s, had already been fascinated by the *jarochas'* pretty feet and twinkling black eyes, but he was astonished on one of his *alameda* strolls to come upon women who were making live, fluorescent jewelry out of fireflies. The insects were gathered out in rural areas by *indígenas* (Indians) who sold them in bulk at the town market. The *jarochas* (peasant girls) who bought them for jewelry making fed them and kept them alive until they could sell them individually or in small sets. The fireflies could be skewered, still alive and flashing, onto a hairpin or placed into fine, transparent little sacks that were sewn onto clothing as ornaments.[4]

Even the Mules Were Lying Down

The soldiers might have missed the bars and the *jarochas* (peasant girls) of Veracruz, but neither they nor their officers missed the heat and the diseases. It had been agreed at La Soledad that they could move inland to healthier climates, so the French and the Spaniards did so. The small British contingent was accommodated aboard ships in Veracruz harbor.

Admiral Jurien's march inland was an eye-opener for the French army. They left Veracruz at six o'clock in the morning, and by noon more than two-thirds of them had dropped out. Jurien, riding back along the road to get some water, was stunned to see most of the world's greatest army collapsed in total fatigue. Even the mules were staggering to the wayside and lying down, exhausted. Many of the roadside dropouts made it to camp during the night, but they had to stop at La Soledad for two days to get themselves rested and reorganized. Eighty more were hospitalized and another two hundred declared unfit for duty. These were left behind at La Soledad, and the rest would need another week to reach Orizaba.

Less than a mile from the center of Orizaba, the relatively flat terrain of the city ended abruptly at the base of Cerro del Borrego. As French soldiers set up camp and corralled their horses nearby, Pierre Saligny and Admiral Jurien gathered a number of local dignitaries and citizens to hear their proclamation: "Mexicans! We have not come here to take part in your disputes. We have come to put an end to them...The French flag has been planted on Mexican soil; this flag will not retreat. Let wise men greet it as a friendly flag. Let madmen fight against it if they dare!"[5]

Fine. The reaction was polite applause from a few and a shrug of resignation from the rest. Orizaba was not a hotbed of liberalism like Veracruz, but neither was it a militantly conservative community like Puebla. Orizaba's conservatism had more of a "take-care-of-business" flavor.

The French were glad to be there, if for no other reason than to escape the unhealthy conditions of Veracruz, where dozens of their soldiers were still hospitalized and hundreds more had been left behind as unfit for duty. The agreement with General Doblado at La Soledad had not only allowed the French to move inland for humanitarian reasons, but had provided a way of thanking Admiral Jurien for having sent medical help after the tragic explosion earlier at San Andrés Chalchicomula.

If the locals didn't mind the French flag flying over their *alameda* (arboretum), which in this case was a public park, the time in Orizaba would serve as a welcome respite for the troops, pending further developments at La Soledad.

Saligny Viewed as a Scoundrel

The British and the Spaniards were becoming quite worried about Pierre Saligny. Sir Charles Wyke told his friends and staff he was convinced that Saligny wanted to overthrow the Juárez government at all costs, because of a combination of his hatred for Juárez and a desire to lick Napoleon III's boots.

General Prim, who realized that his Spanish forces had just been used by the French for cover to get their operation started, wrote to a friend in Paris. Prim confided that he was not surprised that Napoleon III didn't know what was really going on, because he was relying primarily on Saligny for information. The general couldn't understand why Saligny was compromising "the decency, the dignity, and even the honor of French arms..." adding that "the forces of General Lorencez are not sufficient even to take Puebla." He insisted that "the Imperial eagles will roost in the ancient city of Moctezuma when they are supported by twenty thousand more, do you hear? Twenty thousand more men."[6]

Prim went to the last meeting of the three foreign delegations in Orizaba on April 9 and tried to talk sense into Admiral Jurien and his new boss, General Lorencez, but there was to be no reasoning at this point. Jurien and Saligny were both under orders from Paris. Prim's only choice was to pull the Spaniards out of the adventure before they got in over their heads. The joint intervention was dissolved.

Zaragoza Prepares His Troops

Zaragoza, meanwhile, had evacuated his people from Orizaba and withdrawn to his camp at San Andrés Chalchicoluma. There would be no more diplomacy. This was now entirely a military matter. The British and the Spaniards—by engaging the French in prolonged negotiations since December—had given Zaragoza something very valuable: time.

Zaragoza had learned quite a few tricks when the Americans had come through in 1847 and 1848. In particular, a captain by the name of Robert E. Lee had outfoxed dictator Santa Anna's forces by frequently going "off road," lowering artillery pieces down one side of a canyon and hauling them up the other side to approach the Mexicans from behind. Zaragoza decided early on that there would be no traditional head-on battles out in the open. The Mexicans had mobility on their side. They could live off the land, sleep on the ground, and cover three or four times the distances the French could march on any given day. These skills would be tested soon.

4

The Cliffs of Acultzingo

(March 6 through May 4, 1862)

Napoleon's New Man in Town

A festive crowd gathered near the wharf in Veracruz as several French ships pulled into the harbor to unload the reinforcements and supplies sent by Napoleon III. Admiral Jurien had not asked for any reinforcements, but Napoleon had become alarmed when the Spaniards landed their troops prematurely back in December. He didn't want Spain to have the upper hand.

General Lorencez, the new French commander-in-chief, had been added at least in part because of Pierre Saligny's complaints that Jurien had been too agreeable at the negotiating table. Lorencez had orders to stop negotiating and, if necessary, start shooting.

In theory, at least, Lorencez's fresh troops added to the French contingent already in Mexico would give him a force of 7,300 men. Subtracting those who were already sick or who would have to be left to guard the Port of Veracruz would still leave him with 6,000 for the march inland to the capital.

Both Pierre Saligny and General Juan Almonte assured Lorencez that all he had to do was show up in Mexico City and the country would be his. Within a few days, he sent a report back to Paris saying the mission was all but accomplished. No problem.

Then, things started to unravel. First, Lorencez learned that the talks at La Soledad had collapsed and that Admiral Jurien had agreed to return to the coast, wait for the British and the Spaniards to pull out, and then begin hostilities from Veracruz. That had been the agreement. Lorencez would have to move inland quickly and stop Jurien from carrying out the withdrawal. He would need to find some excuse.

Shaky Travel Arrangements

Next, there was the problem of transportation. The locals used mostly small, primitive carts, pulled by two to four mules. Jurien had managed to repair a couple of old, abandoned wagons and commandeer about a dozen more four-wheelers on his earlier trip inland. The sturdy vehicles imported from the United States could handle what passed for roads in Mexico, but when they were fully loaded, it took at least eight and sometimes as many as twenty-four mules to pull them.

The only people who could handle those mules were tough, well-trained Mexican *arrieros* (mule drivers), and they were hard to find. Jurien had tried using Creole sailors from the Caribbean, but he soon found out that they were totally unfit for the job. The horror stories about Jurien's trek inland to Orizaba had already reached Veracruz. Lorencez shuddered at the thought of having those same troops return to the coast and start all over again. It just didn't make sense. He had to stop Jurien at all costs.

Meanwhile Jurien, complying with the terms of the final agreement, had begun pulling his French troops out of Tehuacán and Orizaba. They were stationed at Córdoba, waiting for the Spaniards to pass by on their way to the coast. The details of the agreement had also provided that, as the various forces withdrew to their original lines, the Mexican government would reoccupy the vacated territory and protect any hospitals that the Europeans had left behind.

Lorencez Exploits a Misunderstanding

On April 18, the French were transferring 345 men from one hospital to another in Orizaba. Some of the Mexican forces under General Ignacio Zaragoza saw a number of the Frenchmen carrying their weapons during the transfer and mistook them for an armed unit that should have departed several days earlier.

Zaragoza sent a protest note to General Lorencez, asking that the armed soldiers be removed immediately. Zaragoza didn't know it, but he had just given the French the excuse they were looking for. Lorencez seized the opportunity to claim that he feared the sick soldiers would be harmed or taken as hostages. This was the best excuse he could come up with, and it was certainly better than having Jurien's people march all the way back to the coast. On April 19, he ordered the French army at Córdoba to turn around and head back toward Orizaba.

As the sun came up on April 20, General Prim, along with his wife and child, was leaving Orizaba with the last of his Spanish troops when he met Lorencez and Jurien coming back in the opposite direction.

"What has happened to our hospitals in Orizaba?"[1] asked Lorencez.

Prim had no way of knowing that Lorencez wanted to use alleged mistreatment of French soldiers as a pretext for going on the offensive. He simply stated that he had toured the hospitals with the head physician several times overnight, and that everything seemed all right. The French soldiers, he said, were as safe as they would be in Paris. That wasn't exactly the answer Lorencez wanted to hear, but Prim saluted and went on his way.

Zaragoza, meanwhile, had been tipped off that the French were returning. He was ready.

The strategy would be mostly that of guerilla warfare. His troops would cut supply lines, stage ambushes, kill stragglers, and burn crops and facilities in the path of any French advance. Then they would let yellow fever, hunger, and impassable roads do the rest. Zaragoza would adapt his tactics to the natural terrain and to the native skills of his soldiers, keeping their morale high while doing everything he could do to wear it down among the enemy.

Lorencez's Visions of Grandeur

On April 25, in Orizaba, Admiral Jurien opened his mail to find bad news. He was not only being reprimanded for signing the La Soledad agreement, which called for the withdrawal of French forces to the coast, but he was also being formally recalled to Paris.

Pierre Saligny and General Almonte lost no time in congratulating General Lorencez on his promotion to supreme commander. They assured him that he would meet only token resistance as his newly reinforced army advanced toward Puebla and on to Mexico City.

On April 26, Lorencez acknowledged his promotion and reflected the confidence that Saligny and Almonte had shown in him by sending the following message to the war minister in Paris: "We are so superior to the Mexicans in race, in organization, in discipline, in morality, and in elevation of feeling that I beg Your Excellency to be so good as to inform the Emperor that, at the head of six thousand soldiers, I am already the master of Mexico."[2]

Lorencez was a vain and pompous individual with a Van Dyke beard, waxed moustache, huge braided epaulettes, and a forest of shimmering medals pinned to his chest—but not much of a war record. He had sent a note to Zaragoza apologizing for the misunderstanding on April 19, explaining that his French soldiers were only being transferred from one hospital to another in Orizaba, but the very next day he had stopped Jurien's withdrawal at Córdoba and turned the French army around. He was now back in Orizaba to plan and prepare for his march to Mexico City.

Among other things, he had added 230 wagons to the supply convoy already assembled by Jurien. Now, at last, the French army was ready. They would begin the march early the next day, April 27.

Tough Road

The switchbacks made them dizzy. Sixty-three hundred French soldiers were trudging their way up and up through mountainous terrain leading toward Córdoba and Orizaba. They climbed strenuously around thirty-seven hairpin turns to reach the top of the roadway and enter Mexico's central plateau. The walls on each side of the canyon were almost perpendicular at this point. At the top, directly in their path, was an abandoned jailhouse.

So far, they had seen very little of the enemy. Here and there, some Mexican scouts had been reported disappearing into the woods, and in one small village, they had to wait while a fire was extinguished in the roadway, but that was about it. They stopped for a coffee break—all 6,300 of them.

Then, as they were about to resume the march, gunfire erupted from the ruins of the jailhouse. Within seconds, the entire canyon echoed with the fire of Mexican artillery, which had been waiting atop the cliffs. Lorencez's own artillery was at the very rear of the line of march, where it was useless, so he ordered an Algerian infantry unit known as the Zouaves to charge up the steep incline and capture the jailhouse. The Zouaves were known for their bright, Egyptian-style uniforms and quick-spirited drills, but not for this kind of work. They were not able to silence the gunfire. Lorencez ordered a regiment of cavalry to charge on foot.

Riding in a carriage near the rear of the line of march, French minister Pierre Saligny and Imperialista general Juan Almonte began to feel uneasy as they watched the baggy red pants of the Zouaves snag on the cactus and saw the turban-wearing troops scatter in the underbrush. Only yesterday, they had both assured Lorencez that today's march would be trouble free, and that a victory in Puebla would present few difficulties. Now, it was becoming painfully obvious that the Frenchmen were not accustomed to terrain or long marches like this.

In fact, the soldiers were being forced to do more than just march. They were helping to push some 620 wagons up the primitive, twisting roads, which had been muddied by the melting snow. Many of them were dropping by the wayside, still afflicted by the *vomito*, or yellow fever, which had pursued them ever since Veracruz. This was not fun to watch. Saligny and Almonte knew it would be a long day.

Just as the troops were coming within range of the old jailhouse, a barrage of enemy fire swept down the column. Mexican artillery salvos continued their bombardment from the surrounding bluffs. There would be no response from the French artillery, still placed at the end of the long, winding column.

General Lorencez just kept sending wave after wave of whoever was next in line, until he had fourteen companies all groping for footing and ducking for cover on the hillside. The terrain was backbreaking and the Mexican positions were still not yielding. At five o'clock, just as daylight in the canyon was beginning to fade, word came that the Mexicans had vanished and that the French had finally taken the deserted jailhouse. After three hours of fighting, the cost was two dead and thirty-six wounded.

Lorencez declared victory. Saligny and Almonte were very relieved.

Over the next few days, the French experienced culture shock such as they had never seen before. Whole *indígena* (Indian) villages—Tecamalucan, Atitla, Cañada de Ixtapa, and Quecholac—were deserted, except for the pigs that had been left barricaded inside huts. The soldiers chased the pigs throughout the villages, leaving it up to the officers to figure out how to restore the "superiority of organization, discipline and morality" that Lorencez had claimed.[3]

Whenever one of the *indígenas* (Indians) was caught and held for questioning, the dialogue went something like this:

"Where are the Mexican soldiers?"
"*¿Quién sabe, señor?*" ("Who knows, sir?")
"Were the soldiers here?"
"*¿Quién sabe, señor?*"
"What's your name?"
"*¿Quién sabe, señor?*"
"How many children do you have?"
"*¿Quién sabe, señor?*"

In many of the most remote villages, very few of the *indígenas* (Indians) actually spoke that much Spanish, and those who actually knew it didn't want to "let on." After several hundred years of dominance by the Spaniards, little boys in these villages all insisted that their names were "José" and the girls all claimed to be named "María." The answer to any other question was "*¿Quién sabe, señor?*" but the French had no way of knowing that.

For ten days, Lorencez and his troops followed the mysterious, evasive enemy from one deserted village to another. At least they were in a healthier climate. They could see snow-capped volcanoes in the distance as they marched by fertile farmland, but they still had not made contact with any Mexican forces.[4] This was unnerving to the troops. Letters were recovered from the bodies of soldiers found lying by the roadside that expressed their fears and frustrations to sweethearts, friends, and family members back home.

Some referred to the enemy as "invisible," revealing that the French had often been fired upon, but upon firing back, hit no one at all. Others said that the French had captured or killed no one, but that many of their number had been killed or wounded by an enemy that simply vanished. Friends who fell behind the line of march were never heard from again. The soldiers complained about having to push heavy supply wagons up the winding, muddy roads while the enemy simply lived off the land. Many expressed to the folks back home that they feared they might die before reaching Puebla, let alone Mexico City.

Finally, on May 4, Lorencez reached Amozoc. Puebla was fourteen miles ahead, and the general learned that Zaragoza and as many as six thousand men were prepared to defend it. Lorencez's scouts told him that the streets had been barricaded and that artillery had been placed on many rooftops.

It was time to call a council of war and plan for tomorrow's military offensive against the city of Puebla.

5

Preparations for the Battle

(May 3–4, 1862)

The Approaching Enemy

General Zaragoza had some doubts that the French troops approaching Puebla were actually the world's finest army. He paced slowly as he questioned the members of his war council. Seated around a table in the old converted monastery at the top of Guadalupe Hill that overlooked Puebla were generals Negrete, Escobedo, Rojo, and O'Horan.

General Arteaga had been hospitalized with a wound suffered in the skirmish several days earlier at the Cliffs of Acultzingo. It was Arteaga who had been asked to stage the diversion in the canyon to delay the French advance, find out how Lorencez deployed his forces, and discover whatever else he could about the invaders while Zaragoza concentrated the bulk of his army on the strategic defense of Puebla.

Arteaga's scouts had learned quite a bit about their adversaries. For one thing, the supply train was carrying over two hundred thousand bottles of wine, more than thirty bottles per soldier. If about a third of the 260 wagons that left Orizaba were ambulances, officers' wagons, and those used for cooking and blacksmithing, that would leave about 170 wagons. If one-third to one-half of those were carrying wine, that meant that just 70 to 90 wagons would be carrying everything else for six thousand men: food, ammunition, artillery pieces, whatever.[1]

If nothing else, Zaragoza concluded, the French were very dependent on their supply line. That might not make much difference in the next few days, he thought, but over time it would become more of a liability than an asset. In any case, after pushing all those wagons for more than a week and suffering from disease, fear, and just plain fatigue, the magnificent French army that had landed at Veracruz over the past few months was not the army now approaching Puebla.

33

A Defense the French Could Never Imagine

With his troops deployed in and around Puebla, Zaragoza decided to get a little help from his *indígena* (Indian) friends. He had sent emissaries out to Zacapoaxtla, several days' travel to the northeast, to enlist the services of the fierce, machete-carrying warriors who had helped him during the War of the Reform.

As the recruitment detail made the trip, they noticed that the farther they traveled, the more differences there were in housing, clothing, and demeanor among the local population. As they wound their way through the countryside past the volcano of La Malinche, avoiding Amozoc, they saw isolated huts made of little more than saplings and covered with a muddy form of stucco. A few were made of adobe, sun-baked blocks of straw and mud, with flat roofs made from rows of poles covered with a foot or two of dirt and then perhaps a layer of palm thatch or pine boards. There were no windows, so the doors were the only source of daylight and ventilation.

At first there had been the *campesinos* (country people) in their unbleached cotton pants and shirts without buttons or collars, wearing *huaraches* (sandals) that they had apparently made themselves. The people waved at the wagons with friendly greetings. Farther along the way, both men and women were barefoot, and the men wore only breechcloths. The women wore simple mantles of maguey cactus fiber, which they wrapped around themselves and knotted at the shoulder. The children wore nothing at all. Nobody waved. They stared at the wagons in sullen silence. Some of the men had their hair tied in a style known as *como valiente* (as a warrior), a sign in these parts that each of them had killed at least four men.[2]

It would be even farther from civilization before they would find the Zacapoaxtlas, but it would not be hard to procure their help. After all, the president of Mexico, Benito Juárez, was a full-blooded *indígena* (Indian) himself, and they had fought on his side before.

Ambush the Imperialistas

Zaragoza knew that Imperialista general Leonardo Márquez was headed toward the town with a force of two thousand men, hoping to provide some support for the French, so he ordered General O'Horan's brigade to make sure they never reached Puebla. O'Horan would try to intercept them in Atlixco, about forty miles to the southwest.

Generals Negrete and Berriozábal were with Zaragoza. Negrete was to coordinate everything atop Guadalupe Hill, both inside and outside the two forts. Berriozábal was to be in command of Fort Guadalupe itself, and another commander, General Rojo, was to be in charge at Fort Loreto, a mile or so to the east at the other end of the hill. Colonel Porfirio Díaz would direct the cavalry that because of its mobility would be poised for contingencies.

The French Make Final Plans

In Amozoc, General Lorencez called his officers together in a council of war. He had plenty of expert advice available, but he was known for making up his own mind despite what anyone might tell him.

The road from Amozoc southward toward Puebla ended at a T intersection, where there had once been a tollgate. From there, one could circle Puebla to the east by turning left or to the west by turning right. Straight ahead was Guadalupe Hill, with a steep, forested north slope; there was no road by which to climb to the top from that side. General Juan Almonte had captured Puebla twice and had defended it twice during previous wars, and he warned Lorencez that no one had ever taken Puebla by approaching it from the north.

At the top of the hill was Fort Guadalupe, which had originally been a convent. At the eastern end of the hill, about a mile from Fort Guadalupe, was Fort Loreto. Almonte told General Lorencez that both forts were at a distance so remote from the town that their guns would be all but useless against an enemy that attacked from the opposite side. Almonte and several others advised Lorencez to ignore the two forts and attack from the south, which was not only more accessible but less fortified.

There were some major problems in Lorencez's mind about attacking from the south. One of them involved the commitment of twenty-five hundred Mexican Imperialista forces under General Márquez who were to have helped in the next day's effort. Lorencez had just received word that Márquez's troops had been scattered into the countryside by an ambush earlier that morning. General Zaragoza had dispatched General O'Horan and his troops to Atlixco to intercept the Imperialistas. O'Horan's soldiers had been crouched down in a sugarcane field and hidden in a nearby flour mill as Márquez's forces approached the town. Márquez's men were not that well-trained, so they just panicked and ran.

Protecting All That Wine

Another predicament involved the supply line. Although Pierre Saligny had recommended approaching Puebla from the east, Lorencez sent an officer to tell the minister that such a maneuver would involve not only abandoning the supply wagons, including the wine, but also compromising the security of Saligny and his entourage. "We are compelled by the conditions of our march to remain close to our resources, even at the risk of choosing the point of attack that may not be wholly favorable."

"Very well," said Saligny, settling back in his carriage. "General Lorencez may approach the city as he pleases, but I should consider it a most serious mistake not to profit by the friendly feeling of which I have been informed, and I shall be obliged to report it."[3]

Lorencez's cavalry officers didn't like the idea of galloping blindly into a maze of barricaded streets. They were sure they'd do much better charging up the hill and capturing the forts. That's what they were trained for. The commander of his engineer corps introduced a Mexican engineer, who also favored an assault on the forts. The young engineer testified that there were no obstructions that would stop a spirited charge by French infantry. He added that the moats did not hold water and were partly filled in, and that the walls of the forts were not very solid.

Besides, argued those who favored attacking the forts, the Mexicans would most likely offer a token defense before surrendering. The engagement would last no more than an hour or two, and then there would be plenty of time for a victory parade.

That's what Lorencez wanted to hear. He decided to attack from the north side of Guadalupe Hill.

"Acting French" in Puebla

In Puebla itself, the local elite were actually hoping for a French victory. The town had been a hotbed of conservative activity during the War of the Reform. The population was very pro-European, wearing British clothing styles and speaking their Spanish with a French accent to impress each other. Some of the restaurants in town were even printing their menus in French, although the breakfast specialty at some of them was broiled armadillo.

The sermons in the churches were all in favor of the French, with priests saying that the town was to be "liberated" by the French army, not "protected" by Zaragoza and the Mexicans. In fact, the bishop of Puebla had gone a step further, saying that the French were allies of the Church, and that Zaragoza and his soldiers were excommunicated. Any sacraments or other clerical help for the Mexican soldiers—even if they were wounded—would be forbidden.[4]

Even the wealthier women among the worshippers always wore black, but among their status symbols was their ability to pay for votive candles, which they lighted at the many side altars, to wear shoes, and to sit in the pews. The *morenas* (brown-skinned peasant girls) occupied an area of the floor off to one side of the church. They wore their *rebozos* (coarse shawls) around their heads and chests, covering everything above their waists except their faces. Most wore *huaraches* (hand-made sandals), but many were barefoot.

From a tall array of pipes beyond the pulpit in the main cathedral came the luxuriant sound of the organ. Many of those seated beneath the vaulted Gothic ceiling were seeking reassurance that they would not be harmed in the upcoming battle for control of the city. They were putting their faith not only in God but in the barricades they were building to protect their homes.

Everyone knew that six thousand French soldiers under General Lorencez had reached Amozoc, fourteen miles to the east, and that Imperialista general Leonardo Márquez was approaching with twenty-five hundred more men from the southwest.

Most of the churchgoers were hoping that tomorrow's hostilities would be concluded as quickly as possible. Many were preparing to welcome the French with a victory parade before the day was over.

6

The Battle of Puebla

(May 4–5, 1862)

The *Indígena* (Indian) Messenger

What Pierre Alphonse Dubois Saligny probably wanted more than anything at this moment was a good bath, a relaxing massage, and a stiff drink. France's minister to Mexico knew that the Orizaba-to-Puebla trip should take only three days. After eight days on the road, he had run out of things to say to his fellow passenger, General Almonte.

It can be imagined that Saligny was only too eager to escape the foul-smelling, mud-spattered army vehicle and head for the luxurious hospitality awaiting him at the home of wealthy local conservatives in nearby Puebla. A more suitable carriage for someone of his rank, most likely a four-passenger *Berlina*, a town coach known as a Brougham in England and the United States, was already waiting for him with the French army at its camp in Amozoc, a short distance from Puebla.

As Saligny was about to step up into the more luxurious vehicle, an *indígena* (Indian) came running up, thrust a small packet of hand-rolled cigarettes toward him, said the name "Márquez," and fled. Saligny guessed that he had been chosen to receive this message because he looked as though he were the one in charge.

The packet was obviously for Lorencez. Saligny knew how they sent secret messages this way. He also knew that *indígena* (Indian) runners hid such items in radically ungodly places like their armpits, their crotches, between their toes, or in other unmentionable parts of their bodies. It turned out to be confirmation that General Márquez was approaching with twenty-five hundred men.[1]

Lorencez had sent up camp and sent some scouts over to Puebla to get a quick look at enemy positions while there was still daylight. The detail had returned with the information that most of the Mexican troops appeared to be deployed at the south end of the town, the most likely place for an attack.

Minister Saligny had already written to General Lorencez earlier, intending to provide some upbeat encouragement: "As soon as our troops are in sight of the city, Márquez will appear, all conventional resistance will cease, and the barricades will fall as if by magic. You will make your entrance under a rain of flowers, to the confusion of Zaragoza and his gang. It would be better to enter by the east gate than the one facing you."

Lorencez didn't like anyone telling him what to do, especially people like Saligny who knew nothing about military affairs. No, he would organize the attack, and no one else. Saligny's letter concluded: "In any case, you should have no complications to fear. You may approach the city as you please, but I should consider it a most serious mistake not to profit by the friendly feeling of which I have been informed, and I shall be obliged to report it."[2]

Best Direction from Which to Attack

General Lorencez called a council of war, preparing to announce his decision. Just as the officers were gathering, another note arrived. This time it was bad news. Those twenty-five hundred Imperialista troops under General Márquez—the ones who were supposed to make the barricades fall "as if by magic"—had been ambushed in Atlixco, about thirty miles southwest of Puebla. Zaragoza had sent General O'Horan and his men to crouch down in a sugarcane field and hide in a flour mill. As Márquez's troops approached the town, they were scattered into the countryside. Márquez regretted to say that they would not be able to make it to Puebla by the next day.

Lorencez had a decision to make. From what direction should he approach Puebla? Saligny had recommended the east gate, other officers had suggested circling the town and approaching from the south, and General Almonte, who had both captured and defended Puebla over a number of years, had pointed out that Puebla had never been taken from the north.

Attacking from the east would be giving in to Saligny. That would never do. Circling the town and attacking from the south would stretch out the supply line and make it vulnerable to counterattack. General Almonte had been on the losing side in the War of the Reform, so what did he really know? In Lorencez's mind, it was settled. They would attack from the north.

Let's Attack—But First, a Coffee Break

General Ignacio Zaragoza stared silently through his binoculars, looking down at the road junction just north of town, the one where the old tollgate used to be. It was already midmorning on May 5, and the entire French army had been there about two hours. They had left Amozoc at five o'clock in the morning and had marched for four hours toward Puebla. Now, they were taking a coffee-and-pastry break.

The trip from Amozoc to Puebla normally takes an hour and a half on horseback, two hours by carriage. But this six-thousand-man army had taken almost nine whole days to make the three-day trip from Orizaba. They were surely not counting on the element of surprise.

General Berriozábal was in charge of Fort Guadalupe; General Rojo was at Fort Loreto, about a mile away; and General Negrete was coordinating the activities of both forts, defending all of the territory surrounding them atop Guadalupe Hill. It was approaching 11:00 AM. As soon as the French made a move, they'd be ready.

None of them could quite believe the French move when it finally came. General Lorencez was actually going to try to take Puebla from the north—something that had never been done before.

The Mexicans turned their artillery around to counter this unexpected development. They would be aiming straight down the hillside at French infantry, who would be trying to climb the hill on foot. The French artillery was so far back in line that it might be possible to bombard their infantry for half an hour before they could even get set up.[3]

Some authors claim that General Zaragoza released a herd of stampeding cattle at this point to scatter the French infantry, but diligent research from leading sources does not support this version. Still, the story survives as a popular folk tale among Mexican Americans.

That Cannon Fire Was Not a Welcome Salute!

Down below, the Zouaves were among the French units still under the impression that they were preparing for a victory parade and nothing more. The weather was just perfect: bright sunshine, clear blue skies, and comfortable temperatures stirred by ever-so-slight breezes. The Zouaves were putting the last touches on what they hoped would be an impressive appearance. Dressed in their Arabian-style blue jackets and baggy red pants, they had just whitened their cloth leggings and rewound their turbans. They carefully draped their tassels to one side to achieve maximum flamboyance.

Suddenly—*BAH-OOM!*—an artillery shell landed nearby.

Imperialista general Almonte exclaimed that it was a military salute. "The good citizens of Puebla are saluting our approach," he said.[4]

Lorencez knew better. It was just dawning on him that all those promises and wishful thinking from Almonte, Saligny, and other generals and diplomats were pretty hollow. There would be no victory parade. There would be a tough battle, and he was already into it. The Mexicans had been bombarding his troops for fifteen minutes, and the French artillery was just arriving to set up.

Ten French artillery pieces began returning the fire that was coming from the converted convent at the top of the hill, but not much was happening. Only a few of the shells even reached Fort Guadalupe, much less did any damage. Lorencez ordered his artillery to move closer to the hill to be within shorter range.

The French infantry people were now caught between the dueling artillery forces. The French at the bottom of the hill were firing practically straight into the air. They could not see in a direct line to the fort, and if they aimed much higher, the shells would probably come back down on their heads.

French Artillery Won't Last Another Hour

Zaragoza, meanwhile, was making strategic changes. Colonel Porfirio Díaz's cavalry held the high ground, so they could look down and easily outflank any move by their French cavalry counterparts. The Mexican troops that had been protecting the southern approaches to Puebla were moved to Guadalupe Hill in several ways that the French could not observe. Now, they would be concealed along the hilltop ridge between the two forts, in position and waiting.

At 12:30 PM, a messenger arrived at General Lorencez's headquarters. It was from the French artillery. They had been in place and firing since 11:15 AM as ordered, and now they were saying half of their ammunition was already used up. It would all be gone within the hour.

Lorencez was visibly stunned, but he decided that he could not afford to lose the momentum. The Mexican artillery was still raking the hillside with deadly accuracy, but Lorencez decided that the best way to deal with it was to order another infantry charge—straight up the hill.

At Fort Guadalupe, General Zaragoza was somewhat puzzled by the French. What sort of army would pause for a two-hour, coffee-and-pastry break while marching into battle? Call it overconfidence, call it bureaucracy, but even from a distance Zaragoza and his officers could tell that the Frenchmen's hearts and souls were not really engaged. They appeared to be just going through the motions, expecting just token resistance before their victory parade. From the Mexicans, however, Zaragoza could sense a feeling of allegiance to a cause and a moral obligation that the invaders clearly lacked.

Something the French Never Trained for

Within moments, there were shouts outside the wall of Fort Guadalupe as a few soldiers from the latest wave of French infantry made it to the top of the hill. Gunfire was coming from the woods and from the trenches, not from the fort, as the confused Frenchmen tried valiantly to place ladders against the wall.

Then came something they never could have imagined, even in their worst nightmares.

As the few surviving French soldiers scrambled through the moat surrounding Fort Guadalupe and began to climb their ladders, blood-curdling shrieks and yells resounded throughout the compound. Several dozen Zacapoaxtla warriors, brandishing machetes, swiftly beheaded each of the enemy soldiers who had reached the uppermost rungs. Not a single one of the invaders lived to tell about it.[5]

After three more waves of infantry tried to enter the fort without success, some Zouaves turned left and stumbled onto Fort Loreto. Fleeing uphill, they met five dug-in battalions of Mexican infantry.

Things were not going well for the French. Not only had the Zouaves found themselves outnumbered five to one in their aborted attempt to round the hill toward Fort Loreto, but the Mexican cavalry under Colonel Porfirio Díaz had sent two more companies of French-employed African sharpshooters tumbling back down the hill. General Lorencez had just one more card to play: the Mexicans had not yet seen his cavalry.

It was late in the afternoon when General Zaragoza probably thought God was on his side. As he looked through his binoculars to the west of Puebla, the sky was growing darker by the minute. Every day for the past week or so, there had been a thunderstorm at about this time, and the one that was approaching appeared to be much larger than its predecessors.

Zaragoza sent word to all of his units to let the storm do its work. If there were any Frenchmen still standing when it was over, they would be easier to deal with.

General Lorencez apparently did not have his eyes on the sky. He sent the cavalry charging up the north slope of Guadalupe Hill just before the cloudburst arrived. They were met with drenching rain, thunder and lightning, hailstones, and severe wind gusts that swayed large tree branches all around them. Lost soldiers were crawling and staggering around in the blinding downpour. Horses were slipping and sliding everywhere in the mud, falling over and injuring themselves and their riders.

The smell of gun smoke was mixed with those of mud, horse manure, wet leather, sweat, and blood as Europe's finest army confronted what could only be described as a catastrophe. Ignacio Zaragoza could claim an unexpected but decisive victory. As he later wrote in his report to Mexico's war minister, the French troops fought bravely but lacked strategic command.

As a bugle mercifully sounded retreat, rain-soaked, bedraggled, and confused French soldiers returned to the old tollhouse at a road junction just north of Puebla. The day would go down in history as an embarrassing defeat for the French.

A French Battalion Lost in the Woods

It wasn't over yet.

Not everyone could heed the bugle's call. Wounded soldiers screamed in agony as French medics attempted to rescue them from the hillside in the gathering darkness. French historians would claim that they lost only 462 dead, wounded, or missing, but Mexican author Salazar Monroy says the French retrieved almost all of their wounded and still left 1,139 dead behind on Guadalupe Hill. General Zaragoza's own report claims more than 1,000 French were killed.

The Mexicans were probably more surprised than the French that they had won. They celebrated at Fort Guadalupe by singing songs and cheering wildly. The Zacapoaxtla *indígenas* (Indians) didn't know the words, but they enjoyed the party. Among the songs was "La Marseillaise," which had been banned by Napoleon III when the country returned to monarchy. The tune had been picked up by liberals and revolutionaries everywhere outside of France. Now the Mexicans were using it to taunt the French army which was licking its wounds—within hearing distance—on the plain just north of Guadalupe Hill.

At the height of the victory celebration, someone called for silence. Yes, there was the sound of a bugle coming from the woods nearby. Could it be another French attack? Each man reached for his weapon as General Berriozábal sent out a dozen volunteers to scout the hillside. The scouts found no one during their search, but word later came out that an entire battalion of French sailors had become lost in the woods. Whoever was looking for them had brought a bugler along, but the sailors finally returned to the French encampment on their own.

Mexican author Salazar Monroy claims the Mexicans suffered 490 dead and 210 wounded. Other historians give no figures for the Mexican losses.

French Minister Pierre Saligny, exasperated at Lorencez's incompetence, was already writing to Emperor Napoleon III and including a complete list of the general's mistakes. Others would soon join him. Lorencez would have to eat the words he used in a speech he made before leaving Orizaba, predicting an easy victory and calling himself "the Master of Mexico."

"So much," said one officer, using a quotation from Lorencez, "for being superior in race, organization, discipline and morality."[6]

Zaragoza had guessed correctly: Lorencez didn't have a clue about military strategy. He had just flung his foot soldiers heedlessly up the hill against fortified positions and well-placed artillery, deluded in his belief that no one could defeat his world-famous army. The moral of the story of Cinco de Mayo was that Mexican soldiers could stand up to the best that Europe had to offer, especially when they were under determined and capable leadership. Because of this unexpected but welcome victory, the Mexican people were inspired to persevere.

PART II
A Struggle for the Upper Hand
May 6, 1862, through May 29, 1863

7

The French Withdraw to Orizaba

(May 6–31, 1862)

Lorencez Doesn't Get It

The Mexicans were just as surprised as the French by the outcome of May 5, but General Lorencez was in such denial about the loss that he expected a counterattack the next morning. And the next. And the next. It never came. In Lorencez's mind, the "honorable" thing for the Mexicans to do would be to come down onto the plain and fight on a "real" battlefield. What had happed on May 5 didn't really count.

General Zaragoza didn't see it that way. Zaragoza was well aware of the French reputation as the world's finest army. He knew that he had prepared his defenses well and had fended off an assault on his hilltop forts, but to go down to the plain and fight the French on their own terms was another thing. Many historians quote him as saying that if he had dared to engage the French on May 6, nobody would ever remember what had happened on May 5. As a quotation, that might be hyperbole, but as a fact, it was undeniable. It was not just the morale of his men at stake, it was the morale of all of Mexico. There was no way he would jeopardize the May 5 victory by risking a loss immediately afterward.

Zaragoza wrote two letters to Mexico City: one was to the war minister, saying that the French army had fought with great bravery but that their commander-in-chief had conducted the attack incompetently. That didn't take anything away from the Mexican soldiers, said Zaragoza: "The national arms have been covered with glory. I can state with pride that not once, during the long struggle which it sustained, did the Mexican army turn its back on the enemy."[1]

Zaragoza Wants to "Burn" Puebla

The other letter was to President Benito Juárez. Zaragoza was disgusted with the locals in Puebla, who had backed the French and were lamenting the upset victory by the Mexicans. It was a normal practice of the federal government to compensate local communities for any damages incurred during battle, but Zaragoza opposed such a move this time: "As for money, nothing can be done here, because these people are bad, and above all, lazy and selfish…How good it would be to burn Puebla! The city is mourning the event of the 5th. It is sad to say so, but it is a regrettable truth."[2]

Lorencez Shifts Blame

The mood at General Lorencez's headquarters could only be described as grim. Throughout the camp, hundreds were still milling about in a sort of humiliated daze, looking stunned, overwhelmed, and depressed. Everything they had learned on the drill fields of France counted for little or nothing under the present circumstances. The only sounds that could be heard were those of shoveling as they buried their dead. At first Lorencez had planned to renew the attack begun on May 5, but at this point, even he could sense that there was a morale problem.

On the morning of May 8, Lorencez withdrew his troops to Amozoc, but General Almonte kept insisting that they could still take Puebla as soon as General Márquez reassembled his forces and joined them. They waited in Amozoc through May 9 and May 10, but Márquez never showed up.

That was more than Lorencez could stand. He called the troops together and, without actually naming them, shifted the blame for the massive failure to Saligny and Almonte:

"Soldiers and sailors!…You had been told a hundred times that the city of Puebla summoned you with all its heart and that its population would press on your heels to cover you with flowers. It was with the confidence inspired by these deceptive assurances that we presented ourselves before Puebla."

He told them that it was not their fault, and assured them that they had "given proof, on the fifth of May, of heroic courage."[3]

Not everyone in the ranks accepted Lorencez's argument. "A general," said one unidentified officer, "should be prepared for the enemy to receive his men with gunfire, not with flowers!"[4]

Back down through the deserted villages and past the Cliffs of Acultzingo marched the French army. Finally, General Márquez caught up with them, but Márquez had fallen into yet another ambush and had to be rescued before they could continue on to Orizaba.

The Minister Hits the Bottle

Meanwhile, back in Puebla, Pierre Saligny was found stumbling around in the street with a half-empty bottle in his hand. He had already written to Paris, telling his side of the story about the defeat and blaming Lorencez. When the general found out that Saligny had been discovered totally drunk in public, he threatened to have the minister arrested for affronting the dignity of France.

French soldiers lost no time in spreading the gossip about the quarrel between Lorencez and Saligny, while their officers spent a great deal of time and effort trying to hush things up. The Mexicans got wind of the dispute and embellished the details among themselves and in the press. Cartoons picturing Saligny as a toad in a bottle, steeped in alcohol, began to appear, adding to the overall humiliation of the French.

Even General Zaragoza couldn't resist taking a poke at Lorencez over the situation. On June 12, Lorencez opened a letter addressed to him by Zaragoza. The Mexican commander-in-chief was offering him an honorable capitulation if he would agree to a specific deadline for getting his troops out of Mexico. Said Zaragoza: "I have sufficient grounds to believe, sir, that you and the officers under your command have sent the Emperor a protest against the conduct of Minister Saligny for having misled you into an expedition against a people that was the best friend of the French nation."[5]

Lorencez still resented Saligny enough to answer Zaragoza with a terse note, saying that the emperor had seen fit to confer all political powers entirely on Saligny (which was true), and that any talk of a capitulation offer should be taken up with the minister. Between the cartoons and Zaragoza's letter, both Lorencez and Saligny decided to stop maligning each other before the situation became even more embarrassing.

Sara Yorke Arrives

The end of May was approaching, and the parents of Ogden Yorke, the deceased American embassy employee, were in Veracruz to await the arrival of their daughter from France. Fifteen-year-old Sara Yorke was staying at the home of a member of the French national legislature and was being educated in Paris when news of her brother's death changed the family's plans. Now, after a less-than-exciting trip from France, Sara was about to assume some new duties. She would have to help her expatriate parents cope with not only the loss of one of their sons but with the end of their life back home in Louisiana, to which they could not return because of the American Civil War.

The trip by stagecoach to Mexico City would have to be by way of Xalapa. French and Mexican forces were constantly skirmishing with each other along the route that went through Córdoba and Orizaba. Staying in Veracruz was not an option: Sara had only to look from her hotel balcony down into the street to see the latest victims of yellow fever being carried on stretchers toward the cemetery.

The night before the Yorkes left Veracruz, Sara and her mother were busy sewing little ounces of gold into unmentionable parts of their underwear in the hope that the bandidos along the highway would not think of looking there during a robbery. Sara was well aware that her brother had been killed by bandidos along that same route, via Xalapa and Perote, only a few weeks earlier, and she and her mother planned to offer no resistance.

What the Yorkes didn't fully realize was that the bandidos had long ago figured out the ploy of sewing gold into underwear. Most hotels between Veracruz and Mexico City kept a pile of blankets in the lobby to provide cover when whole stagecoaches full of passengers arrived totally naked.

It was on the second or third night out of Veracruz that Sara experienced something she later wrote that the English language could not possibly describe. As author Blair Niles later put it in her book, *Passengers to Mexico,* "an accident had delayed the stage and the passengers had been compelled to spend the night in a native adobe hut. Cots had been set up for them in the same room. It was, in fact, the only room—with the man of the house, the man's wife, their children, and their various domestic animals, including their pigs. And it was on this night that [a] team of mules put in their heads and breathed over the cots, on one of which Sara lay sleepless."[6]

The Yorke family lived in downtown Mexico City, opposite the Church of La Profesa, on Calle San Francisco near the Hotel Iturbide. When they arrived back in the capital after their long journey from Veracruz, Mexico City was still celebrating General Zaragoza's victory over the French at Puebla on May 5. Still, the many visitors to the Yorke household carried their weapons. They all had horrifying tales to tell, and not one of them would dare to go out at night unarmed. Sara fully realized she was not in Paris anymore.

The News Reaches France

Back in Paris, the news of the May 5 French defeat at Puebla still had not arrived more than a month later. Napoleon III wrote to Archduke Maximilian in Austria that he was just as eager as anyone else to learn what had been going on in Mexico for the past month, but said that General Lorencez had calculated that he'd be in Mexico's capital by May 25. Napoleon was sure that the next mail would bring news confirming the French army's arrival in Mexico City.

It didn't work out that way, of course. Although French newspapers were in denial at first, reporting "glorious victories" in which the Mexicans were "completely defeated," the real story began to leak from other countries, whose diplomats were writing home from Mexico.[7] The Prussian minister in Mexico City, Baron Wagner, sent his government a report that was immediately relayed to the Prussian delegation in Paris. Others followed, and soon Napoleon III could no longer hide the truth. The French public was upset, and the emperor decided to use the anger to his own advantage. He promised to avenge the defeat at Puebla and to restore France's national honor.

Napoleon III thought first of the morale of the French army. Trying to put things in the best light, he wrote to Lorencez and congratulated him on what he had heard was a great success at the Cliffs of Acultzingo. Saying that he was sorry to hear about the apparent setback at Puebla, he wrote, "Such are the fortunes of war, and occasional reverses sometimes cloud brilliant successes; but do not lose heart; the honor of the country is involved, and you will be supported by all the reinforcements you need...Express to the troops under your command my complete satisfaction with their courage and perseverance in enduring fatigues and privations."[8]

Napoleon III wanted his Second Empire to recover in the nineteenth century the power and markets in the world that France had lost in the eighteenth century, so he set out immediately to line up reinforcements. Army officers who earlier had helped him gain power had been eagerly awaiting a foreign adventure like this. They swamped the French War Office with applications.

8

A Mexican General In, a French General Out

(Late May through Early June 1862)

Zaragoza Gets Reinforcements

After all of the casualty reports were in, Zaragoza's scouts told him he had about four hundred more men still standing than did the French. That didn't mean he was ready to go on the offensive.

First, he had sampled the French army twice by now: once at the Cliffs of Acultzingo and once from his forts atop Guadalupe Hill. In both cases, his men had been firing downhill and the French had been poorly led, but this kind of luck wouldn't hold out forever. He still wasn't sure what his troops' capability would be in the open field. Second, he was waiting for General O'Horan's cavalry brigade to get back from its successful ambush in Atlixco, which had kept Imperialista general Márquez out of action. Third, help was on the way from the state of Zacatecas: six thousand new recruits under his old colleague and mentor, General Jesús González-Ortega.

The French had reached Orizaba on May 18. González-Ortega had left Zacatecas on the 19, headed toward Puebla. The sum of thirty thousand pesos was being sent from Mexico City to cover his expenses for the next ten days. Zaragoza could wait.

General Jesús González-Ortega had stepped down as war minister in 1861 to serve as governor of Zacatecas and to recruit men and raise money for the army in that area. As the forces of Spain, Britain, and France began to arrive later that year, martial law had been declared in the cities of Veracruz and Puebla, and in four other states in anticipation of hostilities. Two more states were added in the early spring of 1862, and now, after the Battle of Puebla, the whole country was under martial law.

Ortega's job would be to help Zaragoza pursue the French. The goal was to force Lorencez back to Veracruz and let the bandidos, guerilla bands, and yellow fever each play their part in the ultimate defeat of the French.

Still, Ortega wanted to avoid further bloodshed. He sent a letter to French minister Pierre Saligny and asked if a cease-fire of some sort might be arranged to allow further diplomatic negotiations. He said it would look better for both countries if things were settled with diplomacy, but that in any case, Mexicans would never accept a monarchy. Ortega told President Juárez about his letter, but was politely told to stick to military matters. Pierre Saligny never bothered to answer the letter, and it became obvious that the French intended to resolve the situation with military force.

The Mexican *Soldaderas*

Along with Ortega's new recruits came hundreds of *soldaderas,* women who were motivated by patriotism, employment, support, marriage, or all of the above, and who trudged alongside the men and acted as servants, cooks, nurses, and messengers. Mexican generals in previous wars had tried to exclude the women, only to be told by higher authorities that most of the men would desert or starve to death without them. One thing the army did not provide in Mexico was food. That was up to the *soldaderas.* Now, here they were, not only foraging for food but carrying some of the soldiers' equipment along with their own belongings and sometimes children. Although many *soldaderas* had served in Puebla on May 5, they had not been seen in large numbers like this since the tragic accident at San Andrés Chalchicomula on March 6.

One such woman, forty-six-year-old Ignacia Reachy, had actually started a women's battalion to defend Guadalajara against the French a few months earlier. A friend of General Zaragoza's, she became a second lieutenant and had been transferred to his command when he had taken over for General Uraga in March. She was captured by the French as she covered for General Arteaga when he had been wounded at the Cliffs of Acultzingo on April 28. The Mexicans were still hoping to recover her when Ortega arrived with reinforcements in May and the Mexicans approached the French encampment at Orizaba.

Soldaderas had been part of the Mexican army since the 1810 War of Independence against Spain, where the women had outnumbered the Mexican soldiers two to one. Not all of them were heroic in battle. Some stood sentinel while soldiers slept; others tended horses, cooked for large groups, or cared for the wounded. Still others became arms smugglers, spies (for both sides), prostitutes, or *chusmas* (rabble camp followers).

Many of Ortega's soldiers had been recruited by the *soldaderas*. He knew very well that if the women had not been part of the deal, the men would not have been there either.[1]

French Supply Problems

Transportation and supply lines were still a problem for the French. A major event in Veracruz was still the arrival of the *conducta* (convoy) carrying gold and silver from the inland mines to the coast. As many as sixty wagons, under the whips of expert *arrieros* (mule drivers), would pull into town under military escort, carrying more than one and one-quarter million dollars' worth of precious metals. Over the next two days, the valuable cargo would be taken first to the warehouse of a British firm and then hauled to the wharf. Other businesses had been established to service the rare metals trade, such as vendors of fruits, vegetables, fish, meats, and grain that supplied the transportation firms involved in the exportation of the metallic ores.

Try as they might, the French were never able to figure out how to deal with an acute shortage of horses and mules. They had not brought nearly enough animals themselves, figuring that it would be easy to acquire them upon arrival. The locals in Veracruz, however, had been through situations like this before with the War for Independence against Spain from 1810 to 1821, and again during the American invasion in 1847. Their strategy was to send their wives and daughters to Xalapa and do their maritime trading down the coast at Alvarado and Tlacotalpan whenever an enemy set foot in Veracruz—and they could make animals disappear quickly when necessary.

Admiral Jurien, General Lorencez, and any French commander who followed them could never have the supply line issue far from their minds. The supply line was a tether between the Port of Veracruz and wherever French forces were bivouacked, and their survival depended on its protection at all costs.[2]

Napoleon III's Hidden Agenda

In Washington, D.C., Mexico's Matías Romero, chargé d'affaires, wrote to Secretary of State Seward that the real purpose of the French expedition was now "beyond all doubt." Their real mission, said Romero, was "to subvert the republi-

can form of government now existing in Mexico, and to establish there a monarchy, with a European prince upon the throne…"

Romero reminded Seward that Britain, Spain, and France had all signed an
agreement at La Soledad on February 19, solemnly declaring that they "designed
nothing against the independence, sovereignty and integrity" of Mexico. He said
that the Mexican government, accepting their statement in good faith, had
allowed the foreigners to leave the unhealthy region of Veracruz, "where the
influence of the climate had already decimated them, and would have been sufficient to destroy them without any fighting."

The Mexican chargé d'affaires had harsh words for General Juan Almonte,
whom he referred to as "a degenerate Mexican," saying that as soon as Almonte
showed up, the French had decided not only to ignore the agreement they had
signed at La Soledad, but also the very government they had already acknowledged to be "ruling the country constitutionally." The French, claimed Romero,
were now using Almonte to carry out Napoleon III's instructions to overthrow
the Mexican government, which they now declared was "an oppressive and violent minority."

"This is not the first time," wrote Romero, "that their words are in lamentable
contradiction to their deeds." As further evidence, Romero attached to his letter a
copy of the pronouncement made by Almonte at Córdoba, naming himself as the
head of a government that the French planned to install in Mexico City, "under,"
as Romero put it, "the shadow and under the pressure of foreign bayonets."

Romero asked Seward for "assurances" from the United States that might help
strengthen the determination of the Mexicans to resist the French takeover. He
said he was sure the United States was aware of the gravity of the situation and
that it would not "look with indifference" at the threat of "foreign intervention
and domination" represented by the French.[3]

Seward was not really in a position to pay more than lip service to the Mexican
cause. He had the Civil War going on, and this was no time to pick a fight with
the French. As he said in a memo to the American ambassador in Paris, William
L. Dayton, "We do not desire to suppress the fact that our sympathies are with
Mexico, and our wishes are for the restoration of peace within her borders; nor do
we in any sense, for any purpose, disapprove of her present form of government
or distrust her administration."

Seward told Dayton that President Abraham Lincoln had specifically ordered
that there be no formal communication with the French government concerning
the Mexican situation. "When we desire explanations from France," said Seward,
"or when an occasion shall have arrived to express discontents," Ambassador

Dayton would be called upon to "communicate directly and explicitly" with the French authorities. Until then, said the secretary of state, "it is only prudent" not to raise the Mexican issue.[4]

The Bishop Blames the Liberals

As parishioners sat in the pews of Puebla's cathedral, staring beyond the main altar at the golden sunburst and the white, carved stone angels atop the grand atrium, they took comfort in the fact that the liberals under Zaragoza had not taken revenge against this particular citadel of conservative Catholicism for the local pro-French sympathies. During the War of the Reform, many churches had been ransacked and stripped of their gold, silver, and precious artwork, but not this one. That day, the bishop of Puebla climbed the carpeted stairs to the octagonal pulpit, with its bell-shaped, richly gilded canopy just to the right of the congregation, and began to express his disappointment at the withdrawal of the French forces.

It was all the fault of the godless liberals, the bishop maintained, that the French were unable to rescue Puebla. He pointed out that the Juaristas had simply occupied the two forts atop Guadalupe Hill and, in his view, had done little or nothing to protect the citizens of Puebla from any harm that may have resulted from the battle of May 5. (He conveniently ignored the fact that the citizens were spared from any effects of the battle at all.) The curate was especially incensed at President Benito Juárez's declaration that not only should May 5 be declared a national holiday for the unexpected Mexican victory, but that the town should be renamed "Puebla de Zaragoza" in honor of the triumphant commanding general.

The city had been named Puebla de Los Angeles for three hundred years, and as far as the bishop was concerned, it would stay that way. How dare the liberals presume to speak for us? he asked the congregation. He reminded them that the French had not left Mexico, and predicted that they would regroup and show their superiority before long. They all prayed for the blessed day when Puebla de los Angeles would finally be liberated (by the French, of course). Then they walked beneath the towering arches of the Gothic central nave and out the main doorway into the sunlight of the Plaza de Armas, the town's central square.

Don't Leave Home without a Pistol

Mexico City, meanwhile, was not taking the French army very seriously. People were still going to bullfights and strolling along the Paseo de la Reforma. Shops were filled with luxurious jewelry, silver, and porcelain goods from France, as well as lavishly-embroidered sombreros and silver buttons for *charro* (colorful, rustic Mexican cowboy) suits. Fountains splashed merrily, guitars were strummed romantically, flowers blossomed from balconies, and finely dressed ladies waved their fans. Invasion? What invasion?

That was during the day. After dark, it was a different story, as British journalist Charles Lempriere wrote: "When once the shades of night fall, the Great Gate is closed, and the houses are entirely silent, and guarded as if the city was under martial law…The streets are deserted; and every man carries a revolver."[5]

People walked down the very middle of the street at night, staying away from doorways and alleys. The foreigners were much more apprehensive than the locals. Minister Baron Wagner of Prussia was severely beaten in a street attack, and there was a rumor going around that foreigners would be massacred in great numbers on Mexican Independence Day, September 16.

Ambassador Corwin and the Yorkes

Sara Yorke began to fit right into the expatriate milieu of her parents. Among the many guests visiting their apartment was American ambassador Thomas Corwin. The Yorkes were part of the so-called embassy crowd, and mingled frequently with the diplomats and their families. Corwin loved to tell young Sara stories about how he had grown up in rural Ohio, driving in wagon trains thirty miles to Cincinnati, the nearest town. He claimed that breaking a leg in a wagon accident when he was a young boy had given him time to learn to read. From there, he said, he joined a lawyer's office and later became Ohio's governor, United States senator, Treasury secretary, and now ambassador to Mexico—all because of the wagon accident.

What Corwin didn't tell Sara, but was writing home to Washington, was that French reinforcements were pouring into Mexico by the thousands. Sooner or later, he reported, they would make another try at Puebla. All commerce between Mexico City and the Gulf was now forbidden, so his letters went to Acapulco on the Pacific and then by way of Panama to reach Washington.

Napoleon Makes Some Changes

Two weeks had gone by since Napoleon III's letter to General Lorencez, and some ugly details about the debacle at Puebla were becoming public. This was no longer the quick-and-easy conquest he had imagined.

The Emperor named Élie Frédéric Forey as the French commander-in-chief to replace General Lorencez. Forey, in his late fifties, had helped Napoleon III win his coup d'etat in December of 1851 and was highly regarded for his outstanding performance in the Crimea and in Italy. As he wrote out his detailed instructions for the new commander, Napoleon had nothing but praise for Pierre Saligny, writing that "ever since the beginning of the expedition to Mexico, his dispatches have been earmarked by the good sense, firmness and dignity of France, and I have no doubt that if his advice had been followed our flag would be floating over Mexico today."[6]

Napoleon told Forey that he had seen reports from the Prussian and Belgian consuls in Puebla, along with those of others reporting to their governments, that the city of Puebla was "silent and sad" on the day after the Mexican victory and did not share in the "joy of the Mexican troops." The emperor thus concluded that Lorencez had not been misled by Saligny or Almonte and that "the population awaited us as liberators." He didn't really blame Lorencez so much for losing the battle as for blaming it on everyone else. "Quarrels of vanity" had compromised the French effort in Mexico, said the Emperor, and he wanted no more of them.[7]

Lorencez would not find out about it for at least a month, but Forey and eight thousand reinforcement troops would leave for Mexico on July 28. Forey's second-in-command, General Achille Bazaine, would follow with twelve thousand more.

9

The Battle of Cerro del Borrego

(June 4–14, 1862)

Seeking Weapons for Juárez

Matías Romero continued his efforts in Washington on behalf of the Juárez government. Since there were no weapons factories in Mexico—at least none that could produce the quantity of armaments needed to deal with the French—Romero asked Secretary of State William Seward if the United States could issue an export license and lend Mexico forty thousand dollars for such a purchase. Seward said that the license might be possible, but that lending government money to Mexico would provoke trouble with Napoleon III. With the Civil War in progress, antagonizing the French would be out of the question.

Seward did have a suggestion, though: why not try to raise the funds from private investors? Romero set about doing just that, and within a short time, he collected enough money to place an order with a New York arms dealer. The Mexicans would buy thirty-six thousand muskets, four thousand swords, and one thousand pistols, plus the appropriate ammunition.

When Romero applied to the United States Treasury Department for an export license, there was silence at first, and then a denial. Seward was apologetic, saying that the rejection didn't come from his office but from that of Secretary of War Edwin Stanton. Stanton had ruled that, because of the Civil War, all armament production had to be for the exclusive use of the United States military.

The matter might have been dropped there, but Romero soon discovered that Seward had approved the export of horses, mules, and transport wagons to the French army in Mexico. The French were running into shortages for several reasons: they had not brought enough animals or wagons with them, Mexicans loyal to the Juárez regime were hiding their animals to create a shortage, and others were afraid to sell or rent animals because of the Juárez death decree back in January that would affect anyone caught dealing with the French.

Exasperated, Romero asked Seward why it was all right to sell things to the French but not to the Mexicans. The only reply that Seward could offer was that the United States government needed all the weapons and ammunition but not the horses, mules, and wagons. It wasn't just Seward and Stanton who wouldn't back down; Abraham Lincoln issued a presidential order banning any U.S. arms or ammunition exports for the remainder of the Civil War.

Romero had not run out of options. He had already raised the money, so he quietly began to arrange for weapons and ammunition to be smuggled aboard ships from San Francisco to Mazatlán and other Mexican ports along the Pacific. Even though it was riskier, he also arranged for some illegal gun-running between New York and Matamoros, a port on the Gulf of Mexico that the French did not yet control.

Egyptian and Sudanese Troops

The French were not only short of horses and mules, but of plain, ordinary foot soldiers. Hundreds were coming down with yellow fever, so General Forey decided to try some French Foreign Legion troops, who had performed well in the deserts of northern Africa, to replace regular troops who were more vulnerable to heat exhaustion and diseases.

The legionnaires would probably do well in the tropical climate, but there were not nearly enough of them. The slave trade came to mind, and French authorities already had an Egyptian connection that would provide them with the bodies they needed. Blacks from the Sudan were already being kidnapped by the Egyptians and used for slave labor in Alexandria and Cairo. On paper, Egypt at the time was considered part of Turkey. Foreign governments played along by sending their ambassadors to Constantinople and only assigning consuls to Alexandria. The French, however, had a secret agreement with the sultan's right-hand man in Egypt—known as the khedive—whose family they had supported in the 1830s.

The French had to move quickly and stealthily. A ship carrying troops bound for French Indo-China (now Vietnam) pulled into the port of Alexandria. As usual, the troops got off and headed across the Isthmus of Suez by land, because the canal was still being built. At Suez, they boarded a second ship for the final part of their journey.

What happened next touched off a protest from the Americans. Fifty young black men from Sudan were grabbed from the streets of Alexandria and forced aboard the ship that had just dropped off the French soldiers. Another four hundred fifty Sudanese blacks from the khedive's own army were added, and the frigate *Le Seine* pulled out of the harbor and sailed for Veracruz. American consul William S. Thayer protested to the khedive's minister about not only the slavery issue but also the hostile act toward Mexico. Did this mean that Turkey was also at war with Mexico? The minister indicated the sultan knew nothing about it. When he took his case to Washington, Thayer was told to just forget about it. Secretary of State Seward made it clear that the United States government had enough on its hands with the Civil War, and just didn't want to get involved.

Somebody's Up on the Cliff

During the three weeks that the French army had been in Orizaba, General Lorencez had ordered the building of fortifications out of earth and stone, and had barricades erected all around the town. To strengthen the defense of the town, he had also called in the various units that were patrolling the highway to protect supply convoys between Orizaba and Veracruz. Nothing was overlooked.

Nothing?

Well, yes, there was the four-hundred-foot cliff, known as Cerro del Borrego, rising up over the *alameda* (arboretum) at the west end of town, but the thick vines and underbrush covering the sheer bluff were considered impenetrable. For some unexplained reason, Lorencez decided not to post any sentries atop the mountain overlooking the town.

On June 13, 1862, at about 10:00 PM, French troops in the valley below could tell that there was some movement taking place up on Cerro del Borrego. There was no moonlight. It was pitch black and approaching midnight as Captain Guillame Détric began to lead a detail of seventy-five French soldiers to take over the summit before the enemy could make any kind of move.

They had been climbing for almost two hours when they reached a rock ledge. They couldn't really see each other, but Captain Détrie managed to gather them together for a brief rest, relying on little more than their sense of hearing. As they paused, they heard more sounds above them. Someone suggested that it might be some residents of Orizaba who were hiding up there. Détrie named three men as scouts to climb higher and investigate.

That's when it happened.

They were met with a shower of gunfire directly from above.

As the vertical firefight continued in total darkness, Détrie and several others climbed higher. They stumbled onto a group of men struggling for control of a cannon. Three of them were his scouts. The Frenchmen seized the cannon. As the rest of Détrie's detail joined him near the summit, an hour-long firefight continued with the hidden enemy.

Reinforcements arrived at about 3:30 AM, doubling the strength of Détrie's detail and enabling him to lead a bayonet charge to the top. Détrie was seriously wounded, but he had gained control of the summit. The question was, exactly whom had they been fighting?

Sunrise provided the answer.

It was General Ortega's newly recruited troops who had become disoriented in the dark. Détrie had no idea that there had been two thousand of them, and that most of them had fled in panic. He had led just one hundred fifty, counting the reinforcements, and had lost two dead and twenty-eight wounded.

As dawn broke over the hills, a horrifying scene greeted the citizens of Orizaba. The arms and legs and bodies of some two hundred soldiers hung from tree branches and rocky ledges all up and down the face of the hill.

All of them were Mexicans.

The dead soldiers had been part of Ortega's battalion from Zacatecas. It was quite apparent that they had no idea where they were or whom they had been fighting. Had they been able to hold that position at the top of Cerro del Borrego, the French would have been forced to evacuate Orizaba.

Captain Détrie was decorated, given a promotion, and called a hero. Zaragoza and Ortega withdrew their troops, and the French settled down to contend with the rainy season and await their reinforcements. The battle had not just been for that hill; it had been for the control of Orizaba.

On the morning of June 15, General Juan Almonte posted a proclamation, all but claiming credit for Détrie's victory. He did mention Détrie once, but claimed that what he called the "Franco Mexican" army was fighting for "independence and Mexican nationality," while the troops under Zaragoza and Ortega were defending "pillage and barbarism." He urged the locals to place their faith in his Franco Mexican army and signed the document as though he had been the one in charge all along.[1]

Lorencez Gets Fired

There was a lull of about two weeks, and then General Lorencez received an official communication from the war minister, telling him that Napoleon III was not pleased with the attack on Puebla, especially the timing and the placement of artillery. The emperor was said to deplore the infighting among Lorencez, Saligny, and Almonte—which had been observed and commented on by the enemy. The minister warned Lorencez not to do or say anything else that would upset Saligny, adding, "General Forey will soon assume the supreme command; until then, confine yourself to organizing the resistance and your supplies."

For General Charles Latrille, the Count of Lorencez, the expedition was over—and so was his career.[2]

10

Fighting a Skirmish Dressed in Drag

(June 15 through August 15, 1862)

The Confederates Send an Emissary

Thomas Corwin was not the only American delegate sent to Mexico to represent the interest of the states to the north. The Confederate States of America designated John T. Pickett as its man in Mexico City. Pickett had been the U.S. consul in Veracruz until early 1861, and he knew very well that the North would try to gain the upper hand in trade matters, engaging sugar and cotton entrepreneurs in Mexico to exclude slave labor as a way to stifle the economy of the South.

Whereas Corwin, as he had told Sara Yorke, had grown up as "just a wagon boy," Pickett was the son of wealthy Kentucky parents. Corwin had taught himself to read, but Pickett had been given a fine education. There was just one major drawback to John T. Pickett: he was crude, insolent, and very much a fighter. He had been involved with insurgencies in Hungary and Cuba, and had served as a soldier of fortune alongside William Walker in a number of plundering and pillaging raids in northern Mexico. He had a toughened, heartless disregard for Mexican officials.

Pickett's instructions from the Confederates left him plenty of leeway. He was allowed to ignore the Juárez government and make deals with local authorities wherever convenient. He was urged to recruit private Mexican ships and provide them with arms and ammunition so they could cruise against U.S. ships, both in the Gulf of Mexico and in the Pacific. The attitude was that anything the Mexicans didn't like, at whatever level, could be resolved with a little bribery.

What probably had never dawned on Pickett was that the Mexicans had already made their choice. In a secret meeting, the Mexican Congress had decided that they'd better take sides with the North. The new U.S. ambassador, Thomas Corwin, was already popular for having made speeches as a U.S. senator in the late 1840s opposing a war with Mexico, and he had arrived with a pledge from Abraham Lincoln's government that the United States would not seek any further expansion of its territory.

The South, on the other hand, was perceived as wanting to expand slavery and push for states' rights. Juárez and the Mexicans were trying to build a strong central government, so the states' rights idea was alien to them, and they had opposed slavery all along.

Pickett didn't know it, but most of his correspondence home to Richmond was being intercepted by the Mexicans and by U.S. operatives. Pickett told his Confederate superiors that he thought Mexican military officers should infiltrate and undermine the U.S. army, so that it would be easier to beat, and that they should take extra care not to be captured or they'd have to work for the first time in their lives, either hoeing corn or picking cotton.[1]

In contrast to Pickett, the newspaper *El Siglo Diez y Nueve* claimed the Confederacy wanted to expand into all of Mexico, Central America, and the Caribbean, and to turn the Gulf into "a Confederate lake." Pickett didn't help much when asked if he were seeking recognition. He said that he was there to recognize them, if he could find a government that would stand still long enough.[2]

Working closely with Juárez, Thomas Corwin worked out an agreement that would allow the United States to confront the Confederates in the disputed territory of Arizona. The Yankees would be granted permission to unload troops at the port of Guaymas, on the Gulf of California between the Mexican state of Baja California, and the mainland. Then they would march through Sonora to deal with the Rebels. Pickett was so enraged when he heard that he had been outmaneuvered. He blustered and threatened that if the agreement were real, the Mexicans might expect to see "10,000 Confederate diplomats" cross the Río Grande in retaliation.[3]

Corwin and his top assistant, diplomat Edward L. Plumb, decided they'd better launch some countermeasures: One, warn all Mexican exporters not to let their goods fall into Confederate hands. This was not only because they would never reach the Northern ports where the customers were, but also because Confederate money for the goods would have little or no value. Two, promote use of the direct Veracruz to New York route via Dunbar steamship lines to avoid crossing through Rebel-held territory. Three, flood the area with counterfeit Confederate money to make it worthless. Four, and this may have been the most important, since Pickett loved to get into bar fights, be ready to have him arrested and thrown out of the country at the very next such opportunity.

It wasn't just diplomacy that motivated Corwin and Plumb. Both were investors in companies trying to win contracts to build a railroad across the narrowest part of Mexico between the Gulf and the Pacific. Because of their involvement in those and other projects, they were acutely aware of anything that might jeopardize U.S. business interests. Pickett was one such threat.

A Look at Orizaba

The third highest mountain in North America, and the highest in Mexico, is the Pico de Orizaba, which overlooks the town of that same name from about fifteen miles to the northwest. It has a cap of snow for at least three months of every year. Several rocky streams wind their way through the town, and the sparkling, fresh cold water prompted nineteenth-century German visitors to think about starting breweries there.

Little boys in Orizaba were very impressed with the presence of the French army. Cayetano Rodríguez Beltrán, an author of historical novels in the nineteenth century, pictures the boys as engrossed in military games, marching, executing numerous maneuvers, improvising bugles and drums, firing on imaginary enemies with sticks used as guns, and using recesses during school hours for the development of defense and attack strategy.

Anxious to devote as much time as possible to their pretended battles, the youngsters would rise early in the mornings and go into the streets sounding through cupped hands an imitation of the reveille bugle call. They marched about their chores with a military step, carrying broomsticks on their shoulders as guns.[4]

Utilities, Communication, and Transportation

Veracruz was still the only city in Mexico with gas lighting, but the French were trying hard to get a telegraph connection installed between the coast and Orizaba, some eighteen years after Samuel F. B. Morse first demonstrated its use between Washington, D.C., and Baltimore in 1844. Spy technology was still apparently not advanced enough for the Mexicans to tap in to the French system, because there's no mention of any such intrusion in the various accounts of the conflict between 1861 and 1867.

Although the Spaniards had established Orizaba in the 1500s to protect the highway between Veracruz and Mexico City, it was becoming obvious to the French that the town would never hold all the reinforcements that would be arriving. Thirty thousand soldiers camping next to a town of just ten thousand would be overwhelming. As many as twelve thousand of the additional troops would have to be diverted to Xalapa.

Why Not Xalapa?

There were lots of good things to say about Xalapa. Travelers and historians had been writing about it for decades. After enduring the twelve-hour ride from the tropical lowlands through the rough, desolate *chaparral* (evergreen-forested) region, stagecoach passengers would unanimously say that the air would suddenly begin to smell fresher just over an hour from Xalapa. At three thousand feet above sea level, there was a sense about Xalapa that the threat of yellow fever had subsided or even vanished.

Any stagecoach excursion to Xalapa would enter an area of dark, heavily wooded mountains. The climate was mild in the daytime, still aided by breezes from the Gulf of Mexico, but pleasantly cool at night, as a result of the refreshing air from the mountains.

American soldiers passing through Xalapa in 1847 described it as one of the most pleasant towns in Mexico. They wrote home not only about the beautiful scenery and flowers, but also about the gorgeous, enchanting women. A stroll through the winding, narrow *callejones* (alleys) at night was guaranteed to quicken the pulse of any soldier. The barred casement windows of the houses were like little stages, illuminating the lovely señoritas inside, who were waving their fans, playing musical instruments, or crocheting. The walls on either side of the windows were covered with hanging bougainvillea, adding beauty and fragrance to the setting. Other nineteenth-century travelers passing through Xalapa wrote that they even noticed an improvement in the people as well as in the air quality, referring to the locals as not only more handsome but better dressed and more intelligent than in other areas.

Although residents in the steamy Port of Veracruz could escape to the nearby wooded village of Medellín for recreation on weekends, the wives and daughters of those who could afford it were sent to live in Xalapa to avoid the heat and disease. A merchant who had really become successful would at the very least establish a weekend or summer home in Xalapa, if he were not to move there year 'round, and let his subordinates run the business back in the port.

Coffee was the primary crop grown around Xalapa, but the abundant rainfall also favored the growth of rice, tobacco, bananas, avocados, and sugarcane. There was also a mixture of the plants typically found in both tropical and temperate regions. Apples and peaches grew alongside oranges, limes, and grapefruit. Artichokes and melons were found growing near onions and squash. To the north-west of Xalapa, continuing toward Perote, Puebla, and Mexico City, fruit trees and flowers gradually gave way to forests of oak and taller evergreens. Moss and lichens began to cover the rocks. The scenery reminded many a traveler of attractive mountain areas in Europe or in the United States.

Why weren't people saying these nice things about Orizaba? The roadway from the coast to Mexico City also climbs as it goes through that town, but apparently the change in altitude was not as abrupt and the mixture of tropical and temperate climates was not as prominent, so the same sensations didn't quite occur. To compensate for its runner-up status in the environmental and beauty categories, Orizaba had always been more competitive in attracting commerce and industry. The route from Veracruz to Mexico City was shorter through Oriz-aba than it was through Xalapa. For a stagecoach traveler just passing through, Xalapa was not worth the detour.[5]

In any event, the Mexicans were thoroughly enjoying the controversy that was raging in France as to the value of their military expedition. A spokesman for Napoleon III claimed that the reports from Prussia's minister in Mexico proved that the public was demanding a monarchy, and that the arrival of the reinforced French army was eagerly awaited in Mexico City.

Mexican President Benito Juárez thought otherwise. He wrote to his minister in Paris, M. de Montluc, and told him to forget about trying to reason with Napoleon:

> There is a deliberate intention on the part of the Imperial Government to humiliate Mexico and impose its will on us. This is a truth confirmed by facts; there is no help but defense…The arrival of new and numerous troops has caused no fear or discouragement; on the contrary, it has revived public spirit, and today there is one sentiment in the whole country, the defense of liberty and independence of Mexico…whatever elements may be employed against us, the Imperial Government will not obtain the submission of the Mexicans, and…its armies will not have a single day of rest.[6]

Fighting a Skirmish Dressed in Drag

Meanwhile, the biggest problem for the French army at Orizaba was boredom. Occasional patrols were sent into the hinterlands to chase bandidos or guerilla bands. Mexicans, delighted at the opposition speeches in the Paris Corps Législa-tif, distributed leaflets with quotations aimed at undermining the expedition, and the French commanding officers were distributing leaflets with the rebuttals. This was no way to spend a summer in the mountains.

Among those in the camp at Orizaba were the Zouaves. They were dark-skinned Algerians, Egyptians, and Sudanese who had been recruited—some rather forcefully—from the streets of Alexandria in Egypt. After having been given bright-colored baggy pants and turbans, they had developed a great deal of self-pride and military bearing. They had fought bravely in the earlier battle, despite Lorencez's tactical errors at Puebla.

As the summer of 1862 dragged on, the Zouaves badly wanted to fit in with their French brethren, so they pitched in eagerly to fight another enemy: boredom. There were shows almost every night. Zouave soldiers displayed magic tricks with their turbans, twirled fire with their batons, sang songs, and ate live frogs and snakes.

After watching more reptiles being swallowed than the audience could stand, someone finally came up with the idea of putting on plays. There were plenty of talented soldiers available. It just took a lot of extra courage for those who had to play the female parts. The script of *Michel et Christine*, which had been a hit in Paris just a year earlier, was obtained. Several weeks were spent making costumes, building scenery, and rehearsing lines. The night of August 10 was set for the final dress rehearsal.

What no one had bothered to tell the cast and stage crew was that General Lorencez had ceased sending patrols up into the overlooking hills two weeks earlier. In the general's mind, the Mexicans had learned their lesson from the disastrous Battle of Cerro del Borrego almost two months earlier, and simply would never dare to consider another attack.

A small Mexican patrol on reconnaissance just happened to arrive atop Cerro del Borrego as the dress rehearsal was under way. Finding several cannons, which had not been moved since the night of June 13, they untied artillery shells from their horses and got into position.

As the actors playing Michel and Christine were reciting their lines, several artillery shells came tearing through the roof of the building. There were loud explosions and gunfire all around outside. Cast and crew grabbed their weapons, scrambling to get out the nearest door and run for cover behind rocks and trees. From there, they fired back up the hill at the unexpected—and invisible attackers. The shooting went on for three hours before the Mexicans remounted and galloped off into the darkness.

The next night, the French once again posted sentries atop Cerro del Borrego and all the surrounding hills. The production of *Michel et Christine* came off without a hitch.[7]

11

General Zaragoza Dies

(August through September 1862)

More Mischief from John T. Pickett

Still angered by the deal worked out between Mexican president Benito Juárez and United States ambassador Thomas Corwin regarding the right to unload Yankee troops on Mexican soil, Pickett made a counter-offer. He promised to give back California, Arizona, and New Mexico to the Mexicans. All Juárez had to do was cancel the agreement allowing the Union troops to gain access to Arizona by crossing through Mexican territory. If Mexico didn't cooperate, Pickett warned, Confederate forces would seize the Mexican border state of Tamaulipas within twenty days and join forces with the French.

President Juárez and Ambassador Corwin laughed at the absurdity of Pickett's threats and promises, but both agreed that he must be declared persona non grata and be kicked out of Mexico at the earliest opportunity.

A Toxic Surprise at the Wine Bar

If putting on plays was the diversion of choice for French troops in Orizaba, the small French garrison in Veracruz had another way of fighting boredom: hitting the bars. It wasn't hard to find a lively cantina in Veracruz on any given night. With or without the French invaders, ships were arriving from foreign ports almost daily. The nights were still steamy a full month into autumn, and the sailors needed their drinks and their women. The French soldiers in Veracruz had something their comrades in Orizaba did not have: access to females. For example, three exotic, smooth-skinned *jarochas* (coastal peasant girls), all younger than twenty, served as waitresses and dancing girls at Manuel González' wine bar in Veracruz.

The girls would do a dance set, perhaps La Bamba combined with an erotic blend of bolero and cachoza, that had the troops clamoring for more, and then would serve wine while an organ grinder and his monkeys took to the stage. By some strange coincidence, all three had the first name of "Dolores": Dolores Arellano, Dolores Barajos, and Dolores Carrajal.

Not only had the three Doloreses grown tired of being groped by drunken French soldiers, but the owner, Manuel González, was ready to send the French a strong message. One night, several artillerymen who had enjoyed a somewhat extended happy hour, began to feel severe pains on their way back to the barracks. They staggered into camp in throbbing anguish and were rushed to the French military hospital. The doctors determined that they had been poisoned and ordered enemas for everyone. The soldiers weren't exactly overjoyed at that decision, but it may have saved a few of their lives.

Back at the bar, Manuel had fled, but the girls were still there. They were arrested, along with five others believed to have been involved, and tried by a French court-martial on charges of being accessories to attempted murder. Two of the men were given death sentences, a woman who was said to have supplied the poison got life in prison, and Dolores Barajos was sentenced to ten years of hard labor. Dolores Arellano and Dolores Carrajal were acquitted.

All three girls became famous in the French newspapers. While Dolores Barajos served her sentence at Fort San Juan de Ulua in Veracruz Harbor, the others got new dancing jobs.[1]

Guerilla Warfare Most Effective

Meanwhile, as President Benito Juárez had promised, the French army "would not get a single day of rest." Just as they had disrupted the play rehearsal for *Michel et Christine,* the Mexicans continued to wage guerilla warfare around Orizaba and Veracruz. Mexicans who were found collaborating with the French were killed, French soldiers found wandering alone would be executed on the spot, and any French patrols entering villages between Orizaba and Veracruz were subject to armed attack.

Even outside the Veracruz-Orizaba area, no Frenchman was safe. In Tampico, many miles north along the Gulf coast from Veracruz, the French, who had occupied the town, thought they had control until the locals started stabbing their soldiers in the street.

Generals Zaragoza and González-Ortega agreed that this would be a great time to go on the offensive and annihilate the French before their reinforcements arrived. President Juárez disagreed. He questioned what their fall-back position would be if they were to lose a major military engagement, and insisted that guerilla warfare was the only way to protect valuable troops for later use.

The summer was not quite over and reinforcements had not arrived in any great numbers, but in September the Mexicans suffered a severe blow. General Ignacio Zaragoza, just thirty-two years old, died of typhoid fever. He had apparently picked it up while visiting troops to bolster their morale. By default, General Jesús González-Ortega became commander-in-chief of the Mexican forces.

Ortega was not only a brilliant general but also one of Mexico's most popular politicians. His cheerful, charismatic disposition and remarkable ability to get along with people had earned him enormous public support. In the spring of 1861, when Zaragoza had replaced him as war minister, he had stepped down rather than waste his time working with various cabinet members who were constantly squabbling with one another. Earlier, he had teamed up with Zaragoza on many occasions to defeat the conservatives in the War of the Reform. Now, it was his solemn duty to lead the Mexican army in the current struggle for sovereignty.

Agnes Joy Becomes a Princess

In Washington, D.C., things were not going well for the Union. Yankee troops were defeated in the Second Battle of Bull Run on August 29, and the survivors filed wearily back to the capital. There were ambulances everywhere, and it was hard to raise enough recruits to replace the dead and wounded. These were the dog days of summer, and Washington was in the midst of a heat wave. Even Secretary of State Seward's best horse died of heat stroke.

Despite the heat and the disheartening news from the battlefield, Agnes LeClerq Joy, using just Agnes LeClerq as her maiden name, got married on August 30, the day after the battle. Friends of her younger sister, Ellen, were the bridesmaids, and members of the 31st New York Volunteers, Ellen's husband's unit in the Union army, sat on the bride's side of the church.

The groom was none other than Felix Salm-Salm, the youngest son of the reigning prince of Westphalia. Members of Felix's upstate New York regiment of German-speaking troops sat on the groom's side. The dark-haired prince had a waxed moustache and wore a monocle in his right eye. He was a picture of distinguished elegance.

For Agnes, a dream had come true. She was now a princess, a real live princess. Princess Agnes Salm-Salm. She had no idea that she would eventually wind up in Mexico.

A Little Empire on the Border

President Benito Juárez and his man in Washington, Matías Romero, were trying everything they could to get help from the United States. Juárez had already dismissed any thought of recognizing the Confederacy. He had even published a decree banning any trade with the American Southerners, but there was one city in Mexico that chose to ignore it: Matamoros.

The port city in the northeastern corner of Mexico was just a few yards across the Río Bravo del Norte, the Río Grande to Americans, from Brownsville, Texas. It was controlled by General Santiago Vidaurri. The local people were making fantastic amounts of money from the illegal trade that was passing through town. Weapons and ammunition were pouring into the Confederacy through Matamoros, and cotton, along with other goods the Southerners could no longer export because of the Union blockade, was coming out. Vidaurri's people were not about to give that up.

Vidaurri was governor of the northeastern Mexico states of Nuevo León and Tamaulipas, both of which bordered on Texas. On one hand, he would claim that he backed the Juárez government in Mexico City; on the other hand, he would do whatever he wanted. The Confederates would load their cotton onto barges at Brownsville, clear it through Vidaurri's customs system in Matamoros, and then take it downstream to a small Mexican gulf port called Bagdad and ship it to Europe. At least half a dozen European countries responded with clothing and war matériel.

Matamoros was a busy place. Besides the agents and stevedores of the shipping companies, there were merchants, saloon and hotel keepers to serve them, sailors, prostitutes, spies for both the Union and Confederacy, deserters from both sides of the American Civil War, and several thousand Mexicans who worked as customs inspectors. Before the American Civil War, the population was seven thousand; now it was a thriving fifty thousand.

Texas, just across the river, had been part of Mexico until its war for independence in 1836. It was an independent republic for nine years, it became the twenty-eighth state of the United States, and then it had joined the eleven-state Confederacy, all within a period of about twenty-six years. The Southerners were taking every advantage they could along their extended Texas border with Nuevo León and Tamaulipas, and General Vidaurri was not about to complain. Life was good.

French Reinforcements Arrive

A proud General Élie Frédéric Forey peered through his binoculars from atop one of the nine stone *baluartes* (bulwarks) surrounding the Port of Veracruz. He was observing the last of several thousand troops as they disembarked. Another large contingent would be arriving with General Bazaine in a few weeks.

Right now, the latest group of Zouaves were putting on a great show for the locals. As their ranks flowed down the gangplanks and onto the dock, their sensational maneuvers in their scarlet tassels and crimson-red baggy pants had the crowd mesmerized. Forey hoped they would be as successful in battle.

The fifty-eight-year-old Forey, with a reddish face and prominent white moustache, who had been one Napoleon III's favorites since the coup d'état ten years ago, knew that he had to team up with Pierre Saligny, or else. Failure to do so had been the downfall of both Admiral Jurien and General Lorencez. He knew how to accommodate the emperor; he just had to figure out how to play Saligny.

Satisfied with the arrival, Forey told his officers that the troops were ready to begin their campaign.

Actually, Forey's instructions from Napoleon III were more than just military. General Juan Almonte had already snarled up the situation by publicly proclaiming himself as the head of an interim government sent to set up a monarchy. Forey was to keep Almonte on a shorter leash, diplomatically reducing his self-announced powers while remaining on good terms with him and with any other Mexican general or high-ranking government official who might switch sides to help the French. He was to team up with Saligny as much as possible, but Saligny was to be told that he was reporting to Forey.

Forey's instructions were somewhat Machiavellian in nature. Saligny would hate having to be anyone's subordinate, and Almonte would certainly not enjoy losing his self-proclaimed title as head of state. This balancing act would require both finesse and deceit, neither of which is normally associated with honest, upstanding military commanders.

Forey wasted no time curtailing Almonte's status. One of his first acts was to publish a decree in the newspapers abolishing any government offices that Almonte may have tried to establish. Almonte was ordered to dissolve his ministries, abstain from publishing any law or decree, give up his title as supreme commander of the nation, and limit himself strictly to carrying out the instructions of Napoleon III, as relayed to him by Forey.

Forey was taking the military assignment very seriously, and he did not want to rush into battle as poorly prepared as Lorencez had been. He decided to take a whole month in Veracruz to organize his transportation and supplies. This might have worked in his favor except for one thing: yellow fever. His troops were falling sick, unaccustomed to the tropical climate. When his troops finally marched inland toward Orizaba, many of those who had not been hit by yellow fever came down with malaria. One unit of about two thousand men suffered nine hundred–odd casualties, almost half their original strength. Reports of Forey's dillydallying were getting back to Paris, where Napoleon III was reported to be very depressed.

It was dawning on Napoleon that even though an Assembly of Notables was to be gathered in Mexico City to make it look as though Mexicans were choosing their own government, the rest of the world was not going to believe it—including the Mexicans. Abraham Lincoln had already warned Britain, Spain, and France that any foreign monarchy set up in Mexico backed by European military forces would be considered a hostile act toward the United States, because freeing the continent from any kind of European control had been a top U.S. priority for almost a century. Britain and Spain had already backed off, leaving France with no fig leaf.

Confederates Still Bungling

By now, rumors that Austria's Archduke Maximilian would soon become emperor of Mexico were circulating not only in Europe but throughout both the Union and Confederate states. The Confederates were thrilled at the idea, believing that Mexico under Maximilian would be a friendly ally. Not only would the Confederacy gain recognition, but it could just ignore the United States' Monroe Doctrine and form a military alliance. If the North won, however, any foreign monarchy in Mexico would be at risk.

But no matter how hard the Confederates tried, they just couldn't get it right. First, there was the Pickett matter. After all the put-downs about captured Mexicans working "for the first time in their lives" and all the threats of invasion, John T. Pickett was getting nowhere. In frustration, he sent a letter to the Confederate capital at Richmond, which he was sure would be intercepted. It wasn't the first time, so he sent another one: "I have lost all hope of preserving peace. This government will not retrace its steps. We should at once occupy a military position on the Río Grande and march upon Monterrey…"[2]

Pickett was hoping that the letter would be intercepted and get to Juárez, so that Juárez would reconsider the permission he had given the Yankees to unload troops at Guaymas and march across Sonora to Arizona. Pickett also thought that the Mexicans might begin to fear a Confederate invasion if they failed to cooperate. Then, he started meeting with members of Mexico's old Conservative Party and with various Church officials and others considered hostile to the Juárez government. Finally, he visited the Mexico City office of Northern businessman John A. Bennett, a friend of Mexico's foreign minister, and beat him up. It was not the drunken bar fight that many have claimed, but enough to make him persona non grata.

Pickett took his time leaving Mexico. He not only stopped off to visit and gossip with various Mexican and Confederate political leaders in Veracruz, Tampico and Matamoros, but he claimed that U.S. ambassador Thomas Corwin had set him up. His choice of Pierre Alphonse Dubois Saligny as a traveling partner for much of the journey certainly didn't create a positive image. If Mexicans had been somewhat cool toward Confederates before Pickett's tenure there, they were left somewhat disgusted after his departure.

It wasn't just Pickett's arrogance, belligerence, and heavy drinking that set the Confederate cause back. There was also the well-known craving among Texans to acquire more of the Mexican landscape. In addition, there was the Confederates' obsession with what they saw as law and order—on their terms—near the border, and their strong opposition to what they saw as the special privileges that allowed the Yankees to cross Mexican territory.

Confederate leaders woke up too late to realize that they should have nurtured friendly trade relations with their neighbors south of the border. United States ambassador Thomas Corwin had already been there and done that.

12

A Hurricane and a Valentine's Ball

(Fall 1862 through Winter 1863)

Getting Lorencez off the Stage

The French troops in Orizaba were all wondering when the new commander-in-chief was going to do something. General Forey had issued proclamation after proclamation telling the Mexicans that they should put their faith in the French—whatever that was supposed to mean. Food and supplies were not reaching Orizaba in a timely fashion, and the troops were becoming bored and depressed from the lack of any meaningful activity.

General Charles Latrille, the Count of Lorencez, hardly talked to anyone as a cadre of officers escorted him down the road toward Veracruz. No longer commander-in-chief, he had declined an offer to lead a division under Forey and Bazaine. He was making it quite clear to everyone that he had had enough of Mexico. When he got to Veracruz, it was a challenge for the officers to entertain him at mealtimes. They would all look at one another, trying to figure out what to say to the cold, silent, unhappy man. The end of each meal came as a relief.

First it had been Admiral Jurien. Now, Lorencez was the second commander-in-chief whose career had been wrecked by this expedition, and the French had yet to reach Mexico City.

In order to board a ship headed back to France, Lorencez had to await the arrival of the fleet carrying General Achille Bazaine and his troops. By now, it was late October.

A Special Kind of Hurricane

Then, one night, a gigantic wave swept southward, parallel to the shore. It crashed with a thundering roar onto a rock jetty in Veracruz Harbor. Several more followed behind it. Farther from shore, it was impossible to see the horizon anymore. The surface of the sea was nothing but an endless blur of white foam, being stirred ferociously by the wind. The summer hurricane season had already ended for the Caribbean and most of the Gulf of Mexico, but the local Veracruzanos knew the *norte* (violent storms from the north) season was just beginning.

This was not an evening to venture outside. The streets were blocked by fallen palm fronds and other debris. Large barrels were rolling around, caroming off walls and buildings. Whirling sand stung the eyes and found its way into one's mouth and nostrils. Most businesses were boarded up, especially the ones whose doors faced to the north. Even the cantinas were empty.

At the height of the storm, Bazaine's fleet arrived off the coast. The pilot who managed to make it out to the flagship had bad news: yellow fever was still raging with no letup, the rainy season had just ended but the roads were still muddy and all but impassable, and bandidos prevented most shipments of food and supplies from going inland to Orizaba. It got worse: General Forey had taken only twelve hundred men with him to Orizaba, leaving most of his troops in Veracruz, which was now overcrowded, and making no arrangements to receive Bazaine's people at all. Welcome to Mexico, General Bazaine.

Bazaine made a brief attempt to go ashore with the pilot, but the wind was too strong and the waves were too high. There was no choice but to turn back and spend the night riding the waves of a storm the French had never heard of before—but which the locals called a *norte*.

As dawn broke, the sea calmed down and those aboard the ships could get their first look at Veracruz. In the distance were green hills, but the town itself was flanked by sand dunes as far as the eye could see in either direction. A few church steeples reached toward the sky, and even from a distance, it was possible to see the vultures perched atop the whitewashed limestone walls, waiting for something—or someone—to die. To most viewers, the sight was eerie.

Some officers from ashore approached Bazaine's ship by riding in a small launch. As they came aboard, they confirmed what the pilot had said the night before. Everything was filled up, including the hospitals, and there was steady traffic to the cemetery. It would be best to keep the men aboard the ships until things could be sorted out.

Bazaine didn't object to that advice, but he was determined to get the horses unloaded. There was just too great a risk of injury if they remained aboard the ships for another night, especially with another *norte* reportedly on the way. The jetty with the crane on it was just a pile of unapproachable rocks. It was used to unload fishermen's small craft, but the large, ocean-crossing vessels couldn't get near it. About 700 horses had to be lowered by hand onto scows, floated toward the beach, and then whipped into the water and pulled ashore, bucking and rearing in panic. Through some unexplained miracle, not a single horse was lost in the operation.

Getting the men ashore was another story. Throughout the daylight hours, soldiers threw themselves into the water and paddled madly, crawling up onto the beach or a rock jetty. As night approached, so did another *norte*, more ferocious than the previous storm.

One French officer who kept a journal of the Bazaine arrival was Captain Charles Blanchot. He had supervised the landing of the horses, and now he thought he could catch up on some sleep. That was not going to happen. The house and the windows shook, and the sound of sand being blown through the cracks and whirling in the darkness kept him awake all night.

At daylight, Blanchot climbed a ladder and stepped off onto the roof of the house. A strong blast of wind knocked him to one side, and he found himself sitting against a wall. He couldn't see the sand blowing into his face, but he began to taste it in his mouth. As he got to his feet and looked around, he was totally aghast. Some of the rocky breakwaters had disappeared under the pounding surf in the harbor, and the nearby streets were flooded.

It wasn't long before Captain Blanchot was ordered back to the beach to help with the rescue effort. General Bazaine himself was in charge. Blanchot was to organize several squads to patrol the beach against looters and to guard against bandidos and guerilla fighters, who were lurking in the outskirts of town. Temporary shelters were being set up on the beach for the soldiers who were able to make it to shore alive, but a morgue was also being completed for the corpses that were already beginning to wash ashore.

A third night was filled with the sounds of nature's fury, and both cannon fire and flares were coming from ships in distress. As the sun rose the next morning, there were thirteen ships wrecked in the harbor. The jetties were littered with cases of weapons and gun carriages. The wind had died down, but the hospitals were filling up rapidly as the air once again turned rancid with fever. "The native alone," wrote historian Ralph Roeder, "seemed capable of surviving by some special act of creation."[1]

General Bazaine simply had to play the role of commander. There was no one around, nor was there time, to ask for permission. Within a day or two, he managed to contact General Forey and say that the road to Orizaba was blocked by guerilla bands but that he, Bazaine, just had to get his troops out of Veracruz at the earliest possible moment. He asked for permission to open a second front. Forey agreed, and within a week Bazaine's troops were marching toward Xalapa.

Back in Veracruz, the hearses would be busy for days.

Forey Doesn't Seem to Have a Plan

General Forey's hesitation to act was becoming more and more noticeable, not to just his troops but to the press, the legislatures, and the general public in both France and Mexico. In Puebla, the procrastination was forcing the wealthy elite to conclude that the French were not going to show up in time to "liberate" them at all. Their support was fading rapidly. Pierre Saligny, who had been forbidden to communicate with Paris except through Forey, grew more and more despondent and disagreeable every day. The French papers, detecting Saligny's silence, started to predict that he would be recalled in disgrace. The opposition leader in the French Corps Législatif, Jules Favre, stood up and declared that

-the government was concealing the real purposes for going to war;
-the invading army was led to believe they would be welcomed as liberators;
-not enough troops were sent initially to accomplish the task;
-there was no plan to deal with the responsibilities after a military victory;
-there was no exit strategy.

French prime minister Billault rebutted Favre's remarks, claiming that they had tried to negotiate with the Juárez government, but that the defeat at Puebla showed that the Mexicans could not be reasoned with. The honor of the French flag was at stake, said Billault, and that honor must be avenged. The deputies overwhelmingly approved the funds for escalating the Mexican expedition, and as far as anyone could tell, they were backed by the French public.[2]

General Ortega's Buildup

All of this was giving General González-Ortega time to build up the defenses around Puebla. Ortega ordered that all able-bodied males between the ages of fourteen and sixty make themselves available for that work one day every week, or pay for the labor of a substitute. Ortega not only supervised the project personally, but he also often picked up tools and joined in to help boost morale.

The Juárez administration already had laws on the books confiscating property and money belonging to the Church, but General Ortega knew that many in Puebla were still sympathetic to the French and to the defeated conservative cause. He issued an order that anyone who failed to obey those laws would be tried and sentenced as a traitor. The strategy worked: not only were most of the fortifications completed by November, but Ortega reported to President Juárez that Puebla was extremely well secured and all but invincible.[3]

Romero's Frustration with Americans

In Washington, D.C., Matías Romero, the Mexican chargé d'affaires, did not share Ortega's optimism. Angered by the bureaucratic indifference, evasion, and procrastination of U.S. officials, he wrote to Juárez, suggesting that Mexico cut diplomatic ties with the United States. Secretary of State Seward had ordered that all foreign diplomats go through his office in order to have access to the president, something that Romero knew was aimed directly at him. Whether Juárez severed relations or not, Romero wanted out. He asked Juárez to call him home so that he could at least join the army and be of some service to Mexico.

Juárez recalled Romero, but just long enough to give him a short vacation. Romero would go back to Washington, not just as chargé d'affaires but as Mexico's ambassador. Also, there would be a new game plan: don't worry about Seward and Lincoln. Establish and work through as many other channels as he could: business and political groups, speeches, rallies, banquets, the press, Mexican expatriate organizations, and whatever else occurred to him. Lobby both houses of Congress and leaders of Lincoln's own Republican Party, and build public and political opinion in Mexico's favor that no secretary of state or even president could effectively oppose Mexico. Keep at it for as long as it takes.[4]

A New, Blood-Stained, Anti-Guerilla Leader

Finally General Élie Frédéric Forey was ready to do business. One last detail would be to replace the ineffective Swiss mercenary who was leading the French *contre-guérillas,* or anti-guerilla forces. The group consisted of some of the meanest, toughest, cruelest individuals one could ever find. A few were from France, but most were from other European or Latin American countries. Some were ex-Confederates who had been ruined by the U.S. Civil War, others were former pirates or sailors who had jumped ship, and so on. Their commander, Colonel de Stecklin, spent much of his time and effort running two gunboats up and down the Gulf coast near Veracruz and opening fire on anyone on the beach who looked like a Mexican guerilla fighter or bandido. He was accomplishing very little, especially in dealing with threats to French supply lines from the coast to Orizaba.

Forey saw his chance to make a change on February 14, 1863.

Pierre Saligny's parties were not to be missed, and Napoleon III's minister to Mexico was throwing an extravagant Valentine's Day ball to honor General Forey and his officers, and to thank the local aristocracy for their kind hospitality during the past nine months. Among the guests was the French count Émile de Kératry, who guessed that some of the locals present would stop by their homes after the ball just long enough to change into clothing for guerilla fighting. He wondered aloud how many of them he might see later, hanging at the end of a rope when caught by the *contre-guérillas*. Kératry had left his diplomatic post in Naples, Italy, to join the French army and eventually to become involved with the *contres*.

General Forey took aside an officer wearing the cape and insignia of a colonel. The man looked much older than his forty-eight years. He had a large white beard, piercing blue eyes, and a stern countenance. Colonel Francois DuPin had been in charge of the sacking and pillaging at the emperor's palace in Peking, China, just three years earlier. He had ordered his troops not only to burn the palace and dig up the gardens, but also to destroy all of the emperor's precious antiques. Just a few were destroyed, but then DuPin shipped the rest back to Paris, where he managed to sell them for quite a fortune.

Some fellow officers reported DuPin's behavior to higher authorities and had him dishonorably discharged. There were all sorts of stories about his harshness, terror, and cruelty—even atrocities. Using political connections, DuPin got Napoleon III to reinstate him in the army. Most regular officers would have nothing to do with him, but now here he was in Orizaba.

Forey offered him command of the *contre-guérillas*.

DuPin said he would accept under several conditions. One was that the group had to have special uniforms to improve their morale, which had been lacking under de Stecklin. Another was that they needed the latest in armaments and equipment, but the third one made Forey swallow hard: higher pay than regular soldiers. Forey didn't have much choice, because Mexican guerillas and bandidos practically owned the highway between Veracruz and Orizaba, jeopardizing French supply lines. There would have to be some strong incentives to recruit men for the *contre-guérilla* force, and this was one of them.

Forey agreed, and then he went out to the ballroom to make an announcement: the long-awaited march to take Puebla would begin in three days.

Finally, Some Movement

Forey's announcement was music to the ears of generals Douay, Berthier, de Mirandol, Bazaine, and other top officers. They were all well aware that since Forey's arrival in October, he had made no attempt whatsoever to advance against the Mexicans. His inaction was perceived as dithering, and the troops were getting restless.

Part of the delay in Orizaba was to allow many of the troops to return to good health. So many had been sidelined by yellow fever and malaria that very few units were up to full strength. Now, Forey had 24,300 troops under his command, plus the 2,000 from General Márquez that gave him a total of 26,300. Eighteen thousand of those were infantry, but they were backed by 2,300 administrative personnel, 2,500 artillerymen, 1,400 cavalry, and 450 engineers. Forey's total would exceed thirty thousand if the six thousand troops with General Bazaine in Xalapa were also counted.

For the troops, Xalapa was at first a great relief from the heat and disease of Veracruz, but all the rain and mist that kept the flowers growing for most of the year made the place pretty dreary in the winter. It was cold, and it was not strategically located for military purposes. The locals were keeping their distance, even crossing to the opposite side of the street as Frenchmen approached. As Captain Henri Loizillon wrote home to his family in France, "Not [even] a cat will do us the honor of addressing us."[5]

What was holding up the French advance was not just the fitness of the soldiers but the lack of a transportation infrastructure, which in turn led to a lack of supplies. Feeding 26,000 men in Orizaba and another 6,000 in Xalapa still required sending wagons down to Veracruz to bring back biscuits, which were already known to be rancid when they left France.

One option was to have some of Bazaine's contingent advance just a little farther, up into Perote, which dominated the access to the upper plateau and the rest of inland Mexico. Beyond it was a bountiful wheat-and grain-growing area that would not be nearly as vulnerable to guerillas and bandidos as the roadways going back to the coast. At least that was the plan. Too bad the French didn't think of it until the harvest season was over. The troops, already in a pessimistic mood, became even more depressed when they reached the town. There was nothing cultural going on in Perote, and nothing to talk about except the weather. It was freezing cold at night, and a fierce, skin-chapping wind blew during the day under the cloudy skies. As Captain Loizillon wrote in another letter home: "Perote was a sad little village. Strategic considerations no longer mattered.

Perote was a sad little village on the road to Puebla. Perote was a sad little village on the way to nowhere. Perote was simply a sad little village."[6]

All the French got out of advancing to Perote was more inactivity and more boredom. One officer even wrote home that he had gone to a wake for entertainment. Apparently going to wakes was a popular pastime in Perote and throughout much of Mexico. Captain Henri Loizillon wrote that the deceased happened to be the wife of one of Imperialista general Márquez's officers. The woman had given birth in Xalapa, but had died of exposure after the march to Perote. Loizillon reported that the body was laid out in a hut, with four candles around it.

Loizillon and several companions had stayed for just a short time, but as they got up to leave, a woman begged them to stay. She offered them cigarettes. When they started to decline, she put up such a fuss that they all sat down and smoked in silence. She followed this by passing around a bottle. It finally dawned on them that this was the dead woman's sister, and that she had wanted them to contribute toward the cost of the coffin. They each donated three pesos and left. This was not exactly the exciting military adventure that Captain Loizillon had signed-up for.

Loizillon wrote frequently not only to his parents, but also to one of their friends whose mother had worked in the household of Napoleon III's mother in Switzerland. The parents' friend, Madame Hortense Cornu, said that while her mother worked as a domestic servant, she had spent many happy times as a child playing in the garden with the little prince who later became Napoleon III.[7]

Forey to DuPin: "Whatever It Takes…"

Back in Orizaba, Forey had finally decided what he was going to do about the guerillas. It had been tough enough to defend the supply lines between Veracruz and Orizaba, and now Forey would be extending them all the way to Puebla. Many local merchants in Veracruz and Orizaba sympathized with Juárez and his liberals. They were shopkeepers by day but guerilla fighters at night, destroying bridges and stealing boats, wagons, and horses—doing whatever it took to disrupt French operations.

The worst hotbeds of guerilla activity were little towns like Medellín, Alvarado, and Tlacotalpan. Together, the towns comprised a network of little rivers and streams around Veracruz. The guerillas who were based in these hamlets could intercept just about anything that had been unloaded at Veracruz and was bound for any destination inland. These little population clusters would have to be dealt with more effectively.

All of that would now be up to Colonel DuPin.

13

Icicles in Their Beards

(February 15 through April 9, 1863)

No Progress to Report

In Paris, the French Corps Législatif had decided to postpone the opening of its session until February 15. Surely by then, they thought, the army would have become better acclimated to Mexico, and there would be news of the capture of Puebla to share.

Wrong.

The only force that had made any move was that of Bazaine. The troops had left Perote and marched to—of all places—Quecholac. None of them had been in Quecholac nine months earlier when all the *indígenas* (Indians) would say in answer to every questions was, "*¿Quién sabe, señor?*"

Captain Loizillon wrote home on January 21, and again on February 4, that inaction was still driving them crazy. He said that all of the officers had tried to tell Forey "in every possible way" that "three battalions, two squadrons of cavalry and one battery of artillery could cross all of Mexico without the whole of the Mexican army daring to attack them." The reasoning was that Ortega had confined all of his troops to Puebla "for fear they will desert or disband."[1]

One unlucky colonel was ordered to leave the comfort of Orizaba with his regiment and transfer to Bazaine's troops in Quecholac. Colonel du Barail described the weather in the mountainous area as "Siberian" in nature, and said it reminded him of the stories he had heard about the French retreat from Moscow in the winter of 1812. His unit arrived in Quecholac with icicles in their beards.

Colonel du Barail's regiment was camped out on an isolated plantation, so he adopted a practice that had worked pretty well in Orizaba: put on lots of plays and operettas. Among those attending on several occasions was General Leonardo Márquez. As the month wore on, du Barail had his troops shining the breastplates of their armor until they could see themselves in the reflection, and blowing constantly on the feathers of their hats to fluff them up. They were being told, and many believed, that the feathers would play a key part in battle.

Others weren't buying the business about the feathers, the armor-shining, the cold weather, the boredom, and the misery—none of it. Desertions were increasing. General Forey dealt with the situation by issuing more proclamations.[2]

Now, Forey—still ensconced in his warm, rented mansion in Orizaba—issued an order that was supposed to improve the army's morale:

> Almost nine months ago, a small number of you, marching with blind confidence upon Mexico, met in Puebla an obstacle which you lacked the material means to overcome...The time has not been wasted. The patience which you have shown in preparing your means of action may have been imputed by the deluded soldiers of the government that still reigns for a few days more in Mexico, in the presumption of their easy triumph of the 5th of May, to the fear that they inspired in you. If they have fallen asleep in that fond fancy, let their awakening be a terrible one![3]

There was just one problem. Forey issued that proclamation on February 17, but marching orders didn't come through until March 16, a whole month later. Forey had declared that March 16, the birthday of the prince imperial, be marked as the day that the new operation would begin. Generals Bazaine and Douay were able to see Puebla through their binoculars before darkness on March 16, but the real advance began the next morning.

Acting More like Tourists Than Soldiers

Colonel du Barail felt that things were really starting to happen on March 17:

> During that day we enjoyed the most grandiose of spectacles...The entire ensemble respired splendor, wealth, and magnificence. The road we were following runs along the crests that form the border of the basin, and, rocked by the elastic trot of our mounts and intoxicated by the spring air, we had before our eyes constantly the domes, the belfries, the terraces, the roofs of the town and the panorama of its environs. From time to time an inoffensive cannon shot from the town, or some yet more inoffensive rifle shots from the mounted sentinels on the plain, flavored our pleasures as tourists by reminding us that we were soldiers.[4]

General Bazaine arrived and began to set up the checkpoints along the roads, guarding and occupying land as the troops surrounded the city during the next two days. "This first easy success," said Captain Loizillon, "made everyone's mouth water."[5]

Loizillon said they suspected that—along Puebla's western perimeter—the penitentiary of San Xavier had no artillery, and that the Mexicans were not expecting an attack on that side. He called it an exhilarating day, especially after six months of idleness, and reported that "night fell on a brilliant spectacle, the campfires of the French populating the plain, and rockets rising from the beleaguered town in soaring and luminous signals that communication was cut off and investment had actually begun."

Captain Loizillon wrote that he thought Puebla could be taken by siege in five or six days.[6]

DuPin Begins Operations

When Francois DuPin and his *contre-guérillas* rode into the tiny village of Tlaliscoya, between Alvarado and Tlacotalpan, they were dressed to create fear and awe among the locals.

He was wearing not only his long red and black colonel's cloak, but also a huge sombrero and yellow boots with giant spurs. There were medals all over his chest, a revolver stuck into his belt, and a sword hanging from his saddle. His appearance might have been even more terrifying had not all the citizens of Tlaliscoya turned out their lights. The town was shrouded in pitch darkness. Not a living soul was in sight. As DuPin's reputation had spread from town to town, the villagers had learned to flee and hide long before he even arrived.

"*No hay gente*," said one of his henchmen. "There's no one here."

"Find them!" Dupin ordered.

Within moments, DuPin was seated around a table with half a dozen inhabitants who had been flushed from their hiding places. He informed them that they would be held as hostages until their women produced enough food for his men. At first, they resisted by saying they didn't know where their women were, and that they were all poor and didn't have much food.

"Too bad," DuPin told them. "If the food is not on this table within the hour, you will all be shot." Lights went on all over town as people scrambled to provide the food. This tactic had worked in many small towns along the coast. DuPin usually asked for more food than the men with him could eat, so the villagers would think he had even more men waiting outside of town.

In Tlaliscoya, he wanted more than food. He wanted boats. When they denied having any, he pointed to the docks all along the river and said he didn't believe them. He commandeered the house of a Señor Billegras along the river, taking Billegras and six others hostage. If he didn't have two boats by five o'clock the next morning, said DuPin, he would shoot one of the hostages and burn down someone's house every hour until he got what he wanted. Two men were set free to get the boats, and two boats were at Señor Billegras' house by 5:00 AM.[7]

Confederates Sign a Treaty with Vidaurri

Trying to gain some sort of foothold in Mexico, Confederate president Jefferson Davis sent one of his officials to Orizaba to see if he could work something out with the French. Pierre Saligny liked Davis's proposal for France to team up with the Confederacy by sending troops to occupy Matamoros. It would not only shut down the Juárez government's last remaining access to the Gulf of Mexico and the Atlantic Ocean, but it would keep the United States navy from trying to blockade or even occupy Matamoros. There was just one problem: more than two-thirds of the French navy crews that would be assigned to the mission had come down with yellow fever. They just couldn't do it.

Davis turned next to General Santiago Vidaurri. The Confederates increased their trade through Matamoros and came up with enough money in bribes to make it worthwhile for him to disregard any dictates from Mexico City. Vidaurri signed a treaty with the Confederate States of America. It allowed the Southerners to pursue their deserters across the border into Mexico, and it authorized Vidaurri's people to expel all U.S. agents from Matamoros. Vidaurri was getting even with the United States, which had refused to sell him weapons to fight the French.

Juárez Rallies the Mexican Troops

Just before General Forey's troops left Orizaba to join Bazaine's forces, President Benito Juárez showed up in Puebla to inspect all of Ortega's barricades and fortifications, review the town's defenders, and boost their morale. He called on the Mexican forces to do their best:[8]

"The Emperor Napoleon III persists in inflicting the horrors of war upon a people who have always generously bestowed their favors and sympathies upon Frenchmen…His aim is to humiliate us, and to destroy a free and popular republic in which the privileged classes have been completely removed…Mexico, the American continent, and free men of every nation pin their hopes on you, because you will be defending their cause, the cause of liberty, humanity, and civ-ilization."[9]

The French Army Prepares a Siege

Once again, the French army reached Amozoc, but this time they did not have the forts of Guadalupe and Loreto as their targets. The troops completely surrounded the city, finishing the task by March 16, the birthday of the prince imperial, just as they had been ordered to do.

Finally, General Élie Frédéric Forey showed up at Puebla. His entourage included Mexican Imperialista general Juan Almonte. Forey was said to be all over the place, checking Bazaine's troops to the west of town, Douay's troops to the south, and Colonel du Barail's regiment to the north (there were hills to the east). The French were pretty sure they had the town well surrounded, and that no one would escape.

Not quite.

Fifteen hundred of General Márquez's cavalry troops rode out during the night and switched their allegiance to General Comonfort, the former president of Mexico who had been coaxed out of retirement to act as a backup for Ortega. Most French officers considered General Márquez as a "zero in the left-hand column"—meaning useless. His defectors wouldn't be missed anyway. They ate more than their share of the rations. Puebla was sealed off. Let the siege begin.

Napoleon III believed—and so did generals Almonte and Márquez, who had fought in Puebla before—that an attack on one of the forts protecting the town—Fort Carmen—would be the quickest way to assure success. Forey disagreed, ordering General Bazaine to attack Fort San Xavier, the former penitentiary.

Forey was sure that his 56 artillery pieces would be best suited for the task. What he didn't seem to know, or perhaps care, was that the Mexicans had 96 pieces on the rooftops and another 55 pieces in reserve, giving them a total of 151.

Trying to be helpful, Pierre Saligny was busy getting in the way, assuring French officers that all seven of those forts surrounding Puebla, and all the artillery pieces they had heard about, were nothing more than scenery. Saligny also insisted, as Colonel du Barail later wrote, "that behind them a clerical population was fermenting, awaiting their deliverance impatiently, and ready to fall on the knees before their conquerors." Forey believed him and, wrote du Barail, "because one believes what one wants to believe, and he had no idea of the resistance prepared for him."[10]

Internal Politics Weakens the French Army

What Forey didn't realize was that some of the resistance was surreptitiously coming from his own officers. Forey had by now given his subordinates the distinct impression that he was indecisive and hesitant. He had said over and over again that he had fought enough for glory in earlier European campaigns, and all that he wanted to do was bring peace and happiness to the Mexicans who "needed only order and security" to join the progress of civilized nations.

Whenever French officers needed guidance from Forey, they more often than not found General Bazaine. Bazaine avoided Forey's council-of-war meetings, so if some of the orders issued at those gatherings were distasteful to the officers, he was not the attributable source. His long-range plan, obvious to many, was eventually to replace General Forey. He courted as much favorable attention as he could from Pierre Saligny, to the point where Saligny was convinced that things would be better off if Bazaine, not Forey, were commander-in-chief.

Mexicans Brace for the Assault

Inside the now-surrounded city were the Juárez forces under General Ortega. These forces were not just Mexicans, but included some Spaniards who had deserted General Prim's army, some Englishmen, a few Americans who were avoiding the Civil War back home, and a large contingent of revolutionaries from Europe, who wanted to carry on the fight for freedom against monarchies like that of Napoleon III.

Another woman was among the Mexican officers. She was a lieutenant colonel, having fought bravely at the earlier Battle of Puebla on May 5, and allowed to replace her husband who had been killed in that engagement. Of course, there were the thousands of *soldaderas*, the women who normally accompanied Mexican troops, backing the twenty-two thousand men whom Ortega would command in protecting the city. Not only were all seven forts well staffed and armed, but there were barricades in the streets to thwart the French assault in house-to-house fighting.[11]

More Than Just a Fort

The structure the French were attacking didn't look like a fort to Achille Bazaine. In the general's eyes, it looked more like a prison. It was now March 26, and Bazaine was right. The building the French had been bombarding for the past four days had originally been a penitentiary. It had been built on an American model decades earlier, and now the French were finding it impenetrable.

They had tried everything—laying mines, digging tunnels, launching cannon bombardments—and so far nothing had worked. Not only had the prison and the former convent adjoining it been transformed into one large, formidable barrier, but also the French had found that every house behind it had been well fortified and was crammed with Mexicans determined to fight to the last person.

Bazaine continued to express anger and frustration as he and his small entourage of officers picked their way through the rubble not far from the fort to check on French progress, or lack of it, before darkness fell. Captain Charles Blanchot and several others trudged along behind the downhearted general, taking notes and exchanging glances among themselves. For the mighty French army, this was turning into yet another debacle. The emperor would be nothing less than outraged with another defeat.

In the next instant, there was an explosion.

The screams of Mexican soldiers could be heard. They had been trapped in one of the prison's cells as the French tossed a firebomb through the window to end the day's fighting. Most of those present had not heard anything that desperate since the night they had rescued hundreds of French soldiers from their floundering ships during the *norte* (violent storm from the north) in Veracruz. It was horrifying.

Bazaine decided to send the infantry on the next day. On each of the next two days, his forces were driven back. Finally, on March 29, after the artillery had demolished a section of wall facing them, Bazaine carefully lined up his troops for a final assault. Up in front were survivors of the battle last May, eager to avenge their defeat. The signal to charge would be a five o'clock church bell. As the bell began the five strokes to mark the hour, a great surge rose up from the trenches and charged up the embankment in the face of withering fire. They took Fort San Xavier at a cost of 27 French dead and 189 wounded. Bazaine's second in command was one of those killed. The Mexicans lost about 600 dead and wounded. The French would have kept on going, but Bazaine called a halt. Beyond the fort was a trap: every house was an artillery position.

It's Going to Take a While Longer

With the honeycomb of fortified blocks facing them, the French increased their estimate of a takeover to about eight to ten days. Then, after trying everything they could think of—mines, cannon fire, attacks in the middle of the night—and blasting their way from house to house, they had leveled 4 blocks in two days, with another 154 blocks to go before the entire town would be in ruins. At the end of eight days, only 3 more blocks had been taken.

14

Foreign Legionnaires Fight to the Death

(April 9–30, 1863)

Skip Puebla? Bad Idea

General Forey's siege of Puebla was in its twenty-fifth day, and the Mexican forces defending the town were not about to give it up. Forey finally visited the scene in person. He saw for himself the convents with well-hidden marksmen and the rows and rows of barricades all around them. It was now April 9. Something had to be done.

Forey called a council of war among his top colonels and generals. As Colonel du Barail later wrote, "When a council of war is called, you may be sure that something has broken down. When all goes well, the commander-in-chief appropriates all the glory, but when things go wrong he hastens to share the responsibility with as many others as possible."[1]

The council of war was a disaster all by itself.

Forey said they would try two things at once. They would attack Fort Carmen, as Bazaine and others had wanted to do in the first place, and they would step up their block-by-block assault with heavier cannons and mines. The artillery commander had just been killed the previous day, and the man replacing him had bad news: they were running out of explosive powder for the mines, the eight large siege cannons were all too big to get into Puebla's narrow streets, and the field pieces could do little or nothing against the walls of churches and convents.

Then a young staff officer—who shall remain nameless—came up with what he thought was a very bright idea.

Just forget Puebla.

Lift the siege, evacuate the sick and wounded to Cholula, a few miles to the west, and march on to Mexico City.

Forey thought it was brilliant, and generals Bazaine and Douay didn't want to disagree with the commander-in-chief. They claimed that, yes, their men were tired of all the street fighting, and that this was a good idea. No one else dared to oppose the idea openly, but they all filed out in numbed silence, supposedly pledged to keep the decision secret until General Forey issued orders the next morning.

There were twenty-six thousand French troops surrounding Puebla on this night, but it took less than one hour for Forey's decision to spread throughout the ranks. Alarmed at the outrage and indignation building throughout the camp, officers came running back to headquarters to ask Forey to reconsider. Another top-level huddle ensued. The general reversed himself and moved quickly to counter the angry jeering of the troops.

The young officer who had proposed skipping over Puebla was nowhere to be seen.

Forey decided that Bazaine would move his troops to attack not only Fort Carmen but a Fort Totimehuacan (pronounced toh-tee-may-wah-KAHN) farther to the south, and that everyone else would rotate to another position in the morning.

Élie Frédéric Forey went to bed that night angrier than ever at the "arrogant bastards" defending Puebla. He was determined to get them now at all costs. There would be a sort of "commander-of-the day" routine, hoping to crack the outer ring of forts, prisons, and convents that surrounded Puebla. Each of his generals would get a shot at it, starting tomorrow.

Nine days later, on April 18, Captain Loizillon wrote at the end of the day that "there has been neither direction nor [teamwork] in the siege operations. Every twenty-four hours we have had another general in the trenches; usually he adopted neither the way of thinking nor the method of working of his predecessor;...Moreover, the engineers and the artillery worked each in their own way, without a thought for the whole. Such a state of things was bound to bring bad results. That is what has happened."[2]

A week later, on April 25, it was General Douay's turn. The target for the day was the Santa Ines Convent. The engineers had sunk mines under the roadway the previous day. They were almost ready to blast the convent wall when the Mexicans inside heard the drilling and started to set countercharges to thwart the French effort. As a thunderstorm broke over the area, the French decided that everything would be so soaked that their efforts would be in vain, so they set off the blasts in the desperate hope that the convent wall would collapse.

It didn't.

The wall had leaned over, but beyond it was an iron gate leading to a court-yard. It was raining and dark, and both sides backed off for the night.

Then, when General Douay took over at 6:00 AM, the French began three hours of bombardment to soften things up.

That's when everything started to go wrong.

No fewer than thirty of the French gunners were picked off by Mexican snip-ers from the windows of the convent. At 9:00 AM, the artillery people told Douay something he really didn't want to hear: they were just about out of ammunition and would have to shut down at any moment.

General Douay ordered two columns to dash across the road and begin the attack. Their formations broke as the Mexicans began firing, and Douay decided to abort the mission and call his men back. It was too late: two hundred of them had already wrestled the iron grille out of the way and charged into the courtyard. They became nothing more than targets for the Mexicans, who were firing down at them from three sides.

A clearly unnerved General Douay hugged General Bazaine. It had been a disaster. There would be another council of war to decide what to do next.

The Legend of Camarón

Running out of ammunition at the wrong time had also raised General Forey's anxiety level. Forey realized that his entire operation would be at risk if he couldn't provide his troops with food and ammunition. The commander-in-chief had already detached extra troops from Puebla to guard the wagon trains, but now the bandidos and guerillas had dramatically stepped up their attacks on the convoys.

Forey called on the French Foreign Legion. They had just arrived in Veracruz.

They were approaching the little village of Camarón (which means *shrimp* in Spanish). For a number of years it was called Villa Tejeda, but the name was changed again to "Camarón de Tejeda," by which it is known today. The few authors who have written about it in English refer to it as "Camerone," which is very close to how it's pronounced in Spanish.

The legion had first seen action in the French conquest of Algeria in 1831. After serving during the Spanish Civil War in 1835, it was stationed in North Africa. Now, on the morning of April 30, 1863, the legion's Third Company, under Captain Jean Danjou, was escorting a very important convoy from Ver-acruz. The wagons were bearing ammunition, artillery, food, provisions, and—most critically—three million French francs in gold to pay the troops at Puebla.

Danjou's group consisted of sixty-four battle-hardened legion veterans: Germans, Swiss, Belgians, Danes, Italians, and Spaniards, in addition to the native Frenchmen. They feared nothing. They had taken the legion's oath never to surrender.

Stalking the convoy was a Mexican force of somewhere between twelve hundred and eighteen hundred men, depending on whose account you choose to believe, led by a Colonel Francisco de P. Milán. Regular French troops were guarding the convoy itself, but Captain Danjou's contingent was marching some distance ahead to search for possible assailants waiting in ambush. The legion officers normally in charge of this unit were hospitalized with yellow fever, so Danjou, along with second lieutenants Napoleón Vilain and Clement Maudet, had volunteered to lead this detail.

They had passed through Camarón at about 6:30 in the morning and were cooking breakfast near a location called Palo Verde at 7:00, when one of their sentinels spotted a dust cloud behind them. That could only mean one thing: a lot of people moving rapidly on horseback. They quickly put out their fires and raced toward Camarón, not stopping to retrieve their canteens of fresh water from the pack mules. At Camarón, they encountered several hundred Mexicans who were poised to attack the caravan, and the shooting began.

The convoy was alerted and reversed direction, successfully escaping the ambush, but the legionnaires' pack mules also panicked and fled at the sound of gunfire, taking all the water and extra ammunition with them. By 8:00 in the morning, a few of the legionnaires had already been wounded. Danjou ordered his unit to take cover in a barn, but the Mexicans lost no time in taking over the huge farmhouse nearby, firing down at the besieged legionnaires from upper-story windows.

Mexican Colonel Milán realized that cavalry wouldn't be of much help in taking the barn, so he started to surround it with infantry troops. After a few hours, nothing much had changed. The colonel found a Mexican officer of French heritage among his ranks, and he sent Captain Ramón Lainé with a white flag of truce to see if they could negotiate a surrender.

It didn't work.

Captain Danjou said his legionnaires had plenty of ammunition, and that they'd keep on fighting.

By now, the Mexicans had surrounded the barn and were firing from all sides. It was a hot day, and the legionnaires inside were just discovering that the only canteens they had were filled with wine, not water, because the pack mules had run away with the water as the fighting started. It was going to be a long afternoon.

Although the Mexicans had obvious superiority in numbers, the legionnaires had the upper hand in training and firepower. Most of the Mexicans were of the "national guard" variety. They had left their farms and small businesses just days earlier to help defend their country, while the legionnaires were well accustomed to the sound of gunfire and highly experienced in the art of war. The Mexicans had ball-and-musket rifles, which gave off so much smoke that at times they couldn't see what they were shooting at. The legionnaires were firing percussion-driven cylinders with pointed tips, known as "bullets," and they could see exactly where they were aiming.

In spite of all their technical superiority, the legionnaires were fighting a losing battle. Captain Danjou and Lieutenant Vilain were both dead before noon, and the command fell to Lieutenant Maudet for the rest of the afternoon. Inside the barn, things were going from bad to worse. Ammunition was running out, and the extra supply had vanished with the pack mules. The Mexicans kept charging the barn, and although they were driven back. they were killing another legionnaire or two each time. By 5:00 PM, the legionnaires had already stripped whatever ammunition was left from the bodies of their dead comrades.

The Mexicans knew they had won, but they also knew that the remaining legionnaires intended to fight to the death. They set fire to some straw and threw it into the barn, hoping to bring the matter to a close. The legionnaires just stamped out the burning straw and continued firing through the smoke.

By 6:00 PM, only Maudet and four of his legionnaires were still alive. Each man had only one round of ammunition left. The lieutenant had a decision to make.

"Reload," he ordered. "Then fire on my command and follow me. We'll finish this with our bayonets."

It was going to be a suicide charge.

The Mexican commander, Colonel Milán, ordered his troops to cease fire. All five legionnaires were captured after some brief hand-to-hand fighting, but Lieutenant Maudet and one of his men died of their wounds within a short time. The remaining three were hospitalized, along with the Mexican wounded.

The French later returned to put up a monument at the scene of the battle. For many years, members of the French Foreign Legion have returned each April 30 to what is now called "Camarón de Tejeda" to honor the courage of their fallen heroes. The encounter still stands as the worst defeat in legion history.[3]

15

The French Commandant Wants to Quit

(April 1863)

Fatigue Setting in on Both Sides

Inside Puebla, the main cathedral had been taken over by the Juarista forces defending the town against the hostile French encirclement. Those who wished to attend Mass had to travel at considerable risk down narrow back streets to reach one of the smaller parishes. They could smell smoke and hear gunfire all around them, as they stepped over debris along the way.

At the churches, priests generally deplored the violence and destruction, but most of them blamed it on Puebla's Mexican defenders. If General Ortega's forces would only lay down their arms and surrender, the clerics insisted, all of the terror and agony would come to an end. In the pews, however, the thought was running through many minds that those were not Mexican artillery shells raining down on the town and destroying buildings.

People were hiding in their houses like trapped animals, risking their lives whenever they ventured out to find food. The view from the pulpits in many parishes was that this was all General González-Ortega's fault.

The French soldiers surrounding the city of Puebla were as uncomfortable as the locals who were huddling inside. After each day's failure to capture the town, nights in the French encampments had begun to take on mysterious, shadowy proportions. They knew that Forey should have taken Puebla weeks ago. The soldiers had spent many sleepless nights out on the plains, and the fatigue was beginning to show. Sentries peered out into the darkness with weary eyes, and quivered at the slightest sound. Many of them had the looks of terror each morning as they told tales of the sky spinning and bright lights flashing. Some claimed they had seen fireworks.[1]

The trap set by the Mexicans at the Santa Ines Convent had clearly unnerved the French high command. Generals, colonels, and their staff members gathered at the end of a long, high-ceilinged corridor in the captured Fort San Xavier to sort things out. Captain Blanchot was on call farther down the hallway, but because of the vault-like construction, he could hear almost everything that was being said. He took notes.

The discussion started off in a somber tone, because the French had just taken a lot of casualties during the day. That didn't last long, as generals Bazaine and Douay blamed the losses on the street fighting and the officer who had designed the tactics, a Colonel Auvergne. Shouting broke out as Auvergne claimed that the two generals were not describing them correctly.

That was more than General Douay could take. He shouted back that there was no way that Auvergne, a cripple confined to a wheelchair, could make such an accusation. Obviously, he had been unable to see the outcome. Auvergne angrily defended his plan, but, with all the French losses, the mood was clearly against him. His tactics would never be used again.

What the Captain Overheard

Élie Frédéric Forey had been having a bad day, anyway. What very few of the officers knew was that the general had just received a letter from Emperor Napoleon III. Napoleon told Forey that he had heard it on very good authority—the U.S. ambassador in Paris—that the French army would meet little or no resistance in either Puebla or Mexico City, and that an easy victory was virtually assured in each case.

Then there were the leaflets. Captain Blanchot may not have known about the emperor's letter, but he was certainly aware of the thousands of leaflets that had been scattered into the wind from Puebla, landing where French troops would pick them up. The leaflets were copies of French opposition leader Jules Favre's speech to the Corps Législatif back in September. In the speech, Favre had complained that Napoleon III was concealing the real purposes of the invasion, was not sending enough troops, and did not have an exit strategy. Blanchot wrote that it had been "translated into all languages [and] shipped in bales to Puebla…[where] the besieged showered us with copies."

Generals Bazaine and Douay tried to persuade the gathering to concentrate just on taking the outer ring of forts just as they had done with the old penitentiary, Fort San Xavier, where they were now meeting. They could hold onto those forts without going into any of the neighborhoods. Then, they would just wait for the defenders to run out of food, ammunition, or both. After all, the town had been surrounded for more than six weeks. A Mexican surrender was not a matter of if, but when.

Someone else even revived the idea of abandoning the siege at Puebla and just marching on to Mexico City, where he was sure they'd be welcomed as heroes. Blanchot didn't hear anyone backing the individual, whoever he may have been.

There was a silence. Captain Blanchot could only guess what was taking place. Then, he heard what was unmistakably the voice of General Élie Frédéric Forey.

"Gentlemen," said the general, "before I left France to join this expedition, all sorts of promises were made to me to encourage my collaboration. I asked for various kinds of weapons and equipment, some of which was approved and some of which was rejected. I asked for certain men and officers, again with mixed results. Now, here I am: much of that which was promised to me has never been delivered. I'm sorry to have to say this, but I can no longer take responsibility for this deplorable situation. The bureaucrats in Paris are to blame for this mess. We have done the best we can under the circumstances. At this point, I decline my responsibility, and so can you, if you wish."

Captain Blanchot felt a shiver of panic. He knew that Forey was tired and exasperated, but he also knew that those words should never have been uttered. If any of the officers in that meeting were to testify against him in a military court, Forey could be executed. Just having heard them sent Blanchot's heart thumping. He resolved never to give any sign whatsoever that he had been eavesdropping on the officers' gathering. If anyone told him what Forey had said, he would feign surprise and disbelief.

The discussion rambled on for about an hour, with nothing that sounded like they had reached any kind of agreement.

Suddenly, Blanchot heard General Forey's voice again. "My word! Talk it over among yourselves and come to some understanding." He walked out, passing Captain Blanchot on the way. The top-level staff followed him, stepping over wounded soldiers as they left, and Blanchot noted that Forey apparently never saw the angry stares of either the injured men on the floor or those who were still limping back in pairs from the Santa Ines Convent debacle.

French losses from the failed assault on Santa Ines totaled 335 killed or wounded and 76 captured. Two hundred others who had disappeared into the convent without returning were listed as missing.[2]

Don't Ask Questions—Just Kill Them

Colonel Francois DuPin was still operating from his headquarters near Medellín, about eight miles from Veracruz, and terrorizing the countryside in search of guerillas. One day a man by the name of Perez Lorenzo approached him, claiming to be a fruit dealer from Spain. Lorenzo said that some guerillas had captured his wife and him the previous day, and had forced him to look on while they had raped and killed his wife. He said he knew where to find them.

DuPin took the precaution of tying the man's hands behind his back—just in case it might be a trap. Lorenzo then led them to a campsite where they surprised some guerillas. They killed several guerillas as they attacked, then hung all the rest from nearby trees.

As DuPin's men entered a village a few days later, Lorenzo, who was now traveling with them, claimed that one of the men in the village was a sergeant from the guerilla unit that had killed his wife. DuPin's *contre-guérillas* lost no time in throwing a rope over a tree branch and hanging the individual, without bothering to ask any questions.

After the hanging, Lorenzo abruptly disappeared, never to be seen again. Had he really been who he said he was? Was he a conservative who just wanted to dream up reasons for the French to kill Mexican liberal guerillas? Did he have a personal grudge against the men who had been hanged, and was the story about the wife fabricated to get revenge? DuPin's people never found out, but then they never asked. All that mattered was that they had killed some bad guys. That was their job.

While raiding a banana plantation just outside of Medellín several nights later, DuPin's men found a carbine rifle and some muskets, apparently stolen from the French army. Bringing the plantation's owner, a Señor Muñoz, and his son to the town square, DuPin announced that father and son would be hanged from a large tree in that square the next day. A group of prominent citizens approached DuPin to ask him to pardon Señor Muñoz and his son, but the colonel refused. That evening, many of the town's women got all dressed up in their finest clothes and approached DuPin again, but once again he refused.

Ropes were already swaying from the large tree in the square the next morning when DuPin passed the word that he might be persuaded to pardon the men after all. Within a short time, as many as four hundred locals were parading around the square, shouting, "Long live the intervention! Long live the emperor of the French! Long live the French!" DuPin finally came out of his tent and granted the pardons, freeing Señor Muñoz and his son because the town had "shown so clearly their support for the new order of things."

DuPin moved on. He had other priorities, such as protecting the road to Orizaba and on to Puebla, so that supplies could reach the French troops, and also protecting the little railway line that led from Veracruz to Camarón. To achieve these goals, he would start by burning down every ranch within a certain distance of each route.[3]

Ambassador's Update

At the American embassy in Mexico City, Ambassador Thomas Corwin was trying to keep officials in Washington updated on the situation. He wrote to Secretary of State Seward:

> The progress of the French war presents puzzles to all [who are] not in the Cabinet secrets of the Emperor. It is conceded that he wishes to take Puebla. He has been before that city just one month. It has not surrendered. He has taken Fort St. Javier, [San Xavier Penitentiary] said to be the weakest of those which protect the city, and from that point has made lodgment [a foothold] within the walls, occupying six blocks in that suburb. According to our intelligence, any attempt made to advance has been repulsed…If the French wish to capture Puebla, the reason why it is not done seems to be because, with their present force, they cannot. Reinforcements from France, to the number of 3,000 or 4,000, lately landed at Vera Cruz, are now on the march to join the army at Puebla. It is surmised that General Forey awaits the arrival of these troops, and will, when they reach him, make a more vigorous assault…The Mexicans' last and surest hope lies in the establishment of our old Union, which they believe would exert a controlling influence against the occupation of this country by any monarchy of Europe.
>
> Your obedient servant,
> Thomas Corwin[4]

Forey Regrets His Words

General Forey remained somewhat detached from the day-to-day siege of Puebla. Sitting in his tent at the French camp about half an hour's ride to the west, he was still depressed about the failure of his troops to take Puebla and move on to Mexico City. He regretted his remarks about declining his responsibility. They had been uttered in frustration, and he had been trying off and on to convince those to whom he had spoken that he really didn't mean to say that he was quitting.

No one picked up on it. What would be the point? They all knew they were stuck, at least for now.

16

Bare Buttocks in a Convent Window

April 25–29, 1863

He Would Have Captured Mexico City by Now

Just when everyone thought things couldn't get any worse, Pierre Saligny showed up.

The minister had stayed behind in Orizaba for a while, but he arrived just as Forey and the officers were sorting out the Santa Ines disaster. His entourage consisted of five carriages, one of which was filled with women. Captain Blanchot was assigned to find housing for the group. He later wrote that Saligny had very good taste in women.

Another individual who showed up unannounced was a finance inspector from Paris by the name of M. Budin. Blanchot at first thought that Saligny would extend the courtesy of sharing his quarters to Budin, but Saligny would have nothing to do with him. The man wound up sleeping in a soldier's tent.

The French officers trying to carry out the siege may have argued among themselves about many things, but not about Saligny. To all of them, he was rude and overbearing—a complete pain in the buttocks. In Cholula, just west of Puebla, where Church officials had fled the siege, he bragged to a number of officers that he could have taken Mexico City by now with just a platoon of cavalry.

Saligny and Forey got into some pretty good arguments about whose fault it was that Puebla had not yet been captured.

"What were you doing since you have been here," asked Forey "not to know that the Mexicans would defend themselves like the Spaniards in Saragossa [Spain]?"

"It's your own fault," replied Saligny. "You soldiers think of nothing but wounds and scars, crosses and grades. You should have left Puebla and marched on the capital, where we would have settled the Mexican question."

106

The situation in general was bad enough, but Saligny's comments added to the sting. An angry Élie Frédéric Forey started holding several councils of war a day, resulting in more shouting and arguing. One discovery emerged from all the bickering: the unnamed officer who had proposed dropping the siege at Puebla and moving on to Mexico City had been coached by Pierre Saligny. It was beginning to dawn on many in the top command that Saligny, after helping to demolish Lorencez's career, was doing the same thing to Forey. That would make room at the top for General Achille Bazaine.[1]

The Forey-Saligny disputes and the stormy councils of war weighed heavily on the morale of the troops—as well as their knowledge of the hundreds of dead, wounded, and missing—but there was one incident that wounded French pride more than any other. General Douay's troops were crowded into trenches, fifty men deep, across the street from the convent, awaiting the signal to charge, when a woman appeared in one of the windows and displayed her naked bottom. She stayed there for a while, until some of the soldiers started shooting at her. Then, she disappeared, leaving with them only a memory of the kind of insult no Frenchman could ever forget.

Agnes Lobbies the Army Chief of Staff

Back in Washington, D.C., Agnes Salm-Salm was feeling a bit nervous as the maitre d' hotel escorted her to a table in the Willard dining room. She was to have lunch with the nation's top military man, the War Department's provost marshal-general, as she sought to save her husband's job as an officer in the United States army. Prince Felix Salm-Salm knew nothing about this. She had told him she was just coming from New York to visit her sister. Any thoughts about Mexico had not yet entered her mind.

The problem was this: most of the enlistments in the German-speaking unit where Felix had been serving were about to expire. Felix had been told that if he couldn't recruit seven hundred men to replace them, he would not be needed as an officer. Agnes was going to ask if some men could be transferred from other units to help Felix meet his quota.

As they talked over lunch, it turned out that Governor Yates of Illinois was in town. The governor had reported that he was ready to hand over a promised company of soldiers from Illinois, but that he still lacked qualified officers. What if Agnes's husband Felix were to be named commander of the new unit with the rank of colonel? And, to make the offer more attractive, what if she were to be named as a captain with a staff to care for wounded soldiers?

As she rode in the carriage toward Union Station, Agnes couldn't believe her good fortune. She had kept her husband's career alive. The hardest part would be to tell Felix.

Ortega to Comonfort: Last Chance

At about the same time, General González-Ortega wrote to General Comonfort, saying that the city of Puebla could endure the siege for just one more week—maybe eight days—if there were no relief. Comonfort indicated that a rescue convoy was on the way and urged Ortega to hold out as long as he could. Comonfort, a former president of Mexico, was not much of a team player and preferred to follow his own priorities. In reality, the aging Comonfort also lacked the strategic leadership skills to intervene on Ortega's behalf. Just the hope that Comonfort might come through, though, dampened any expectation that the Mexicans were about to surrender.

General Forey knew that Ortega had presidential aspirations. The Mexican Constitution provided that, as chief justice of the Supreme Court, Ortega would be next in line to succeed Juárez as president. Forey's representatives at the occasional prisoner exchanges between the French and the Mexicans dangled the possibility of Ortega's being named president. Ortega didn't take the bait. He replied that as long as the French were involved, he was not interested. He refused an invitation to meet personally with Forey.[2]

Corwin to Seward: It's Not Over Yet

It was now May 1, and the French had been pounding Puebla for more than six weeks. In Mexico City, American ambassador Thomas Corwin wrote once again to Secretary of State William Seward in Washington: "Nothing has occurred to change the general aspect since my last letter to the department. The French army has been before Puebla forty-five days…Small detachments of troops are reported from day to day to be fighting in houses and streets, hand to hand with the Mexican troops…General Comonfort, with a force of 15,000 of all arms, is at, or near San Martín, a short distance from Puebla."[3]

Under the arrangement set up by President Benito Juárez, General Comonfort was supposed to defend Mexico City if the French were to choose that as their target; Ortega's forces would come to his rescue. Since Ortega was defending Puebla, it was Ortega's expectation that Comonfort was supposed to come to the rescue. So far, Comonfort had been unsuccessful in getting through.

That evening, Corwin dropped by the Yorke family apartment on Calle San Francisco. Just as all other visitors, he carried a revolver. It wasn't safe to go out at night unarmed.

Sara Yorke and her family had heard Corwin tell many times about the Battle of Cinco de Mayo the previous year, and how the French now had Puebla surrounded for a second try. On many nights in Mexico City, they would hear random gunfire and shouts of *"¡Mueran los Franceses!"* ("Kill the Frenchmen!"). There were even rumors that all foreigners, not just the French, would be massacred if the Mexicans won a second time at Puebla.

"You don't hear them shouting *'¡Mueran los gringos!'* ('Kill the gringos!'), do you?" said Corwin. He contended that the French had been camped outside Puebla for forty-five days, earning their reputation as the spiteful invaders. They had nothing to show for it, and the anniversary of last year's Mexican victory was fast approaching.

"President Juárez has persuaded General Comonfort to approach Puebla with about fifteen thousand men in some kind of rescue effort," he told the Yorkes. "They have a large convoy of wagons bearing food," he said, "and that's what worries me. The French will no doubt take this as a signal that hunger is about to become the determining factor, and they'll hold out accordingly. We should know the outcome within the next few days."[4]

On the night of May 5, General Comonfort made what would be the first of several attempts to get the food convoy into Puebla. The French repelled the attack, as they did again on the night of May 6. Corwin had been right: Comonfort's persistence led the French to conclude that hunger, indeed, was taking its toll.

Just Use Spanish in the Dark

General Bazaine picked up on the cue. On May 7, he went to Forey and asked for permission to lead a night attack on Comonfort, who was just ten miles west of Puebla. The two men argued for some time, but finally Forey gave in. Bazaine took some French troops and some Mexican Imperialistas out on the road toward Mexico City. After dark, he cut across country to where Comonfort's troops were camped out near the village of San Lorenzo.

When the French troops were challenged by Comonfort's sentries, Bazaine had one of the Imperialistas answer in Spanish. It worked. Once past the sentries, they climbed the hill and scattered the rescue forces in all directions, food wagons and all. Bazaine's people returned with twelve hundred prisoners and eight large cannons. He would have chased Comonfort's troops to the gates of Mexico City if he had had about three more battalions, but that was the part of the argument he had lost with Forey.

Still, the rank-and-file French soldiers gave Bazaine credit for the breakthrough, and he became the folk hero of the army. Colonel du Barail took notice, writing that "the soldier, happy and proud to feel himself commanded by a real warrior, lavished on him the proof of blind and unlimited confidence. But, as always happens, his popularity was carved at the expense of that which the commander-in-chief might have obtained. They were compared with one another, and that comparison was not in favor of General Forey."[5]

Forey's lack of presence among the troops was not helping. Whenever he showed up, which was not often, he was perceived as cranky, harsh, and repressive. Behind his back, he was referred to as "the old man"—someone whose prime had passed—and who now was somewhat out of touch.

The troops' perception of Bazaine, especially after the successful raid on Comonfort's troops, was much different. As Colonel du Barail wrote, "What a difference from General Bazaine! Day and night, in the trenches, in the bivouac, he was seen moving about without pomp or embarrassment or escort, on foot, his cane in his hand, good-natured, talking familiarly to everyone, joking with the soldiers, listening to them, explaining to them what they had to do and how to do it, and walking, in short, very skillfully toward his goal."[6]

Bazaine's breakthrough and his charismatic approach put a new robust vitality into the French effort. It wouldn't be long, now, until the expected Mexican surrender. To keep up the pressure, Forey ordered new attacks on forts Carmen and Totimehuacan.

17

More Than a Year Later, Puebla Is Finally Taken

(May 8–29, 1863)

Hope Runs Out for General Ortega

On the morning of May 8, General Ortega's people learned the sad news: there would be no rescue convoy. They were already down to slaughtering horses, mules, and dogs to stay alive. Rats were next on the list, and some of the soldiers were said to be already roasting them on sticks over open fires.[1]

Ortega managed to get a message off to General Comonfort: they would attempt a mass breakout from Puebla on May 14. Comonfort was being asked to stage an attack from the outside as a diversion. May 14 came and went, and Comonfort's people never showed up, so the attempt was called off.

On May 15, Ortega contacted General Forey and arranged for an evacuation of all the noncombatants. At six o'clock the next morning, the exodus began. Starvation was written all over the faces of the women, children, and elderly men as they trudged through the gate and headed westward on the road toward Cholula. Many French soldiers were seen crying at the sight of the ragged, famished individuals who passed by them. Some even offered their own rations of bread, and looked the other way as children reached for corn in horses' feeding bags.

At one o'clock in the morning on May 17, the city of Puebla was rocked by a series of explosions. Ortega's troops were destroying their weapons, or at least some of them. The French later found more than a hundred cannons still in good condition and more than seventeen hundred rounds of ammunition. At five o'clock that afternoon, Forey received a note from Ortega that the town was his.

The 12,500 prisoners taken by the French included more than 11,000 soldiers and noncommissioned officers, 1,179 administrative and support staff, 303 commissioned officers, and 20 generals. The siege had lasted for sixty-three days.

What were they to do with all those prisoners? The Imperialistas told Forey that all the officers should be executed by firing squads, but the general immediately rejected that suggestion. He respected not only the way Ortega had so skillfully defended the town for nine weeks, but the humane treatment received by French soldiers captured during all of the fighting.

Forey decided to release the officers if they would sign documents promising not to take up arms against the French. Unanimously, they refused, so Forey ordered that all of them be sent to prisons in France. Of the regular soldiers, five thousand agreed to become Imperialistas under General Márquez, another four thousand were sent to work on the railroad still under construction from Veracruz toward Mexico City, and the remaining two thousand were put to work cleaning up Puebla and taking down all the barricades.

On May 19, Élie Frédéric Forey rode on a beautiful white horse at the head of the parade, waving and smiling as though the entire victory had been accomplished only through his daring and innovative leadership. Marching behind him were several thousand French soldiers who knew better. Many of them believed that if it had not been for General Bazaine's night patrol that scattered Comonfort's rescue convoy, they might still be hopelessly engaged in an endless assault around the edges of this town. When Ortega surrendered, Bazaine's popularity among the troops soared.

The clergy were waiting at the cathedral door. In their eyes, General Forey was "the deliverer," the one who had finally saved them from the clutches of all those godless Juaristas. As Forey soon realized, the priests were the only welcoming committee he was going to see. There were no local officials on hand to greet him, nor cheering crowds in the streets. The entire town was all but dead.

To start the religious celebrations, a *Te Deum* (Mass of praise) was sung in the cathedral to honor Forey and his army. Forey's top generals and other high-ranking officers filled the pews all around him. Farther back in the pews, soldiers whispered to each other. Many were praying that they would get back on the road to Mexico City the next day. It had taken them nine weeks to get into Puebla. Some of them had already concluded that if they were to give the Mexicans time to set up another defense like the one they had in Puebla, that's how long it might take the French forces to get into the capital.

The young soldiers' prayers were not about to be answered. It was May 21, and General Forey was still in Puebla for a third day, taking in all the pomp and circumstance that the clergy could muster. The ordinary soldiers found themselves taking care of all the refugees who had been evacuated to Cholula, five miles to the west.

Many conservatives and French sympathizers had fled from Puebla to Cholula at the beginning of the nine-week siege in March. They were overjoyed at the French victory. They were joined in Cholula by clergy who had retreated after the surrender. As Cholula mounted three days of all-out celebration to honor the French army, priests staged events that ranged from the almost carnival to the almost operatic. The streets were filled with statues and relics. *Indígenas* (Indians) fervently beat their chests and threw themselves to the ground. Musicians with various levels of ability, or lack of it, wandered everywhere, playing by ear at an occasionally painful volume. More than one soldier concluded that if anything could make enemies for Mexico, it was the music.

If it were not the music, then perhaps it would be the food. Several of the locals slaughtered goats on the ground at the side of the road. The blood and the entrails spilled all around as women tended fires nearby and chopped feverishly at searing-hot chiles. The smoke drifting over the village was enough to bring tears to any Frenchman's eyes. It was safe to say that almost all the soldiers declined to partake in the feast, regardless of the sincerity with which it was offered.

After three days of Cholula's nonstop fiesta, French general de Mirandol decided that he had endured enough. He ordered a cavalry patrol to disperse the crowds.

General Forey, meanwhile, remained in Puebla. He would stay there for two whole weeks.

Prisoner Head Count Comes Up Short

On May 22, long lines of defeated Mexican officers waited to be checked in for trips by stagecoach or wagon to Veracruz, where they were to be put aboard ships bound for France. Each was to step up to a table, sign a document promising not to escape, and board a vehicle.

The Mexicans had unanimously refused to sign a pledge not to take up arms against the invaders, but simply disappearing was another issue. At some point, it dawned on the French officers who were supervising the operation that the line was too short. Of the 1,508 officers who had surrendered five days earlier, only 950 had signed a "no-escape" pledge. Of the others, 558, including 4 generals, had already fled. No one really wanted the job of telling General Forey.

Ortega and His Generals Escape

Things got worse as the convoy bearing the prisoners headed toward Veracruz. Lower-ranking officers were being marched on foot, but Jesús González-Ortega and several other generals were being transported in heavily guarded carriages. Reports were reaching them that those on foot were being abused by the French soldiers who had drawn this dreary assignment. Probably, the Frenchmen realized they would wind up back in steamy, disease-ridden Veracruz while their comrades would proceed to Mexico City, and they were taking out their frustrations on the prisoners. Ortega was so outraged by the cruelty and lack of discipline among the French captors that he decided to renounce the "no escape" pledge he had signed. He made plans to slip away.

At Orizaba, while he and the other generals were being held at the former convent of San José de García, a unique opportunity presented itself. Some vendors had been allowed to sell provisions to the prisoners, and the generals quietly began expressing interest in certain items of clothing so that they were able to put together simple disguises. The trick was not to look like a general but more like someone visiting a son or nephew among the other prisoners. The guards had not been told who the generals were, and didn't care to find out, which helped Ortega and the others to simply walk away when the circumstances were favorable, probably with a smile and a *"¡Muchas gracias!"* ("Thanks a lot!") on the way out.[2]

One hundred ninety-three superior officers also disappeared, along with 772 lower-ranking aides and noncoms. Out of 1,508 originally captured, only 530 were still in custody when they were finally loaded onto the ships bound for France. Among the generals who got away, Mariano Escobedo and Porfirio Díaz (who had been promoted by Zaragoza after the first Battle of Puebla) would play even more prominent roles in the conflict later on.

Before moving on, Captain Henri Loizillon got another letter off to his parents. As he reviewed the outcome of the nine-week siege, he couldn't help grieving over the loss of some of his best friends. He admitted to feeling guilty about losing track of them and all but forgetting them before it was all over. Maybe it had been the need to preserve his own sanity in the face of all the suffering. Even so, he began to wonder why they had lost their lives.

He noted that the ground all around Puebla was still littered with copies of that speech by Jules Favre. The French government, in a clumsy attempt at rebuttal, had flooded the town with copies of the speech by Prime Minister M. Billault. Monsieur Billault had claimed that the Mexicans would be guaranteed the freedom to elect their own government, even if they were to choose Benito Juárez.

Benito Juárez? If that were the case, thought Loizillon, what had the French army been fighting for all this time? To reinstate Juárez? If Billault meant what he said, it conveyed, to Loizillon at least, that the whole project had been totally absurd. Something else didn't seem right: if Puebla were supposed to be the most pro-French city in all of Mexico, someone was going to have to explain why it took sixty-three days to subdue the place.

Loizillon was not the only one having confused or negative thoughts about Puebla. Minister Pierre Saligny, the one who had predicted a quick victory, couldn't pile enough harsh criticism upon Forey and his generals. He blamed them for the long, drawn-out siege and the mass escape by hundreds of captured Mexican officers on the way to Veracruz. All the French generals came in for criticism, except Bazaine. Saligny liked Bazaine. Achille Bazaine had managed to distance himself from Forey, and he was good at telling Saligny only what the minister wanted to hear. As a result of what he was hearing, Saligny believed that he and Bazaine were in close agreement with each other.

Élie Frédéric Forey was another story. As the Mexicans liked to say, "Every monkey to his own rope!" Forey admired General Ortega as a soldier. He was glad that Ortega had escaped, and would gladly have recommended that he be part of the new provisional government Saligny was putting together—if he could entice Ortega to surrender. It didn't seem to matter to Forey that neither Saligny nor Ortega was likely to go along with such a scheme.

All We've Conquered Is a Stretch of Roadway

Captain Loizillon was assigned as part of an advance team to line up housing for the French army in Mexico City. Upon hearing that Juárez had withdrawn—or was about to withdraw—his government from the capital, Loizillon wrote, "We shall be masters as usual only of the points we occupy. After eighteen months of war, we shall have conquered the road from Veracruz to Mexico City; that will be the result."[3]

18

Reactions to the Fall of Puebla

(May 28–31, 1863)

Mexican Forces Regroup

As the news from Puebla reached Mexico City, President Benito Juárez put the capital under martial law. He issued a proclamation calling for the population to prepare for a vigorous defense and began recruiting additional forces to make a last stand. Juárez accepted the resignation of General Comonfort, whose forces had been scattered by Bazaine before the fall of Puebla. Generals Ortega, Escobedo, and others who had escaped in Orizaba would soon arrive to carry on the struggle for Mexico's sovereignty.

General Ortega, moving carefully to avoid recapture, began his journey at Huatusco, a small town along the Gulf coast southeast of Veracruz, and traveled cross-country by way of Xalapa to the tiny village of Teziutlan, in the mountains just northwest of Perote. He was accompanied by generals Llave and Patoni. Other Mexican officers who had escaped French custody were gradually regrouping in order to get back into the fight against the invaders.[1]

DuPin Called on the Carpet

Aboard a ship in Veracruz Harbor, Colonel Francois DuPin angrily denied any connection with the escape of 978 Mexican officers. French navy officials were distressed at receiving only 530 of the 1,508 officers originally captured. Their question to DuPin was essentially, "Where were you when we needed you?" They chastised him for being obsessed with terrorizing little fishing villages and not paying attention to protecting French supply lines and preventing the escape of prisoners.

DuPin was still smarting from the criticism when he gathered with his henchmen later. He vowed to retaliate against those who had so far managed to evade and humiliate him. There was no way to get the prisoners back now, but nobody was going to blame their escape on him. The violence and atrocities would escalate until he got more respect.

Silent March by Moonlight

The news of the Puebla defeat reached Mexico City during the day on May 30. That night, as Sara Yorke sat with her family in the drawing room at their apartment on Calle San Francisco, they heard the tramp, tramp, tramp of marching feet. There was no music, not even drums. Nobody was calling out orders.

As she stepped to her window, Sara could see what was left of the defeated Mexican army passing by on its way to the Zócalo, or main plaza. They were not singing or even talking to each other as they marched along with their women, the *soldaderas*. Most of them were dressed in loose white shirts and baggy trousers, carrying only muskets and ammunition boxes over their shoulders.

Where were they going? Were the French right behind them in hot pursuit? Had Juárez decided to rally them and make one last stand to defend the capital? None of those who watched them trudging along in the moonlight knew the answer. Sara called it "a strange weird sight."[2]

Mexican Government Leaves the Capital

Porfirio Díaz was among the first of the escaped generals to reach Mexico City. He and several others met with President Juárez and confirmed his worst fears. The defeated Mexican soldiers trudging into town numbered only about six thousand at best. Forey and his victorious French troops numbered more than twenty-five thousand. If Juárez were to defend the city, the local residents would have to suffer through something similar to what the citizens of Puebla had endured. Even then, Mexico City was neither barricaded nor as well armed as Puebla had been. It was possible the French could prevail in under twenty-four hours.

President Juárez announced his decision before an emergency session of Congress on the morning of May 31. He would move the government and all major federal officials to San Luis Potosí, some two hundred miles to the north of Mexico City. He pledged that he would continue to resist the French intervention and never surrender. Congress voted to grant him extraordinary powers for the duration of the conflict.

The firing of a cannon at three o'clock that afternoon announced the Congress's final adjournment. An enormous crowd gathered in the Zócalo to hear announcements about the actions taken. Juárez did not want to give the appearance of panic. He deliberately waited until sundown to conduct the flag-lowering ceremony at its usual hour, but behind the scenes government officials were packing for departure that very night.

At the Yorke apartment on Calle San Francisco, a courier arrived with a message from Ambassador Thomas Corwin, confirming that the Mexican government was moving the capital to San Luis Potosí. The American embassy would not be moving with them. It would be shut down until further notice, and Corwin himself had already been granted a leave of absence.

President Juárez appeared on the balcony of the Palacio Nacional with his ministers and his military staff. Men raised their hats. Women lifted up their children. A color guard and a number of troops presented arms as the national anthem was played and the flag was lowered, just as it would have been on any other day. As the flag was handed to Juárez, he kissed it and shouted, "¡Viva Mexico!" ("Long live Mexico!"). The crowd echoed his call in a tumultuous voice. Then, Benito Juárez went directly downstairs, climbed into a waiting stagecoach, and rode northward through the night.

Along with Juárez in the stagecoach were members of his cabinet. His wife and eight children (Manuela, Margarita, Felicitas, Jesús, Josefa, Soledad, Benito, and José) followed in several carriages.

Fears of Mob Violence

As the caravan disappeared, many foreigners were afraid that mob violence might arise. There were cries of "Mueran los Franceses" ("Kill the Frenchmen"), and for many of the locals in the crowd, all foreigners were considered Franceses.

Then, too, without any police force there might be rioting and looting. Many of those present well remembered the "Tiger of Tacubaya"—General Leonardo Márquez—who had carried out the hospital massacres during the War of the Reform. Márquez's men were part of the Imperialista forces now serving along with the French, and there were fears that if his contingent arrived ahead of the French, they might set out to massacre anybody whom they suspected of being a Juárez supporter.

Something would have to be done to prevent both mob violence and possible atrocities by the Márquez troops. At the very least, foreign embassies and consulates would have to think of protecting their own citizens.[3]

Veracruz Is at Greater Risk

There was also trouble brewing in Veracruz. General Forey had called up so many French soldiers to carry out his operation at Puebla that the port city had been left in the hands of Sudanese and Egyptian troops, who spoke neither French nor Spanish. While the Puebla siege was in progress, eleven French officers and at least half the black troops from Africa and the Caribbean had died of yellow fever. A Captain Grandin from Colonel DuPin's *contre-guérilla* unit reported that without the Sudanese and some black engineers from the Caribbean islands of Martinique and Guadeloupe, Veracruz would have been left almost entirely defenseless.

As Richard Hill and Peter Hogg write in their book *A Black Corps d'Élite:*

> The streets [of Veracruz] were alive with soldiers and sailors of many countries whose tented camps outside the wall received overflow from the city barracks. But the town had a dried-up appearance; the public square was devoid of vegetation, something abhorrent to the French concept of a town square as a place of beauty and repose with shrubs and lawns and, of course, a band playing on Sunday afternoons. For the sensitive, the dust stirred up by the winds made the streets a torture for the eyes. The place to stay, according to the unanimous verdict of Europeans and Americans, was the Hotel Diligencias in the main square, if only the guests would refrain from spitting on the floor and loudly gambling all night.

The French had apparently assumed that the African troops could withstand the climate and the diseases of Mexico's tropical coastline, but seventy-one of them had been taken to Fort San Juan de Ulúa, which had been converted to a hospital, upon arrival, and fifty-two of them died within the first two weeks. Mexican food didn't suit their digestive systems, and it didn't help that they had been transported below decks in the hold of a ship that had no portholes and that had not been cleaned since it carried horses and mules on the previous trip.

A French army doctor found the African troops to be extremely dejected and reported that "the majority are in a state of stupor…" Yellow fever was not the only medical problem. Many of them were diagnosed with typhus, tuberculosis, and tapeworm. These were the troops Forey had been counting on, not just to defend Veracruz but to guard the railway and escort the trains. Clearly, the general would have to deal with this problem before moving on to Mexico City.[4]

An Alternate Seaport on the Pacific

It was not hard to imagine that the French would become frustrated with Veracruz and begin to search for alternatives. One strong possibility was Mazatlán, Mexico's largest Pacific west-coast seaport. Californians had been coming and going from that side of Mexico for decades. Among them was an American expatriate mining engineer and businessman, who had owned a mine in the western Sierra Madre range, in the little town of Copala on the road to Durango. Frederick G. Fitch knew his business would suffer if the French took over Mazatlán, so he had begun a project to fortify the town in May of 1863, just before the fall of Puebla.

Another factor was beginning to have an effect: world opinion. Newspapers like the *Times* of London, Madrid's *La Iberia,* and even the Paris newspaper *Le Temps* praised the Mexicans for their heroic defense of Puebla during the sixty-three-day siege. Very few papers criticized General González-Ortega as a military commander or thought that General Comonfort or even President Juárez may have contributed to the defeat. Overwhelmingly, stories about the fall of Puebla applauded the Mexicans rather than the French.

As Mexican historian José M. Vigil put it in his *Resumen Integral de México A Través de los Siglos,* "The valiant defenders of Puebla succumbed, not to the arms of a powerful enemy but to the horrors of hunger and the lack of munitions of war. A town had been lost, but the honor of Mexico had been saved."[5]

PART III

French Generals Are in Charge

May 30, 1863, through March 31, 1864

19

Mexico City Awaits the French Arrival

(First Week of June 1863)

Foreign Legations Patrol the Capital

It would be several days before General Forey and the French army arrived from Puebla, but Mexico City needed some interim security to guard against criminals and anarchy. Edward L. Plumb and fellow diplomats from a number of foreign consulates and embassies had suddenly become the Mexico City police force by default. President Juárez's overnight departure had forced them to organize a seven-hundred-man security group to protect their own nationals and to try to keep some law and order.

There were the expected questions about rioting and looting, but those who had been in town for more than five years were most concerned about Leonardo Márquez. They recalled for the gathering how the general and his troops had massacred hundreds of unarmed civilians in hospitals and government offices. There had been no discipline at all, they said. Márquez's people had simply gone on a rampage.

The Prussian vice consul stood up. His name was Franz Bahsen. He strongly urged the group to send a delegation to General Forey, asking for assurances that Márquez's troops would not be the first to enter the capital. Bahsen insisted that the delegation include someone who knew firsthand the story of the atrocities committed four or five years earlier. He said that General Forey must be made to realize that all of the countries represented in the seven-hundred-man security group were making the request on behalf of their citizens. Bahsen warned that if any such massacres occurred this time, France would share the culpability and the shame for such atrocities.

Bahsen got a standing ovation.

Twelve diplomats volunteered for the assignment and left immediately to prepare for the trip toward Puebla. They planned to intercept General Forey along the way.

Foreign Delegation Appeals to Forey

As the delegation of diplomats made their way toward Puebla, they came across the French advance guard led by General Bazaine. They told him what their mission was, but he pointed out that his troops were already at the front of the army, which followed them, and that further changes in the lineup would have to come from General Forey. As the foreign emissaries reached Puebla, the locals had already reverted back to openly supporting the French. A number of them, recognizing that the group was a diplomatic contingent, shouted to them, "Long live France! Death to Juárez!"

Forey was not as cordial in his reception of the delegation as they might have hoped, saying that he couldn't just change the army's marching orders to suit the preferences of people in Mexico City. It took some convincing, but after he heard about Márquez's earlier atrocities and was told that France would share the blame if it happened again, he agreed to hold back Márquez's troops until he received confirmation that General Bazaine and the advance guard had actually entered Mexico City.[1]

Mexico's Man in Washington Wants to Quit

In Washington, D.C., Matías Romero was packing up to go home. The bright-eyed, twenty-six-year-old chargé d'affaires at the Mexican Embassy was despondent over his lack of progress in lining up U.S. backing for the Juárez government south of the border. Besides, Romero had not been receiving either his paycheck or money to cover the expenses involved in mounting an effective campaign to influence United States' policy. He planned on joining the army.

Romero knew that the Americans were all absorbed in their Civil War. He had made endless presentations to Secretary of State William Seward, but both Seward and President Abraham Lincoln were afraid to risk a war with France over the Mexican intervention while the conflict with the Confederacy was still in progress. He had made friends with people like California senator James A. McDougall and with the chairman of the Senate Foreign Relations Committee, Charles Sumner. McDougall not only sponsored a resolution alerting the Senate to the repercussions of the French intervention in Mexico, but relayed a great deal of Senate gossip about Mexico to Romero.

Chairman Sumner got as far as bringing Ambassador Thomas Corwin's proposed loan treaty up for a vote, but when it was defeated, he told Romero that the Mexican situation would have to wait until the Civil War was resolved. Sumner didn't want to anger the French, and he couldn't afford to defy Secretary of State Seward. After a while, Romero concluded that with no pay and no operating budget, and with Seward and Sumner as major obstacles, he might as well go home. He wrote in his notes,

> The public men of this nation are blind in this respect. The emperor [Napoleon III] has deceived them like children. Through the medium of his dentist, an American citizen, Napoleon assures them that he is a friend of the Union and desires its reestablishment and indicates to them that they must fear England. Although he has failed to keep his word and even his sworn promises, they believe in his sincerity on this occasion. Even his decidedly partial conduct in favor of the South, acknowledged by President [Jefferson] Davis…and by Secretary of State [Judah] Benjamin in correspondence recently intercepted by this government, is not sufficient to persuade them otherwise. I do not have the remotest hope that McDougall's resolutions will be approved by the Senate.

Romero decided that it was time to return home to Mexico. He sent his resignation to President Benito Juárez.[2]

20

Finally, the French Enter Mexico City

(June 8–15, 1863)

A Staged Grand Entrance

Some of the sergeants were having a hard time keeping their men in line as the first waves of General Bazaine's advance guard entered the capital on June 8, 1863. They were "ooh-ing" and "ahh-ing" and whistling at the young lady standing on a balcony overlooking Calle San Francisco as the sergeants tried to march them in some kind of order toward the Zócalo in the center of town.

Sara Yorke had just turned sixteen, but since she had been brought up in Parisian high society, she looked just like the girls back home in France. The troops just couldn't keep their eyes off of her. Some of them pressed their fingers to their lips and blew kisses. Sara just smiled and waved.

Not all of the inhabitants were waving or even smiling. As General Forey arrived two days later, in a parade flanked by Imperialista general Juan Almonte on his right and Minister Pierre Saligny on his left, the commander-in-chief was totally oblivious to the passive resistance being shown by the locals. What Forey saw were occasional small crowds, which had been hastily organized by Bazaine's military police and other advance troops. He was being showered with the flowers and applause that Almonte and Saligny had promised General Lorencez a year earlier. Eduardo Ruiz, in his book, *Triumphs and Tragedy: A History of the Mexican People,* describes the occasion: "Old criollo fogies, remnants of the Santa Anna years, stepped out onto the balconies of their palatial homes to applaud their liberators, while *mochos* (Catholic fanatics,) yelled and waved handkerchiefs. Squat and pompous like some impersonator of the Romans, Forey believed that the whole nation was kneeling in gratitude, oblivious to the spectators who watched from afar."[1]

No one dared tell Forey that these highly contrived events did not exactly express the true sentiment of the public at large. He sent a telegram to the minister of war in Paris claiming that "the entire population of this capital welcomed the army with an enthusiasm verging on delirium." Actually, the delirium belonged to Forey and to no one else.[2] As Captain Loizillon later wrote, "The people were attracted by curiosity rather than enthusiasm. The places where we were applauded or showered with flowers were rare, and those few demonstrations had been organized by the police and the commander of the city. Nevertheless, the commander-in-chief has taken all this for true coin, his vanity preventing him from judging things at their true value."[3]

Time to Hear the New Rules

On June 11, Forey gathered his officers together and told them there would be some limited freedom for the press. Catholicism would be the only "officially recognized" religion, but the clergy and their conservative backers would be required to "tolerate" other religious practices. But, said the general, those who had bought Church land seized earlier by the Juaristas would not be forced to give it back to the Church, at least not for now. All issues surrounding that controversy would have to be settled at some later time.

Forey continued, announcing that they were going to choose an "Assembly of Notables" to form an interim government. Finally, he came to something the officers cared about: housing. Many of those who had arrived with Bazaine had been put up in filthy, run-down hotels, four or five to a room, with most sleeping on the floor. The rest of the officers had to sleep in tents, along with the troops, outside of town. That was all about to change.

Families of good character, ordered the general, meaning those with the biggest houses who had servants, would be required to accommodate French officers in their homes. The others, he added, would also be required to house as many soldiers as their facilities would allow. The officers were to serve as models, said Forey, and be on their best behavior. They were to make friends with the families wherever possible. They were also to escort young women who came from good backgrounds to the theater and other social occasions, just as they had successfully done in Orizaba a year earlier.

Among those "families of good character" were the Yorkes. They were asked to receive two young naval officers and their orderlies. Years later, Sara Yorke Stevenson wrote in her memoirs that she had opposed such a move, but then, "they turned out to be perfect gentlemen, and completely won us over by their unvarying good breeding under shabby treatment. Before long we were, and remained, the best of friends."[4]

It wasn't just the young officers who were being amiable and mannerly with Sara and her sister. The officers' two orderlies were busy making love to the family's *indígena* (Indian) servants.

New York Times Triggers Anti-French Outrage

Not only did Northerners in the United States act with dismay when they learned that the French had entered Mexico City, but the *New York Times* published an English translation of a brochure from France that called for an attack on the Americans. The pamphlet's author was quoted as saying that the French expedition would make Mexico more civilized and would yield exceptional commercial advantages. To really succeed, however, the French were urged to join the Civil War in support of the Confederacy. The paper's readers were outraged.

A columnist for the newspaper, Vine Wright Kingsley, claimed that the pamphlet had been written by someone widely known as an unofficial spokesman for Napoleon III and was most likely prompted by the emperor himself. Kingsley warned Secretary of State William Seward to drop his appeasement of Napoleon III and get ready for a possible war with France.

Mexican Church Leaders Test the Limits

It wasn't long before Church leaders began to test their limits with the French. They began to seek the return of some of their lost privileges and authority. Captain Loizillon wrote home to France:

> We had no sooner arrived than the clergy began to ring all the bells to make up for the constraint they had suffered under the Juárez government, which had fixed the hours when the bells might be heard. Since then we have been deafened. Under Juárez, processions were forbidden as they are in France. Last Thursday the clergy asked permission to hold the procession of the *Fête-Dieu*. The commander-in-chief not only consented, but attended the procession with all his officers. The Mexicans looked for all the world as if they were mocking us. All that we lacked were tapers in our hands."[5]

Ortega Escapes an Attempted Murder

Meanwhile, General Jesús González-Ortega, who was still a fugitive, escaped with his life when three soldiers who had been assigned as his escort tried to rob and kill him. He had met with General Doblado in Guanajuato on June 12, and was heading from there to San Luis Potosí to confer with President Juárez. Doblado provided the three-man escort because Ortega was carrying five hundred ounces of gold, which had been taken from Puebla. Generals Llave and Patoni were still riding along with him, and Ortega asked Llave to help him carry some of the gold. Some of it fell to the ground as the soldiers watched, and the three immediately began plotting to kill the generals and steal the gold. General Llave was lagging somewhat behind Ortega and Patoni as the attempt began on June 14. Llave was shot in the back but managed to shout a warning to the others. All three generals managed to escape by galloping away at full speed.

Once they arrived in San Luis Potosí, Ortega planned to resume his duties as president of Mexico's Supreme Court, which would put him next in line for the presidency. Within a few weeks, it was determined that he was more urgently needed in his former post as governor of Zacatecas, since the state had been declared under siege as the French drew closer and closer. He assumed the post, although it was to cause constitutional problems later on.[6]

French Support Dwindling Among Conservatives

Back in Mexico City, the enthusiastic backing of the French that had been expressed by monarchists, conservatives, devout Catholics, and the clergy was already beginning to fade. Not only had they learned of the decision not to give back Church lands seized earlier by the Juaristas, but they were told that this was what Napoleon III wanted. The so-called Assembly of Notables ratified the policy.

To many who had originally backed the French takeover, the refusal to return confiscated Church property was a complete surprise. To the many rich and powerful members of the Assembly of Notables who had already bought Church property or who had close friends or relatives who had done so, it was no surprise at all. Some of them had spent more than forty thousand pesos to acquire their real estate, and they were not about to give it back.

Juárez's Strategy to Wear Out the French

To the north in San Luis Potosí, Benito Juárez unfurled the Mexican flag over his temporary capital. He issued a proclamation in which he stated that the French would soon recognize that the Republic is not confined to Mexico City or Puebla. The invaders, he said, had aroused a noble pride—the love of independence and democracy—and the sense of right and strength among the whole of the Mexican people. If the enemy continued to concentrate its forces in just one point, it would be weak in all others, he asserted. However, he said, if they dispersed their forces, they would be weak everywhere.

But, as historian Ralph Roeder points out, "manifestos favor their authors." Juárez knew that the main body of Mexican forces had been defeated at Puebla. Not only had General Comonfort's rescue brigade en route to Puebla been scattered by Bazaine within half an hour, but many of Comonfort's soldiers had simply switched sides when captured and turned their guns against the very people who had been their comrades less than a day earlier.

Juárez also knew that he had to change the focus. The French wanted to count battles won and cities taken. The Juárez strategy was to engage in guerilla warfare over an area so wide that the French wouldn't know which way to direct their fire. He would cut their communications, harass their supply lines, and through a never-ending series of hit-and-run tactics, force them to overextend themselves. Also, he would stall for time until the French started developing political problems with the Church and among themselves as they attempted to decide how best to run the country. It would be a test of endurance.

Even Captain Loizillon sensed that the French wouldn't be able to please everybody. "The reactionaries think themselves masters of the situation," he wrote. He predicted that the Church would keep pushing for the return of the property seized under Juárez and for the return of authority to the clergy. Despite the best intentions of the French, Loizillon knew that all of that would be impossible. "The result," he wrote, "will be that we shall have the reactionary party against us, and that we shall maintain ourselves here only by force."[7]

21

Napoleon III's Offer to Maximilian

(June 16 through August 21, 1863)

The French Army's Charm Offensive

As a military band played in the background, General Élie Frédéric Forey handed out candy and toys to many of Mexico City's children. Some had been brought by their parents while others had wandered there on their own. Many of the children approached the old gentleman with the bushy white moustache out of curiosity. Forey let them sit on his knee, and allowed them to play with his sword and the medals on his uniform. The general was trying his best to show how he wanted his officers and troops to make friends.

Some of the officers started producing plays, the Zouaves resumed their frog-eating and sword-swallowing displays, and other units of the French army pitched in with serenades, *tertulias* (social gatherings for conversation or entertainment), picnics, and a host of other entertaining events. Ordinary soldiers were buying up grammar books and memorizing romantic things to say to the local señoritas, such as "*Eres la preciosita de mis ojos*" ("You're a precious sight to my eyes") and "*Te quiero más que ayer y menos que mañana*" (I love you more than yesterday and less than tomorrow").

Forey Is Mesmerized by the Church

General Forey didn't notice—but others did—that he was being swayed by the dramatic, welcoming pageantry put on by the Catholic Church and the clergy. One of those who took note was Colonel du Barail, who like most career military officers normally avoided politics. He later wrote:

> The 10th of June marked the triumph of the French army, the 11th marked the triumph of the Clerical party…A monster procession was organized for

131

that day, and nothing was neglected to give it an incomparable effect. The triumphal arches of the day before served for this new parade, which was escorted by three squadrons of cavalry and three regiments of French infantry, and which was hailed with the same enthusiasm, the same flowers, the same acclamations, and the same smiling women. The politicians of the army and the French mission thought that we were going too far and throwing ourselves too much in the arms of the Clerical party.[1]

That was just the beginning. Every Sunday from that point on, an entire division of the French army attended military Mass at Mexico City's main cathedral. While one regiment of soldiers occupied the pews inside, batteries of artillery and regiments of cavalry were posted outside. As the Mass was celebrated, a general outside in the square led the troops through the various maneuvers prescribed for each stage of the religious service taking place inside.

Colonel du Barail sensed that Forey was walking into a trap. Du Barail admitted that it was going to be all but impossible to keep a balance between Mexico's clericals and liberals: "The Clericals," he wrote, "were not far from demanding restoration of the Inquisition, and the Liberals the expulsion of everything that wore a cassock."

Saligny Appoints Right-Wing Radicals

Pierre Saligny played his part in the new scheme of things as well. He figured that it would be too difficult to form a legislature with delegates who would have to travel great distances from other cities, having members from liberal strongholds would only cause trouble, and that the *indígenas* (Indians) didn't care to participate in government anyway. He decided that an Assembly of Notables could easily be identified from among the two hundred thousand residents of Mexico City. In his view, this assembly would adequately represent the country's population of eight million.

On June 16, 1863, General Forey officially nominated Saligny's list of thirty-five notables. They, in turn, appointed a three-man regency to rule Mexico until Maximilian—or whoever the emperor was going to be—showed up to claim the crown. The three regency members were General Juan Almonte, retired General Mariano Salas, and the newly elected archbishop of Mexico, Pelazio Antonio Labastida. Labastida was visiting Rome at the time.

The three regents did not impress Colonel du Barail or Captain Loizillon. Colonel du Barail said the name of the seventy-year-old Salas "would not encumber the pages of history," and Loizillon referred to him in one of his letters as "a mummy unearthed for the occasion." Loizillon called Almonte "a reactionary of little value" and the substitute who was sitting in for the archbishop still en route from Europe, as "a vigorous man who immediately set foot on the others and who directs everything." Almonte was supposed to preside over the group.[2]

Forey, Saligny, and Almonte were all quite satisfied with the new appointments. The one who was not satisfied was Napoleon III. He had been telling Forey and Saligny all along to include all honorable men in the provisional government, not to stack it with members of any particular faction or to make commitments that would leave the Church or any other special interest calling the shots. Instead, he learned after-the-fact about Saligny's ideology-driven choices.

To Forey, one of the first signs that the regency was overstepping its authority came when the triumvirate issued a proclamation if its own. The manifesto said that the Church no longer had an enemy in the state, and that all remaining issues with the provisional government would be settled shortly. Suddenly, priests began showing up in houses that once belonged to the Church, admonishing the tenants to stop paying rent to their landlords. Anyone who ignored the warnings would be forced to pay a second time to the Church when it regained possession.

An angry General Forey dispatched Almonte and Saligny to get the bishop out of bed before dawn one morning with a warning of his own: back off. The bishop was to keep his mouth shut and not issue any more proclamations. After all, he was only supposed to be substituting for Archbishop Labastida, who would be returning from Europe shortly.

The thirty-five conservatives who had been chosen to form the Assembly of Notables were all given brand-new frock coats, imported directly from France. Various high-ranking civil servants and members of the Imperialista military were provided with elegant new suits and uniforms. Most of the prominent and wealthy conservatives in town fell in love with the French. They responded to the army's parades and pageantry by staging extravagant balls and parties of their own to welcome and honor Forey and his officers.

The poor and middle classes saw through the whole thing. Among themselves, they were saying that all the candy and toys, the shows and picnics, and the frock coats and uniforms were all part of an elaborate façade, stage-managed by the French. There were no open protests, and the cries of "*¡Mueran los Franceses!*" had stopped. General Forey continued happily along, totally oblivious even to the existence of most of Mexico City's *Chilangos* (nickname for natives of Mexico City).

On June 28, it was the French army's turn to stage a ball. The invitation read, "The officers of the French Expeditionary Corps in Mexico request the honor of your presence at a Military Ball to be held on the twenty-eighth of June at the Teatro Nacional. Festivities will begin at eight o'clock. Respondez S'il Vous Plait."[3]

The French army Corps of Engineers had really outdone themselves. The Teatro Nacional (National Theatre) had been made into a virtual forest. As the guests entered the cavernous hall, they discovered that the engineers had brought in several hundred wagonloads of dirt and had planted trees all around the periphery of the dance floor. Brightly colored lanterns hung from the branches, and rustic decorations adorned the walls and tables. This would be an unforgettable Military Ball.

Public Whippings for Not Tipping Your Hat

The gossip at the tables during the military ball was that Napoleon III had sent General Forey a letter backing Pierre Saligny on the flogging issue.

Those who were just hearing the news acted with disbelief, many with eyes widened in astonishment.

Their worst fears were confirmed. Church processions would be back in the streets full time, and any Mexican who didn't tip his hat when the cross went by would be whipped in public. Forey didn't think that was the best way to win friends and influence people, but Saligny had apparently written to the emperor and forced the point. The general had just received word on the day before the ball.

Flogging wasn't the only issue causing friction between General Forey and Minister Saligny. As a matter of fact, Forey himself had written to Napoleon several days after Saligny had done so. Forey was having second thoughts about the group Saligny had chosen to become the Assembly of Notables. In his letter, he tried—too late—to distance himself from Saligny:

> I am sorry to see that the government is placing itself in too great a dependence upon the clergy. I can understand that it should honor religion and the ministers of religion, though in this country they are not always worthy of honor. The people are devout and bigoted to the point of fanaticism, and it is good policy to respect and even honor what it respects and honors; but it is to be feared that, whereas the government which has been overthrown has gone too far in the spoliation and ill-treatment of the clergy, the present one may go too far in the opposite direction. If it places itself under clerical domination, as it seems to intend, it will be following a reactionary policy, and will not rally round it moderate men who are truly but simply religious.[4]

As a matter of fact, Napoleon III had already decided to bring Forey and Saligny home. It wasn't just the dueling letters from the general and the minister, nor the choices for the regency and the Assembly of Notables. By mid-July, there was some unsettling information from a confidential source that no one else would ever suspect. The little girl who had played with Napoleon III as a child, Madame Hortense Cornu, was a friend of Henri Loizillon's family, and she was also receiving letters from Captain Loizillon.[5]

Madame Cornu became alarmed at not only the stories of "indignities and stupidities of which we are impotent witnesses," but at the ways in which the Church was manipulating the French authorities in order to recover lost power. For example, clergy were intimidating people who had bought Church land under the Juárez reforms, warning that the land would have to be returned. Local ordinances had already been published in Mexico City prohibiting work on Sundays and forcing everyone to kneel as the Holy Sacrament was carried through the streets.

"As you see," wrote Loizillon, "we are in full reaction, and no one is surprised by it, since it could not be otherwise with the constitution of the provisional government." According to the captain, religious practices were being restored in Mexico that had already been abolished in France. "We stand by and watch," he wrote, "as if it did not concern us." Madame Cornu took the letters directly to her old friend Napoleon. It would certainly concern the emperor.

Napoleon III Summons Forey and Saligny Home

It dawned on Napoleon that many of his top officers had only been telling him what they thought he wanted to hear, to protect their own jobs or to promote their own views. The letters shown to him by Madame Cornu were from an obscure captain who had nothing to gain and a lot to lose, but they had a ring of truth to them. Just to test many of the claims, Napoleon sent copies of the letters—without Loizillon's name—to General Bazaine for comment. Bazaine was discreet: he said the complaints about Forey were a bit harsh, but did not dispute the rest of the findings.[6]

Even before Bazaine would have a chance to reply, Napoleon had begun to initiate some changes. He had his new foreign minister, a Monsieur Drouyn de Lhuys, write to Saligny and tell him that the emperor felt that he had completed his assignment in Mexico and wanted him to return to Paris. "His Majesty wishes," wrote de Lhuys, "to receive from your own lips information which could contribute to clarifying his decisions." Forey's letter of recall was also in the mail, telling him that he had done such a great job that he was being promoted to mar-shal of France. "A Marshal of France," said the emperor, "is too great a personage to be allowed to struggle with the intrigues and details of administration." Forey was to hand things over to Bazaine and return to France, so that he could receive the honors due to him and enjoy the fruits of his success.[7]

If Napoleon had bothered to proofread his letter, he would have noticed that he had also referred to General Bazaine as a marshal. Forey read it and became very upset. He could see through the flowery language, and he realized what was really going on. Since the emperor had left it up to him as to when to turn the reins over to Bazaine, he would delay as long as possible.

What Forey didn't realize at first was that Napoleon was already bypassing him, sending confidential instructions to Bazaine as though he were already in charge. The emperor's first order to Bazaine was to take care of the Church prob-lem. Let them know under no uncertain terms that the "sword of France" is the ultimate authority, and no one else.

Reassure the rest of the population, said the emperor, that none of the factions that had previously divided the country would influence any decisions by the French administration. Tighten security and establish order so that people felt safe before worrying about the small details of what kind of government will emerge. Above all, don't chase Juárez for now. Stay close to your base and don't do anything that would require sending more troops. Juárez will probably with-draw to remote parts of the country to gather support, but it would be unwise to undertake a pursuit at this time.[8]

Maximilian Fears a Northern Victory in U.S. Civil War

At Miramar Palace in Austria, Archduke Ferdinand Maximilian eagerly opened the envelope containing the telegram from Mexico City. "Archduke Max," as his subjects called him, had been having difficulty making up his mind for more than a year about whether to accept the offer to become emperor of Mexico. In the telegram, General Achille Bazaine informed him that the Assembly of Notables, appointed by Forey, had offered him the Mexican throne.

Maximilian was still not sure. He wrote to Napoleon that he'd been hearing reports about Northern battle victories in the American Civil War. He was afraid the United States would invade Mexico shortly after that war was concluded. He wanted to start off his reign as emperor with treaties in hand from both France and Britain that would guarantee their support if he were to be attacked within the first fifteen to twenty years. He awaited Napoleon's reply.

Those Northern battle victories by now included the Battle of Gettysburg and the capture of Vicksburg, Mississippi. If Napoleon had been hoping that the British government might somehow come to his side and recognize the Confederacy, those hopes were beginning to evaporate. Those who were well informed about the progress of the Civil War were now seeing the increased likelihood of a Northern victory in the long run, but cautioned that it wasn't over yet.

Agnes Salm-Salm Builds Influential Contacts

While her husband was busy recruiting more soldiers for his Union army unit, Princess Agnes Salm-Salm spent much of the summer of 1863 as a house guest of *New York Herald* publisher James Gordon Bennett, his wife, and his son, James. The Bennetts had homes both in New York City and at Port Washington on Long Island.

There was much to see and do at the country estate. The younger Mr. Bennett had a stable of fine racing horses, was active as a yachtsman, and was also as a breeder of hunting dogs. He presented Agnes with a black and tan terrier puppy from one of his kennels, and she promptly named it Jimmy, in honor of both young James and his father.

The dog was still small enough as a puppy that Agnes was able to take him home in her pocket and to bathe him in her wash basin.

Diplomatic Blunder by the "Mexican Empire"

In Washington, an envelope arrived for Secretary of State Seward. The letterhead read, *Palace of the Regency of the Mexican Empire.* A man claiming to be the "Under Secretary of State and Foreign Affairs" told Seward that Mexico had adopted as its new form of government "a limited monarchy, with an [a] hereditary Catholic prince as its sovereign." The new sovereign's title would be "Emperor of Mexico." The crown, according to the letter, was to be offered to "his imperial and royal highness, Prince Ferdinand Maximilian of Austria, for himself and his descendants." If for some reason Maximilian could not serve, France's Napoleon III would nominate somebody else.

Seward was outraged. Whatever had happened to Napoleon III's promises that he would only collect the debts Mexico owed to France but would not take over the country? Seward kept his composure. He and President Lincoln still had a Civil War on their hands. Even with the summer's victories at Gettysburg and

Vicksburg, this would be a poor time to take on the French. He would continue to play a waiting game.[10]

Guerilla Leader's Wife Threatens DuPin

Despite the success at Puebla and the occupation of Mexico City, the French still had to contend with guerillas and bandidos in the countryside. Colonel DuPin and his *contre-guérillas* continued shooting and hanging those whom they suspected of underground activity, sometimes punishing whole towns to underscore their message. Learning that guerillas might be meeting in the village of Cotaxtla, about halfway between Veracruz and Córdoba, DuPin's men galloped toward the tiny hamlet where guerilla leaders were gathered at the home of Señor Molina, a local businessman. All of the guerilla leaders' horses were tethered to a railing in front of the house. As someone warned them of DuPin's approach and they all rushed to untie the animals, Señor Molina hastened their escape by grabbing a machete and chopping through the ropes. DuPin saw only the dust cloud the guerillas had left behind as he entered the town.

DuPin captured Señor Molina, along with a cousin, and searched the house, finding letters that had been exchanged between Molina and the guerilla leaders. As Molina's wife pleaded for their lives, Señor Molina and his cousin were executed as she looked on. She remained calm as the two were being shot, but approached DuPin as he was mounting his horse to leave.

"Colonel," she said, "you will die within a week."[11]

22

The Emperor's "Popular Vote"

(July through August 1863)

Napoleon III Moves to Regain Control

Things were getting out of hand.

First, thought Napoleon III, Saligny and Forey had set up an Assembly of Notables and a three-man regency without running any of the names by him first. Then General Almonte had the audacity—again without consulting him—to offer Maximilian the throne of Mexico. The first he had heard of the offer was a telegram from Maximilian, saying that he suspected Almonte and the regents were acting on their own. What Maximilian wanted was some evidence that the Mexican people as a nation, not just the handpicked government, actually wanted a monarch.

Once again, Foreign Minister Drouyn de Lhuys was asked to write a letter, this time to Bazaine, diplomatically telling the general that the provisional government now had to be put to the citizens of Mexico for a vote. Drouyn de Lhuys was aware of the overwhelming illiteracy in the country, but he instructed Bazaine to work something out that would fit with Mexican customs. He also urged Bazaine to reverse some of the policies that had been advanced by the regents, especially those that would restore property and authority to the Church.

The army was very happy about Bazaine's promotion to commander-in-chief, but even his staunchest backers wondered if he would ever be able to undo the damage done by Forey and Saligny. Bazaine began by forcing Saligny and Almonte to issue a proclamation that the regency had no intention of giving any property back to the Church.

Saligny and Forey, meanwhile, were still resisting calls to return to France. Saligny wrote to Napoleon III that he was staying in Mexico for the time being, explaining that Forey had assured him his services were still needed. The emperor wrote back that he was to return home as soon as possible. Napoleon had his war minister write to Forey ordering him back to Paris, but Forey put the letter in his pocket and acted as though he had never received it.[1]

General Bazaine versus the Church

Bazaine had another adversary to deal with. Archbishop Labastida arrived back from Europe. The general had met him earlier when Labastida was bishop of Puebla, and he knew the man was articulate and well informed, but Bazaine wrote back to Paris, "Unfortunately his [Labastida's] ideas are those of the Roman clergy, almost those of the Spanish clergy at the time of Philip IV, minus the Inquisition; we cannot count on his intervention to reach a solution by conciliation...If we let him have his way, we would soon have another Rome in the New World."[2]

Priests were already refusing to give last rites to anyone who had bought Church property unless their families and survivors agreed to give the property back. Bazaine had to intervene in many such cases, ordering bishops in a number of dioceses to perform the last rites. When they refused, he forced Labastida and the other regents to discipline them.

Last rites were just one of many issues over which Bazaine was forced to confront the clergy. There was the time that the wife of one of Bazaine's officers showed up at Mass dressed as fashionably as though she were in Paris. This was in stark contrast to the Mexican women who attended services heavily veiled and dressed in black, sitting only on the floor. The priest in charge of the Mass was so shocked that he flicked an obscene gesture toward the French officer's wife.

The husband complained to the priest's superior, who admitted that the priest's behavior was inappropriate but said that the way women dress in Paris was not acceptable for attending Mass in Mexico. He claimed that priests in his diocese could actually refuse to admit women to Mass who dressed that way.

Bazaine had to take a stand. He wrote to Archbishop Labastida, saying that French Catholics were just as good as Mexican Catholics, and that French women were entitled to wear the same kind of clothing to Mass in Mexico that they wore in France. He made it clear that there would be repercussions if Labastida did not order his clergy to admit them.

It didn't end there. Archbishop Labastida convened a meeting of the regents to try one more time to retrieve Church lands that had been confiscated under the Juárez regime, and Bazaine came striding in with an armed escort to block the move. As his Zouave guards looked on, Bazaine ordered the regents to ratify the titles of the current landowners and to uphold the earlier nationalization of

Church lands by Juárez. Almonte and Salas went along, but Labastida refused. Bazaine then dismissed Labastida from the regents.

The archbishop retaliated by ordering the excommunication of all government officials who had been appointed by the regency and by ordering church doors closed to all French soldiers on Sunday. Bazaine said he would blast the cathedral doors open with cannon fire if French soldiers were not admitted, or if any of the government officials were excommunicated.

Archbishop Labastida slept in a different house every night for the rest of the week, fearing that he would be arrested. Bazaine wouldn't play the game; he knew the archbishop would become some kind of a martyr if he were arrested, so he simply banned the publication of the excommunications and waited.

Sunday morning came—and the church doors were open. Labastida had finally backed down.

Confederate Nightmare: The French Also Want Texas

In Richmond, Virginia, Confederate President Jefferson Davis and his secretary of state, Judah Benjamin, were getting nervous about the rumors that France might be expanding its Mexican empire to include Texas. French consuls in both Texas and Virginia were asking almost identically worded questions about whether or not Texas really belonged in the Confederacy. Secretary Benjamin was pretty sure the idea had been floated by Pierre Saligny. Saligny, as the French ambassador to Austin when Texas was a republic, had always been against Texas joining the United States.

Secretary Benjamin wrote to a Confederate agent by the name of John Slidell, asking him to check out the rumors, but the letter fell into the hands of United States' officials at sea and wound up on Secretary of State William Seward's desk. Seward asked the U.S. ambassador to Belgium, General Henry Sanford, to investigate. Sanford replied that Napoleon III still harbored the thought of expanding Mexico back to its old boundaries, and that the questions being asked by the French consuls were evidence that the idea was alive and well.

The Confederacy's man in Belgium confirmed the fears of President Davis and Secretary Benjamin: "He [Napoleon III] will remain anxious for us to believe that he is silently our friend. Mexico first, and then Mexico as she was previous to her dismemberment is the resolutely and faithfully cherished end at which he aims." In other words, Texas just might be up for grabs.[3]

Forey and Saligny Still Dragging Their Feet

September was fast approaching, but Pierre Saligny and Élie Frédéric Forey were still getting in the way. Since neither one wanted to go home, both were using various ways to delay their departure from Mexico. Since Napoleon III had indicated in his letter to Forey that Forey had some discretion in choosing the exact date of his return, the general chose to ignore what was a diplomatic courtesy and take the emperor's instructions literally. Soldiers were singing songs in the barracks as to when he would finally get the hint and leave.

What Forey really wanted was to be there in Mexico to hand over the government to Maximilian. He thought that his task would not be complete until he did so, and he was hanging on in hopes that such a development might occur. He received a sterner letter from the war minister, ordering him home, but he chose to ignore it and tell no one.

An open letter appeared in a Mexican newspaper, congratulating Forey on his promotion to marshal. The letter also suggested that he use the occasion to send the French army out into the countryside to pacify the rest of Mexico, and show everyone that he had awakened from his apathy. He was stung by the word "apathy," and responded that Mexican roads were not in any shape to support an army with cannon and munitions in this season. Furthermore, the general insisted, he was the one who had successfully outlasted the defenders of Puebla for nine weeks. Nobody was going to tell him what to do.

Even though he wrote to the emperor that he'd rather endure another siege of Puebla than to "be moderator of these people who do not want to be moderated," he still just couldn't let go.[4]

23

General Bazaine's Crackdown

(September through October 1863)

Expenses Mount as Spies and Liberals Infiltrate

With Saligny called home and a new minister to Mexico appointed, Napoleon III was awakening to another problem with the Mexican expedition: finances. His finance minister totaled up the bill and discovered that the French had spent 172 million francs as of September 9, 1863, and so far they had very little to show for it. The emperor instructed the Marquis de Montholon, Saligny's replacement, to meet with the Regents in Mexico City and work out a plan to reimburse France for its expenses. A team of French financial experts was dispatched to go over the books in Mexico and look for belt-tightening opportunities.

General Bazaine sent reports twice a month, indicating that the army was doing its job and would have control of the entire country within a few months. However, he complained that the regency and the Assembly of Notables were causing problems.

General Forey, still trying to assert some kind of authority, ordered that all Mexicans entering the capital be brought before the authorities and be forced to sign sworn statements that they would keep the peace.

The liberals reacted by holding clandestine meetings in the suburbs. The village of San Angel was one such base of operations, and so was nearby Tlalpan. Before the summer was over, three French soldiers had been killed in Tlalpan.

Forey took a number of Tlalpan residents hostage and warned that they would be killed if the village did not pay a steep fine. If there were any more attacks on French soldiers, he decreed, others would be executed. If that didn't put a stop to the violence, Forey warned that the town would be destroyed. This was not exactly promoting the sense of friendship and good feeling that Napoleon III had hoped for.

It wasn't just the suburbs that were giving Forey trouble. All foreign embassies and consulates were suspect, especially those of Peru. Forey and the regents had identified four locations where the Peruvians were providing sanctuary for some of Juárez's people. Shortly after that, they discovered that Peruvian ambassador Corpancho was passing information via diplomatic pouches to the Juárez forces in San Luis Potosí. They gave the Peruvian delegation three days to get out of Mexico City and eight days to be out of the country entirely.[1]

DuPin Suspects a Security Leak

On September 29, Colonel Francois DuPin stopped in at the army paymaster's office in Veracruz. As he filled out the paperwork to pick up the payroll for his men, he told a number of people that he would be leaving on October 1 to return to La Soledad. He mentioned to all of them that he would be taking the two o'clock train. That was not true. He was fabricating his schedule to test for a possible leak.

As the train chugged along between two high banks in a wooded area near La Pulga, it was derailed. The Sudanese and Egyptian soldiers who had been assigned to guard the train climbed out of the overturned coaches, only to be fired upon by guerillas from both sides. Some passengers were also killed.

Several of the survivors said that a woman had arrived and asked if DuPin had been killed. No one knew if the woman was Señora Molina—the widow of the businessman from Cotaxtla—but whoever she was, she learned that DuPin had secretly taken the six o'clock train that morning.

At Last, Forey Gets the Message

"The Bear" finally gave in.

That's what all of the officers were calling General Forey. He had been walking around for weeks with the letter from the war minister telling him to return to Paris, but his vanity had prompted him to delay in hopes of having the chance to pass the government over to Maximilian. Forey was teased, he was the target of sniping and gossip, and he was the object of songs and stories the soldiers made up about him. According to an old Mexican saying, he was "a zero in the left-hand column," useless. As Captain Loizillon wrote in one of his letters home, "In refusing to hand over his command to General Bazaine, Marshal Forey shows himself to the end what he has always been, a vain nonentity. He thus impedes future operations, since General Bazaine needs material time to prepare the expedition and to begin a new liberal policy. M. Forey, in fact, has attained the apogee of his reputation by retarding operations even by his departure."

Colonel du Barail had been promoted to general by this time, and although he had backed Forey throughout the siege of Puebla, he now had to admit that "his [Forey's] situation was becoming false and bizarre. He no longer commanded. He no longer received anything from Paris."

The postmaster helped to nudge Forey's decision-making process a bit by referring everything addressed to the "General Commander-in-Chief" to Bazaine. When Forey showed up to ask about his mail, there was nothing there for him.

Élie Frédéric Forey finally got the hint. It took a lot longer than anyone else had wanted, but he finally left for France during the first week of October 1863. Younger officers endured his rambling speech at the farewell ceremony. For some of the older ones, it was the end of an era, but others simply pitied the Bear as he heaped praise upon General Achille Bazaine. Then, he mounted his horse and rode off toward Veracruz, surrounded by the appropriate escort. First it had been Admiral Jurien, then General Lorencez, and now General Forey had become the third French commandant to be vanquished by Mexico.[2]

Mexican Conservatives Visit Maximilian

At about the same time, a delegation arrived at Miramar on October 3, 1863, to invite Archduke Maximilian to accept the Mexican crown. They had stopped off in Paris, where they were joined by expatriates José María Gutiérrez de Estrada and José Hidalgo. Prominent among the group was the ultraconservative Father Francisco Xavier Miranda, who was still hoping to get the lands previously confiscated by the Juárez regime returned to the Church. Both Forey and Saligny had warned him before the delegation left Mexico that he was to hold back on that issue until they were sure that Maximilian was fully committed.

Maximilian still didn't want to commit. He wanted to see a popular referendum and a vote of ratification by the Assembly of Notables and by the regency. In fact, he expressed some concern as to what extent the notables and the regency actually represented the people of Mexico. Maximilian had seen the resolutions of support presented on behalf of sixty-six towns, but he was also aware that these were all tiny villages in and around Mexico City and Veracruz.

General Bazaine, upon hearing that still more votes were to be rounded up, prepared the army to do the job, with fixed bayonets and an armed escort. British diplomat Charles Wyke joked that they'd be visiting towns "inhabited by two Indians and a monkey" to gather them.[3]

"Father of Weather Bureau" Petitions Maximilian

Word of the delegation's offer to Maximilian spread quickly. Among those who saw an opportunity was Confederate scientist Matthew Fontaine Maury. It was Maury who, before the Civil War, had started the United States Weather Bureau when he had been an oceanographer for the U.S. Navy. Now, he was writing to Maximilian to congratulate him on his invitation to become Mexico's emperor.

As he wrote about the things that he and Maximilian had in common, Maury began dropping hints that the Confederacy might not last and that he could be more useful under Maximilian's administration than in his present post. In particular, he was interested in commanding a Mexican navy under Maximilian. He told the archduke that the Confederates had ordered an ironclad ship built in England but could not get it released because of the Foreign Enlistment Act. He said that with a fleet of ironclad ships, a new imperial regime could not only control the Pacific coast of North America but could also reclaim California for Mexico.

Maximilian was intrigued. He would get back to Maury.

Bazaine Launches a Field Campaign

For the French army, the intermission was over. No more military balls, no more parties. With Forey gone, Archbishop Labastida subdued—at least for now—and Maximilian asking for a more representative plebiscite, Bazaine saw his chance to mount an offensive to pacify the countryside. On October 25, 1863, he set out with twelve infantry battalions of five hundred men apiece, six cavalry squadrons of a hundred horses each, and various units of artillery and engineers.

The objective was to wipe out Juárez's ragged, ill-equipped troops and to prepare for Maximilian's arrival as emperor. Bazaine divided his Mexican Imperialista forces into two armies. General Mejía was to capture San Luis Potosí, while General Márquez was to take control of the central Mexican province of Michoacán. Within three weeks, Mejía held San Luis Potosí. Ten days later, Márquez had overrun Michoacán and was occupying the city of Guanajuato. The French followed behind them, collecting signatures in support of Maximilian with the help of local clergy and a prominent display of weapons. Many of those signing the petitions had never heard of Maximilian before.

The French and their Imperialista comrades occupied town after town, but something strange was happening as they moved along. Everywhere they went, guerilla forces reentered the towns they had just left, and life went on as though the French had never been there.

General Mejía had hoped to capture President Benito Juárez as he entered San Luis Potosí, but Juárez had been tipped off and had moved his government to Saltillo. Nonetheless, Bazaine and his generals had to come up with some signatures so that Maximilian could be satisfied that he had been elected by the will of the people. The campaign continued.

Internal Squabbles Plague the Juárez Government

While his government had been headquartered in San Luis Potosí, things had not gone very well for Benito Juárez. Only four foreign countries still maintained legations in Mexico, but Corpancho of Peru had already been thrown out, Corwin of the United States had been called home, and the diplomats from Ecuador and Venezuela could not move their embassies to the north and abandon their people in Mexico City.

Not only was Juárez doing without friends, he was doing without money. The French had been collecting all of the revenue from the customs houses for almost two years, but Juárez was not ready to give up. His poorly equipped guerilla bands would come down out of the mountains and attack French convoys and army patrols frequently enough to send a clear message: the French had not yet "pacified" the country, and they were not about to do so anytime soon.

As Bazaine and his French troops moved north, Juárez and his government kept one step ahead of them. The French moved from Mexico City to Querétaro, and then to San Luis Potosí, Saltillo, and finally Monterrey. Juárez and his supporters kept just ahead of the French. Although this was no time for the liberals to be fighting among themselves, a dispute broke out that put the Mexicans at an even greater risk. Things were going badly as Bazaine advanced, and former Foreign Minister Francisco Zarco began to publish his doubts about the Juárez team and its ability to hold things together. This touched off a wave of finger-pointing. To regain control, Juárez wanted to form a new government that would consolidate the talents of General Manuel Doblado and Foreign Minister Manuel Zamacona, along with Zarco if he could possibly agree.

Doblado didn't want to go along with the plan if it included Zamacona and Zarco. As the military commander for the area, Doblado ordered the two men to leave San Luis Potosí. Juárez revoked the order and tried several times to persuade General Doblado to cooperate, but when a new government was announced on September 8, 1863, Doblado was not a part of it.

Con Artists Want to "Sell" Mexican States

As if the internal disputes were not enough, some swindlers were on the move, hoping to exploit the confusion. One such scheme involved a fellow by the name of José Domingo Cortes, who showed up at the United States consulate in Havana with a note from Thomas Corwin saying that he "appeared to be a gentleman." Cortes claimed that he was the governor of Sonora, and that he represented a separatist movement from his home state plus the Mexican states of Sinaloa, Chihuahua, Durango, and Baja California.

Cortes managed to get a letter from U.S. consul Thomas Savage, introducing him to Secretary of State William Seward. His plan was to take the letter to Washington and present Seward with a plan to take all five of these northern border states and annex them to the United States.

In Mexico City, Chargé d'Affaires Edward L. Plumb became aware of the plan and warned Seward's son, Frederick, that he had never heard of Cortes. He also sent word to the State Department that he had learned from Mexico's consul in New York that Cortes was a fraud. Cortes, according to the consul, had been a member of dictator Santa Anna's army and had later been kicked out of Puebla by General Ignacio Zaragoza.

Mexican ambassador Matías Romero got into the act, forwarding letters from the governors of Chihuahua and Sinaloa. One of the governors said he had never known Cortes, while the other said he was a known troublemaker from Spain. Both said that he never held any elected or appointed office that they knew of in Mexico.

Romero and Juárez decided to just let Cortes twist in the wind. They left him stranded in New York, not allowing him back into Mexico nor seeking to expel him. Cortes later published stories in New York alleging that Juárez had twice tried to "sell" the Mexican state of Sonora to the United States, but by then nobody was really paying attention.[4]

24

Women Must Leave the Train

(Late October through Mid-November 1863)

The Princess Pulls the Emergency Cord

Among the units under General William T. Sherman's Union army regiment was the 68th New York Volunteers. They were ordered to Nashville, Tennessee, under the command of their colonel, Prince Felix Salm-Salm. Felix's soldiers already knew his wife, Agnes. They called her the "Soldier Princess." She had prepared for this assignment by buying two sets of riding habits as well as two sets of jackets and ankle-length skirts that looked somewhat like army uniforms. With her new clothing and her little black and tan dog, Jimmy, she was ready to follow Felix's troops wherever they went.

As Sherman's regiment boarded a troop train in Nashville and headed for Alabama, a guard came through the cars and shouted that "all women must leave the train." He was not about to listen to any argument. At that very moment, Agnes saw some officers from the 68th New York Volunteers still standing out on the platform. They knew who the Soldier Princess was, and it was no problem for them to smuggle Agnes and Jimmy onto a wooden bench in the very last car—packed with soldiers—so the guard wouldn't see them.

As the train made its way southward toward the war zone, Agnes saw burned-out houses and overturned train cars. There were deeply wooded areas where the enemy might be lying in wait, but Agnes saw herself as a soldier now. Somehow, she managed to fall asleep despite all the rumors she was hearing of outrageous acts committed by the Rebels.

Suddenly someone nudged her awake with the news that Jimmy had jumped off the train. As she looked out the back, the tiny image of the dog was disappearing in the distance. There was just one thing to do: grab the red handle and yank the emergency cord. Everything came to a screeching halt as soldiers ran down the tracks to retrieve the dog. Then, the train carrying General Sherman's regiment on its way to do battle in Alabama resumed its journey. Soldiers in each car were laughing in disbelief when they found out why there had been an unscheduled stop.[1]

Maximilian Wavers, But It's Too Late

At Miramar, Archduke Maximilian was beginning to have second thoughts about his agreement to become an emperor. Britain's Sir Charles Wyke dropped in on him after returning from a visit to Mexico. Wyke, who had been sent by his government to take a look at the French intervention, was not impressed. He warned Maximilian that aligning himself with the clerical party or with the Regency would guarantee failure. He recommended dissolving both the Regency and the Assembly of Notables and starting from scratch. Mexico, advised Wyke, should be allowed to vote—and not at the point of a bayonet—whether it wanted a monarchy or not.

Napoleon III was opposed to Wyke's advice. He had invested far too much already, and starting over would be the same as admitting a mistake. As Napoleon put it, "In France it is no longer possible to be mistaken." He was under pressure to accommodate the business community. As a result, he was talking not only of imposing French financial agents upon Maximilian's new imperial government, but also of possibly claiming the mining-rich state of Sonora, adjacent to Arizona at the United States border, for France.

As soon as he heard that a delegation of Mexican expatriates in Europe was on its way to Miramar to offer the crown, Austrian emperor Franz Josef summoned his brother, Maximilian, to Vienna. Among other things, Franz Josef said the delegation had no authority from Mexico's imperial government, and that any meeting with such a group could not be listed as an official public event. It would only be considered a private conversation, without any sort of government approval.

Furthermore, according to Franz Josef, Maximilian would be naïve to go to Mexico without the guaranteed support of both England and France, the world's only major naval powers, if things were to turn sour. If Maximilian were simply to accept Napoleon III's terms as they had been presented so far, he would be viewed simply as a French puppet. The guarantees would be even more crucial if one were to consider the likely victory of the Union over the Confederacy in the American Civil War. Both Lincoln and Seward were opposed to a monarchy, so an unfriendly army along Mexico's thousand-mile border with the United States simply could not be ignored.

There's no record of whether Seward put him up to it or not, but the American consul from Trieste dropped in for what was supposedly an informal visit with Maximilian. The consul told Maximilian that if the French army were not withdrawn by Napoleon III when the Civil War ended, the Gulf of Mexico would be blockaded, all contact with Europe would be cut off, and an American army of seasoned veterans would help Benito Juárez kick out the invaders.

That did it. Maximilian didn't react during the consul's visit, but later he picked up his pen and began writing to Napoleon III, demanding more than just a gentlemen's agreement of support. He wanted a signed tripartite treaty, guaranteeing that both France and England would defend his empire in Mexico for at least the first fifteen, if not the first twenty years.

There was no way Napoleon III could agree to such an alliance. He chose not to respond to any of Maximilian's letters on the issue. Having already used up most of his goodwill with England and Spain during the 1862 invasion of Veracruz, he proposed floating a loan for Mexico in Paris—one that Austria would guarantee. Austria's Franz Josef would have none of it.

Maximilian's mother-in-law had been through all of this before. Her nephew, Otto, had been overthrown as king of Greece. The same powers that Maximilian was asking for protection were the ones that had promised to back Otto in Greece. Instead, at the last moment, they sent only one English destroyer to help him escape. Archduchess Sophia predicted that the only way Maximilian could step down as emperor of Mexico would be by dangling at the end of a hangman's rope or by facing a firing squad. There would be no ships from European countries standing by to rescue him, regardless of any treaties or agreements. She had been against the whole Mexican adventure from the start, and she made her views very clear when Maximilian and Charlotte visited her in Vienna.[2]

Ortega Wants to Be Mexico's Next President—But When?

Having reshuffled his cabinet, Benito Juárez proceeded with a military shakeup. With General Comonfort as war minister, Juárez reorganized the army into five divisions. General Doblado, who was no longer in the cabinet, would command a division of four thousand men based at Guanajuato. General Porfirio Díaz, with three thousand men, would be in charge of the eastern division. Similar divisions were to be headed by generals Uraga, González-Ortega, and Berriozábal. The terms of all of Mexico's Supreme Court members except one would expire on December 1, and because elections were not possible, Juárez said he would name the replacements.

The one Supreme Court magistrate whose term did not expire for another five years was General Jesús González-Ortega. Because of the War of the Reform, there had been no election in 1860, but Juárez had been elected president in June of 1861. Mexico's Constitution stated that if elections were not possible, the chief justice of the Supreme Court should assume the presidency when the term of the incumbent expired. González-Ortega was the chief justice, and he was waiting for Juárez's term to end so that he could become president.

The question was, exactly when did Juárez's term end? Was it on December 1, 1864, or December 1, 1865? González-Ortega wrote to Foreign Minister Lerdo for clarification. Juárez and Lerdo sensed a possible challenge from González-Ortega. They answered that the Constitution specified that a president's term ended on December 1 in the fourth year after his election. In Juárez's case, that would mean 1865. Juárez and Lerdo breathed a little easier when the general yielded to their reply. It had bought them some time, but they knew that González-Ortega had the presidency on his mind. Sooner or later, he would be back.

Romero Becomes Ambassador—But Don't Talk about Mexico

Matías Romero returned to Washington in October of 1863, this time as Mexico's ambassador and not just as the chargé d'affaires. Prior to the ceremony in which he presented his credentials to the president, Secretary of State Seward warned him not to make any mention of the current situation in Mexico. Although President Lincoln's speech was full of warmth and praise for Romero personally, neither man uttered a word of any substance about Mexico itself.

Romero had already made plans to bypass Seward, whom he regarded as deliberately turning a deaf ear toward Mexico or its problems. Instead, he planned to work with right-wing Radicals from Lincoln's Republican Party to force Seward's resignation and possibly even Lincoln's defeat in the presidential elections of 1864. Romero and the Radicals shared the view that there was some kind of connection between the French intervention and the Confederacy. They saw it as a conspiracy to undermine the United States.

One of Romero's closest allies, Congressman Thaddeus Stevens, warned that the French had occupied Mexico to "strike this Republic now in our troubles..." He continued,

In a few years, if we remain united, we would become a match for any or all of the despots of Europe. If this nation were broken into fragments, and two or three republics were to rise upon its ruins, we should be a feeble people, incapable of self-defense. The Old World would shape our institutions, regulate our commerce, and control all our interests. Free trade would bring with it the destruction of our manufactures, the prostration of our commerce, and finally dictate the rulers who should sit upon our thrones.

As an example, Stevens pointed to the French occupation of the Mexican port of Guaymas, just south of the border with Arizona. He claimed that they were just getting into position for a future attack on California. Finally, he blasted Secretary Seward, who was already a scapegoat of the Radicals, by blaming him for what Stevens called "the moral cowardice of the Foreign Department."[3]

Romero, meanwhile, had rented a large house in Washington, D.C., and lavishly furnished it. He began hiring and training a team of personnel to entertain influential people who could back his cause. The new ambassador spent much of the fall of 1863 staging rehearsal dinners to be sure that the real ones would come off smoothly. He began to avoid Seward and the State Department. If Romero couldn't get what he needed for Mexico through normal government channels, he would try some other ways.

Don't Tell Bazaine about His Wife

In Mexico City, one of Bazaine's staff members was handling his mail while the general was in the field near San Luis Potosí. He was absolutely astonished when he opened an envelope and found a letter from a woman in Paris with some scandalous gossip. It seems that Madame Bazaine was having an affair with an actor. The actor's mistress—or former mistress—had not only written to the general about his wife's affair, but also had told the actor that she had done so.

The actor told Madame Bazaine, who then went straight to Napoleon III to confess everything. The emperor moved quickly, ordering the post office to intercept the letter.

It was too late. The letter was already on the high seas, headed for Mexico. No order from Paris could possibly reach Mexico City in time to prevent the letter from reaching Bazaine's headquarters. The emperor was worried that the news would distract Bazaine from his duties as commander-in-chief. Luckily for both Napoleon III and General Bazaine, the aide decided to burn the letter and say nothing about it.

A few weeks later, another letter arrived from the war office. Madame Bazaine had died. General Bazaine took some time off to mourn the death of his faithful spouse.[4]

25

The Guerilla War behind the Scenes

(January through April 1864)

The Hunt for José María Carbajal

Things had improved for the French in the area between Veracruz and Orizaba. Thanks to contingents from such places as Austria, Belgium, and Egypt, they were better able to control the main supply routes. However, they soon discovered that the guerillas had simply moved north and were attacking outposts in the state of Tamaulipas, near the border with Texas. French soldiers were being murdered in the streets of Tampico, and many more were dying of yellow fever, forcing the French to temporarily evacuate the garrison there. As they did, guerillas moved in to capture the town.

Colonel Francois DuPin was ordered to leave the base he had established at Camarón and shift his *contre-guérillas* northward into Tamaulipas, closer to the U.S. border, to chase down the bandidos and guerillas that had moved there. One of DuPin's toughest adversaries was the guerilla leader known as José María Carbajal. Before the American Civil War, Carbajal and his men had been bounty hunters for Southern slave owners, capturing runaway slaves in Mexico and returning them to their masters. He was known for cruelty, like DuPin, but he was loyal to Juárez.

During the few weeks that Carbajal's guerillas held Tampico, they held courts-martial for all of the locals who had worked or served in office for the French, ultimately hanging them in the town's main plaza.

When the French finally returned, DuPin was given the task of tracking and killing Carbajal. He set out with 285 men, hoping to surprise Carbajal, but found that the guerilla leader was waiting for him with 1,200 men at the little town of San Antonio, Tamaulipas. There was a fierce battle, which cost DuPin 11 dead and 32 wounded, but his forces finally won, scattering Carbajal's men into the countryside.

As the smoke cleared, there was just one problem: they had not caught Carbajal. They had shot two horses out from under him during the battle, and they were certain that he had been badly wounded, but somehow he had escaped. Carbajal knew the territory, so he made it to a swamp where he hid all night, despite his wound. At dawn, when DuPin's people gave up the search and left the area, he crawled out of the swamp and made his way to Soto la Marina, Tamaulipas.

As DuPin and some of his officers arrived in Soto la Marina two days later, they were greeted by the United States' consul for the area, who invited them to his home for dinner. The consul, Don Martín de Leon, revealed that he was Carbajal's cousin, but said that he did not sympathize with the guerilla leader's behavior or his political inclinations. He told DuPin's men that they had just missed their fugitive by one day, saying that Carbajal had stopped by to get treatment for his wounds and to get a fresh horse before heading toward Monterrey.

Don Martín was lying. His cousin, José María Carbajal, was hiding in a vaquero's hut elsewhere on the ranch while the consul entertained his guests. If DuPin doubted Don Martín's story, he knew better than to start trouble with a representative of the United States government. After his guests left, Don Martin brought his cousin a horse, and Carbajal rode away to find his men.

The Games Diplomats Play

In Washington, D.C., the rehearsals were over. Matías Romero began to hold formal dinner parties aimed at winning the hearts and minds of the capital's political elite. On January 21, 1864, he staged the first of sixteen such events, and by the end of sixty days, he had included every cabinet member and almost all of the leaders of both the House and Senate.

In Paris, there was an extravagant reception for Maximilian and Charlotte, with far more pageantry than normally given to an archduke and archduchess. U.S. ambassador William L. Dayton had already asked the State Department how he should conduct himself for the event, and was told not to show up if Maximilian were being presented as Mexico's emperor. Dayton didn't have to worry about it; the French knew that as a religious man, he did not attend social events on Sundays. Maximilian's reception was on a Sunday.

Maximilian Labeled as a "Cabbage Head"

Those who already knew Maximilian were aware that he was a big spender, a man who knew little or nothing about money. He was always in debt. When he met with Napoleon III, he agreed to a treaty that would break Mexico financially in order to pay the bills for the French military, without even considering the costs for an imperial government. He agreed that Mexico would pay France 270 million francs to cover the costs of the invasion so far, through July 1, 1864. The French army would keep twenty-five thousand soldiers in Mexico until Maximilian could replace them with a Mexican military. The French Foreign Legion would provide eight thousand legionnaires for eight years. All claims presented by Pierre Saligny to the allied commissioners at Veracruz would be paid off, and so would the claims of the Swiss banker named Jecker, who had loaned money to Miramón's government before Juárez had come into power.

Mexican diplomat Jesús Terán, upon learning the terms of the treaty, wrote to Juárez, "What man of any dignity would have agreed that 25,000 Frenchmen should remain in Mexico, not under his orders but under a general named by the French emperor? This treaty confirms the opinion I have already given you about the archduke; he is what we call a cabbage head."

Napoleon III also made it very clear to Maximilian that he was not to recognize the Confederacy. The French emperor realized that the South was going to lose the Civil War, and the effort had to be switched to patching things up with the United States. Also, said Napoleon, Maximilian should not bring up any problems about Mexican priests or property when he visited the Pope. Any discussion of clerical matters should wait until Maximilian reached Mexico City.

A very unpleasant surprise awaited Maximilian when he returned to Miramar from his visit to Paris. He was asked to sign a "family pact," renouncing all his inheritance rights to the Hapsburg fortune and giving up for himself and all of his heirs any rights of succession to the Austrian throne.

Maximilian was stunned. He said he would refuse the Mexican throne if it meant having to yield to the family's demands. His declaration managed to upset just about everyone who thought the Mexican arrangement had been completed. Diplomats, politicians, and royalty from several countries—especially Austria, France and Mexico—were all in an uproar. Charlotte was summoned to Vienna, Austrian emperor Franz Josef showed up at Miramar, and Napoleon III was totally outraged. Napoleon sent Maximilian a telegram on March 28, 1864, saying that it was too late to back out. Maximilian had signed an agreement, and, wrote Napoleon, "a family quarrel cannot prevent your Imperial Highness from undertaking your exalted mission."

After a great deal of tough bargaining, Maximilian was able to keep his family inheritance money, but not his succession to the throne. They simply agreed to find him a "worthy" position back in Austria if he ever left the throne of Mexico.

The New Emperor Cries at His Send-off

On April 14, 1864, the port at Miramar was filled with delegations that had come to say good-bye. Ten thousand citizens of Trieste had signed a farewell message, large crowds threw flowers, and fishermen came in their boats to salute their departing archduke and wish him well. Maximilian was so moved by the send-off that he couldn't speak. He got all choked up and cried.

To the sound of a twenty-one-gun salute from the shore, the Mexican flag was raised on the frigate *Novara*. Napoleon III had sent the French frigate *Themis* as an escort; Maximilian's brother, Franz Josef, had sent a contingent of Austrian soldiers; and Carlota's father, King Leopold, had sent some Belgian troops. Bands played, flags waved, and crowds cheered as the *Novara* set sail along the coast for a brief stop in Italy, where Maximilian and Carlota were to receive the Pope's blessing before heading across the Atlantic to Veracruz.

Señorita Pepita: Talk or We'll Hang You

The cat-and-mouse game between DuPin and Carbajal continued, involving Soto la Marina, Tamaulipas, and the nearby town of San Fernando. The French had managed to shut off Juárez's last port on the Gulf of Mexico by taking over Matamoros on the U.S. border. The only way the weapons smugglers could deliver their goods to the Juárez forces was to dump them on deserted beaches near San Fernando and Soto la Marina.

DuPin and his *contre-guérillas* decided to concentrate their attention on San Fernando, but none of the locals wanted to talk. The unanimous silence among the inhabitants aroused DuPin's curiosity, and he finally got one of them to reveal some of the gossip. The man told him that, a few days earlier, Carbajal and his men had been seen loading supplies into a barn at the top of a bluff overlooking the beach just outside of town.

Making their way to the barn, DuPin and his men came upon quite a cache: besides four hundred tons of gunpowder, they found four thousand bullets and shells. All of the ammunition had markings showing that it had been manufactured in the United States. There was too much in the barn to move it anywhere, so they just rolled it all over the bluff and into the waters of the Gulf.

In another part of Tamaulipas, the French tried to organize a local government in Ciudad Victoria, but Carbajal and his guerillas warned all those who had been chosen as members of the town's Council of Notables not to attend the first meeting of the council. Those who did, said Carbajal, would be executed as traitors under President Juárez's decree. DuPin learned of Carbajal's threat and provided an armed escort to be sure that the notables would show up for their inaugural session.

Also in Ciudad Victoria, three of the locals managed to get two French soldiers into a house, where they shot them and butchered them with machetes. After catching the perpetrators, DuPin rounded up all of their relatives and forced them to watch as the three were executed in the town's main plaza. Then he had his *contre-guérillas* burn the house to the ground.

As DuPin left Ciudad Victoria and headed eastward toward Soto la Marina and the Gulf, he passed through the tiny hamlet of Croy. He expected to encounter another guerilla leader by the name of Ingenio Abalos, but apparently Abalos and his men had been tipped off and had left the town a few hours earlier. DuPin located the mayor, who not only told him that the guerillas were waiting with an ambush on the way to Soto la Marina, but that a local señorita by the name of Pepita was Abalos's mistress.

Arriving at Pepita's house, the *contre-guérillas* displayed a rope, suitable for hanging, as DuPin took a watch from his pocket and placed it on the table. He told the señorita he'd give her five minutes to tell him everything about the ambush, or she would be dangling at the end of the rope. Pepita remained silent, but she kept looking toward the door. DuPin and the officers in the house with him took out their revolvers and pointed them at her. She looked frightened, but still did not speak.

DuPin told Pepita that her five minutes were up and ordered his men to hang her. As she felt the rope being placed around her neck, she gave in and told them all about the plans for the ambush.

The colonel realized that Pepita would make an excellent hostage. He forced her to walk just ahead of his men, and ordered two of them to keep their pistols aimed at her back. As they passed by the place where Abalos and his men would have staged the ambush, the guerilla leader saw his mistress being marched along at gunpoint and called off the attack. DuPin and his men arrived in Soto la Marina unharmed, where they released Pepita.

Juárez to Ortega: "If You Can't Take the Heat,..."

While all of that was going on near the Gulf of Mexico, General González-Ortega was having a rough time holding his army together. He was able to slow the French advance sporadically in places like Aguascalientes, San Luis Potosí,

Zacatecas, Durango, Chihuahua, and Coahuila, but he could not stop them completely. He desperately wanted some kind of victory.

Finally, he decided to go on the offensive near a town called Majoma in the state of Durango. It was a serious mistake. In fierce and bloody fighting, he suffered an overwhelming defeat. President Benito Juárez wrote to his son-in-law, Don Pedro Santacilla, who was living in the United States, that Ortega had all the advantages but "did not engage all his forces but only a small part, which fought heroically, and the other, which was the larger, remained drawn up and retired in order…"

Juárez claimed that most of Ortega's men never fired a shot, and that Ortega had allowed them to disband when they had retreated about twenty-five miles from the enemy and were not being pursued.

Ortega did not answer Juárez directly, but offered a number of excuses to those who would listen. He claimed that the troops were just plain worn out after long marches through the desert, and that no amount of discipline would have prevented them from disbanding. He withdrew to Chihuahua to await further orders. None came. From Juárez, there was just silence.

General Ortega began to feel uncomfortable. While no one can be sure exactly why—perhaps advice from his friends, fear for his life, or the desire to be somewhere beyond Juárez's reach—he wrote to Juárez asking for permission to leave Mexico. Ortega claimed that he felt he was not accomplishing very much in Chihuahua, and said that he wanted to travel to the United States to recruit American volunteers, and then return to some other part of Mexico where he could more effectively confront the French.

Juárez was relieved. He would have Ortega out of the way for now. Request granted.

Friends of Romero: Five Hundred Dinner Guests, Sixteen Speeches

In New York City, Matías Romero's Washington dinners and all of his lobbying had finally paid off. At the corner of Fifth Avenue and Fourteenth Street stood Delmonico's Hotel and its new restaurant. There was a grand ballroom, a Chinese room, and a very popular room with blue satin furnishings known simply as "The Blue Room." Two of the rooms had been reserved for a reception, a third for a testimonial dinner, and a fourth just for the orchestra and dancing. The dinner on March 29, 1864, was in honor of Matías Romero.

The menu was in blue satin with gold lettering, and the dinner included no fewer than ten courses. Halfway through the meal, Dinner Chairman James W. Beekman proposed a toast to President Abraham Lincoln, to which prominent lawyer David Dudley Field replied. After the dinner, President Charles King of Columbia College proposed a toast to Benito Juárez, to which Matías Romero replied. Other prominent individuals among the five hundred or so guests were William Cullen Bryant, John Jacob Astor III, Hamilton Fish, William E. Dodge, and George Folsom. There were sixteen speeches, all showing support for Mexico's fight to drive out the European monarchists, and all regretting that the United States government was tied up with the current Civil War. However, all of the speakers emphasized that the Southern rebellion was about to be crushed in a massive offensive during the coming summer, and that the United States would then be free to help the Mexicans defeat their invaders.

Matías Romero told the gathering that he could see the day when "our common interests, political as well as commercial, will give us a common continental policy which no European nation would dare to disregard." He and the others—whether they mentioned it by name or not—were referring to the Monroe Doctrine.

On this same evening, March 29, 1864, the latest newspapers which had just arrived from London reported that Maximilian and Charlotte had visited Queen Victoria, among others, and were now on their way to Mexico.

PART IV
The Emperor of Mexico
April 1, 1864, through July 15, 1867

26

Maximilian's Arrival: All Those Parties

(May through December 1864)

Embarrassing Welcome for the Emperor and Empress

This was certainly no way to greet royalty, but then again, it was five o'clock in the morning of May 28, 1864, and they were three days ahead of schedule. The streets of Veracruz were empty.

Emperor Maximilian's ship, the *Novara,* had been anchored in Veracruz Harbor since about noon on May 27th. The French naval commander had come aboard to tell them they should have dropped anchor among the French ships, and that by staying where they were, they'd all catch yellow fever. He went on to tell them horror stories about bandidos along the highway to Mexico City, and claimed that Mexican general Porfirio Díaz was plotting to ambush and kill them along the way. Maximilian just stood there and listened to the admiral with what one of his aides later described as sarcastic tranquility. Welcome to Mexico.

General Almonte was supposed to have met them at dockside, but he had been waiting in Orizaba, not only to avoid picking up some disease, but because he wasn't expecting them for another couple of days. Local authorities went to fetch Almonte, and by the evening of May 27th, he came rushing on board with all sorts of apologies.

Almonte recommended an early morning start for their inland journey, so they decided to have dinner aboard the ship. After all, they had brought chefs with them from France, along with the finest foods and wines. This would be the last chance to enjoy a fine dinner before several days of cross-country travel to Mexico City, and there was no urgency to go ashore.

The orange reflection of the rising sun highlighted the tips of the waves in the bay, as small boats rocked at anchor. The imperial party—after hearing Mass on deck—was rowed ashore at 5:00 AM. Small groups of fishermen didn't even bother to turn their heads as they dragged their nets up onto the beach. A couple of triumphal arches had been quickly put up at dockside overnight, and someone had apparently been paid to fire off a few rockets. Other than that, some of Maximilian's aides described the reception as excessively chilling. Almonte had grabbed a couple of reluctant local officials, who offered the royals the key to the city, and then the party was hustled off to the railroad depot. There were no crowds to greet them along the way. Charlotte had tears in her eyes. Maximilian just looked straight ahead.

The French had managed to build the railroad inland as far as Paso del Macho in order to get troops and supplies quickly out of the disease-ridden tropical zone. The emperor and empress boarded the train and seated themselves on woven straw benches. The venetian blinds had been closed to shade them from the already-glaring sun. It took a while to get started, because the royal entourage included eighty-five people, with more than five hundred pieces of luggage.

Leaving Veracruz in silence, they passed marshes and sand hills dotted with scrub growth and an occasional cactus. Wild cattle wandered about, with skinny white birds standing on their backs picking out the bugs. After about twenty-five miles, the train stopped at La Soledad. Almonte had lined up a band, which played airs while breakfast was served in a rickety wooden building surrounded by grass shacks. As the locals stared in curiosity, Maximilian made a little speech in Spanish.

It was only about another twenty miles until they came to the end of the line at Paso del Macho. It would be carriages from now on for everyone. An English traveling carriage had been brought from Europe for the royal couple, and there was a phaeton for the ladies-in-waiting, but stagecoaches, which the Mexicans call *diligencias*, were lined up for everyone else. Each was pulled by eight mules. Charlotte was uncomfortable, since her head frequently banged on the ceiling and her arms and shoulders rubbed against the sides of the carriage. She was also quite apprehensive as she watched for what she thought might be suspicious spots along the primitive roads that, at times, were only dried-up stream beds. She admitted that she would not have been surprised "if Juárez himself had appeared with some hundreds of guerillas." Her guess wasn't that far off: the regular mail coach, on its run from Mexico City to Veracruz, had been held up that very same day.[1]

The carriages bumped onward through the ruts, the drivers furiously whipping and shouting curses while little boys ran alongside, throwing rocks at the lead mules. Maximilian was fascinated as the convoy headed inland through tropical jungle growth. He saw large stands of banana trees, mango groves, and tall coconut palm trees. Occasionally they passed primitive huts made of bamboo sticks; each one was surrounded with beautiful planted flowers. Children were usually nearby, playing with coconut shells or other objects improvised as toys. There was something else the new sovereigns could not avoid seeing: the hundreds of roadside graves of French soldiers who had died of yellow fever on the march inland during the initial invasion.

This was the rainy season, and deep in the forest a deluge triggered a flash flood along the roadway. The carriage just ahead of the royals turned over at the edge of a ravine. Maximilian's minister of state and five others managed to escape with their lives by climbing through the windows. Then a wheel of the English traveling carriage broke. The emperor and empress would have to continue the journey in a coach still labeled *"Diligencia de la República"* ("Stagecoach of the Republic").

They had hoped to reach Córdoba by nightfall, but the rain and the other mishaps delayed them by many hours. At the height of the thunderstorms, soldiers with lighted torches were placed atop the carriages, but the heavy downpour quickly extinguished the flames. They finally arrived in Córdoba at two o'clock in the morning. The welcoming committee consisted of a few dozen soaked and bedraggled *indígenas* (Indians), waving fistfuls of wilted flowers and shouting *"¡Viva!"*

It was pretty clear that the *indígenas* (Indians) had no idea why they were doing this, or who Maximilian and Charlotte were. A loud thunderclap close by made everyone duck. The rain continued unabated. Charlotte was crying.[2]

Grand Entrance to Mexico City

What a change two weeks can make.

After spending time in Orizaba and Puebla en route to the capital, Maximilian and Charlotte finally arrived in Mexico City at noon on June 12. It was a bright, beautiful sunny day, with not a cloud in the sky. More than a hundred carriages bearing the finest-dressed women from wealthy Mexican families met the royal entourage at a town outside the capital. Accompanied by almost five hundred men on horseback, they escorted the new emperor and empress into the city. Sixty more coaches with high-ranking government and church officials followed.

The parade was led by Imperialista captain Miguel Lopez and his Mexican Lancers regiment, followed by groups of French Chasseurs d'Afrique and French Hussars. General Achille Bazaine himself rode alongside the royal coach.

The first order of business was a *Te Deum* (Mass of Praise) at the cathedral, after which Maximilian and Charlotte walked across the Zócalo, or main square, to the Palacio Nacional, which had been vacated by Benito Juárez. More than a hundred thousand onlookers cheered their arrival.

Nonstop Fiestas

By the first week in August, even though the summer was not yet half over, the French troops were exhausted. It was not from combat.

Emperor Maximilian loved parties. There were more bullfights, plays, opera performances, balls, and receptions in the seven weeks since Maximilian had arrived than during the entire first year since General Forey had ridden into town. The emperor really wanted to identify with his new subjects, to the point of wearing a sombrero at bullfights and cheering with the crowd. He even practiced twirling a lariat. Half an hour's drive from the Zócalo by carriage was the old castle at Chapultepec, which had been the summer home of the Aztec emperors. The royal couple moved to the castle within eight days after their arrival, hiring so many hundreds of workers to renovate the place that no one else in Mexico City could find skilled workmen to do anything else.

Country Estates—and a Gardener's Daughter

While Maximilian spent his time searching for a country estate, Charlotte spent hers working on various decrees about road building, mining, education, public health, and so on, all to be issued in the emperor's name. Maximilian finally settled on an estate in Cuernavaca, about thirty miles south of Mexico City, which had been owned by the silver-mining tycoon Joseph Borda back in the Spanish colonial days. Borda had created a palatial home surrounded by trees, gardens, ponds, stone walls, and terraces to rival some of the palaces of Europe, but it had fallen into disrepair during Mexico's fight for independence from Spain. Maximilian eagerly looked forward to fixing it up.

They had another residence about three miles outside of Orizaba, which they named Jalapilla. Maximilian preferred the warmer climate there, but he was unable to visit as often as he liked because of the long journey. With all the residences to keep up—and the staff required to operate each one—the emperor's household expenses after one year came to $1.5 million (in U.S. dollars), about fifty times what the tab had been for President Benito Juárez.

Charlotte didn't particularly like the country estates, and Maximilian often found himself entertaining without her at Cuernavaca. It was well known that Maximilian and Charlotte did not sleep together. Historians disagree on whether this was from a "social disease" that he had picked up during a trip to Vienna or Brazil years earlier, or whether Charlotte just imagined that she had caught something from him.

In Cuernavaca, the emperor's bedroom opened out onto a secluded garden, and rumors soon began to circulate about his ongoing affair with the gardener's eighteen-year-old daughter.

Cultural Enrichment: A Nude Ballet Performance

General Bazaine had already begun to encourage cultural links between Mexico and France, and Maximilian continued such efforts. He ordered books from France, knowing that upper-class Mexicans had always learned to speak French. Before 1864 was over, seventy-seven pianos had been shipped from Le Harve to Mexico. French plays were staged in Mexico City, many attended by General Bazaine as well as by the emperor and empress.

One thing the new regime was interested in but was never able to attract from Europe was famous opera singers. Not only were the singers afraid of yellow fever and bandidos along the highways, but they had all heard about the company of French actors that had been stopped along a desolate stretch of roadway outside of Orizaba. Several of the men in the company had been killed, and others had been pinned down on the ground with their hands tied behind their backs. Then, the bandidos had forced all of the women to strip down and dance naked under the moonlight if they wanted to escape with their lives.

Biographer Jasper Ridley refers to the above group as "French actors" in his 1993 book, *Maximilian and Juárez*, but in his footnotes, he lists a book by J. J. Kendall as one of his sources. The Kendall book, *Mexico Under Maximilian*, was written in 1871 by a former British captain who had served as a major in Maximilian's army. Kendall says that a "friend" who was in charge of the Imperialista post at Córdoba received a report of bandidos attacking three *diligencias* (stagecoaches) between Córdoba and Paso del Macho. Arriving at the scene, the "friend" reportedly told Kendall that he had seen the same attack but said it was an opera company, and that company members were singing their parts rather than dancing them at gunpoint.

In any case, news of the incident not only infuriated Maximilian but also dampened European singers' desires to perform in Mexico. Mexico's emperor would have to settle for French-speaking theater groups from Martinique and musicians from Cuba.[3]

Although Maximilian managed to get telegraph lines hooked up around the country, he was less successful in extending the railroad from Veracruz to the capital. Guerilla fighters kept blowing up the tracks and killing the railway workers. Proclamations were issued almost daily from Chapultepec Castle for one project or another, but very few saw completion.

Romero's Dinner Speeches Are Published; Maximilian Is Targeted

Just two weeks before Maximilian and Charlotte had sailed from Europe, Mexico's man in Washington was giving that rousing speech to five hundred VIP guests at Delmonico's Steakhouse in New York. Matías Romero and fifteen other speakers predicted a Union victory in the Civil War and said they'd turn next to pressing the U.S. administration to enforce the Monroe Doctrine by ousting the invading French army from Mexico. To be sure that Maximilian and his French backers got the point, Romero had all sixteen speeches published in both English and Spanish and distributed freely throughout the United States and Mexico.

Romero didn't stop there. Intensively lobbying Congress, he got a U.S. senator to propose a resolution demanding the immediate withdrawal of all French forces from Mexico. The Senate Foreign Affairs Committee chairman blocked the measure, saying that it would not help win the Civil War but might push France into backing the Confederacy. Romero then turned to the House of Representatives, where he won a resolution saying that it would be against American policy to recognize a monarchy in the Western Hemisphere, especially one established by the overthrow of a democratically elected government.

If Secretary of State William Seward were still reluctant to confront the French over their violation of the Monroe Doctrine, Matías Romero had carefully built a support network of influential friends, not only in official Washington but also among commercial interests in major U.S. cities. He intended to use them all.

Maximilian Backs off Church Leaders

As Maximilian would soon discover, the problems of relating to the Union and the Confederacy were relatively small compared to the serious discord he had inherited with the Roman Catholic Church. Perhaps some kind of backing could have been worked out during his visit with the Pope, but Maximilian followed the advice of his brother, Franz Josef, and of Napoleon III. He avoided the topic of confiscated Church lands in Mexico during his time in Rome.

Within weeks after his arrival in Mexico, a leading French priest who had close connections to Napoleon III warned Maximilian that if he continued the practices of Benito Juárez and the liberals, it would lead to ruin and anarchy. Maximilian resented the pressure being put on him and told the cleric, Abbé Domenech, that if he were not a priest, he would be expelled. Domenech wrote to a friend who would pass his letter to the French Foreign Minister—and perhaps higher—that "Mexico is on a volcano: the Emperor and Empire used up; the insurrection triumphant."

It wasn't that Maximilian had any sort of record of colliding with the Church—as did Napoleon III who had a history of such conflicts—but he did feel strongly about religious toleration and was already committed to retaining the confiscated Church property. He had put together a nine-point plan for relations with the Church in Mexico, which envisioned a state-supported Catholic Church but with toleration of other faiths. In lieu of returning the confiscated Church properties, the government would pick up the salaries of the clergy.

That didn't set well at all with the papal nuncio, who continued to demand nothing less than the return of all confiscated lands to the Church and the restoration of authority to the clergy. Maximilian sent Empress Charlotte to try to move the nuncio from his rigid stand, since she was the daughter of a Catholic king and the granddaughter of a Catholic queen. She spent two hours with the nuncio but got absolutely nowhere. She later wrote in frustration to Napoleon's wife, Empress Eugénie, that "nothing has given me a better idea of hell than that interview, for hell, too, is no more nor less than a blind alley with no way out."

At that point, Maximilian decided to just deal on a "take it or leave it" basis with the Church. He waited until two days after Christmas, and then issued a decree confirming the main points of the Juárez rules: freedom of worship for all beliefs and validation of property rights for those who had acquired Church lands under Juárez.

The nuncio left Mexico in a huff, returning to Rome. He was never replaced during Maximilian's regime. Conservatives were appalled, distancing themselves from the imperial government, and the clergy kept a low profile, regarding Maximilian with suspicion and hostility. The loss of support from conservatives and the Church did not bode well for the success of an imperial Mexico.[4]

Colonel DuPin Must Go: The Atrocities Are Piling Up

Another problem quickly surfaced for the new emperor: DuPin was getting out of hand. The *contre-guérilla* leader was chasing Pedro Mendez, one of the most terrifying liberal guerilla chiefs, and DuPin's response was to commit even more horrible atrocities than the man he was trying to catch. Pedro Mendez's trademark costume was white breeches with a black vest, an enormous sombrero, extravagantly fashioned spurs on his boots, and a revolver at his waist. Just to be sure he was not mistaken for anyone else, he wore green eyeglasses. He was considered so cruel and terrifying that no Mexican would dare to be seen helping the French in areas where he was on the move.

DuPin had been following Mendez for months, sometimes spotting him at a distance but always arriving too late to capture him. At one point near Victoria, Tamaulipas, DuPin's people came upon the corpses of French soldiers and local collaborators hanging from the trees. A cross atop a fresh grave bore the sign "Death to the French murderers." As one of DuPin's men angrily tore down the sign, a bomb exploded and killed him. DuPin's *contre-guérillas* scattered for cover, running right into the ambush that Mendez and his men had set up in the immediate vicinity.

DuPin was so enraged by the surprise attack that he decided to escalate the violence in an all-out effort to annihilate Mendez and his followers. He established a base in Tampico and raided outlying villages from there. Whenever he captured individuals suspected of collaborating with Mendez, he had them brought to the town plaza in Tampico and hung them from trees during the early part of the evening, when the square was crowded with locals taking a stroll. He'd leave the bodies there all night, facing toward the Gulf of Mexico, and take them down in the morning.

Even for citizens who were pro-French or pro-Maximilian, that was too much. They sent a delegation to Mexico City and complained directly to Maximilian. Empress Charlotte had also been hearing horror stories about DuPin's activities and added some criticism of her own. Maximilian referred the complaints to Bazaine, who ordered DuPin to conduct courts-martial before executing anyone.

That must not have done much, because the complaints just kept on coming. Maximilian knew he had already lost the support of the Church and the conservatives, and the backing of those moderate people in the northeastern part of the country was vital. He insisted that Bazaine remove DuPin from his duties. At first DuPin's men were angry over the loss of their leader, but Napoleon III moved quickly to replace him with the Marquis Gaston de Gallifet. Colonel Gallifet had been seriously wounded during the siege of Puebla, but he was already a national hero in France for his part in the Crimean War and had been awarded the Legion of Honor. He had wanted to even the score over what happened to him at Puebla. Now, at thirty-three, he was rested and ready to return to Mexico.[5]

27

General Bazaine and the Teenage Señorita

(January through June 1865)

Prince Salm-Salm Becomes a U.S. General

In the American Civil War, General William T. Sherman had concluded his famous "March to the Sea," ravaging the Georgia countryside from Atlanta in the interior to Savannah on the Atlantic coast. He occupied Savannah on December 21, 1864. It was a sort of Christmas present for President Abraham Lincoln as the Civil War approached its final months.

Among those up for a promotion after Sherman's successful campaign was Colonel Felix Salm-Salm, who had been commanding the 68th New York Volunteers. After some weeks of delay, Agnes Salm-Salm decided that she'd better make the rounds in Washington, D.C., to be sure that Felix would be advanced to the rank of general. The nomination was to go through Secretary of War Stanton's office. Agnes had a lot of friends in the House, the Senate, and the president's cabinet, and she knew her personal effort toward Felix's interests would certainly help move the paperwork along. Arriving three days after Lincoln's inauguration for a second term, she spoke with two generals and three senators the first day. She sent many telegrams, and she traveled to Albany to see New York's governor. One way or another, Felix would get his promotion.

The "Mexican Robin Hood"

Even with Colonel Gallifet now leading the French *contre-guérillas*, Mexican liberal guerilla activity was still plaguing the country. Maximilian was worried that guerillas and bandidos would eventually overwhelm the French army if he didn't stamp them out. Not only were the guerillas still active in Tamaulipas, but now they were causing problems in the state of Michoacán. That was less than a hundred miles from Mexico City. Something had to be done.

The terrain of Michoacán was much more challenging than that of Tamaulipas. Tall mountains and deep canyons were covered with thick forests. Torrential rainstorms and raging whitewater streams made advancement by an army—especially an army of outsiders—virtually impossible for much of each year.

Michoacán was home to the "Mexican Robin Hood," Nicolás Romero. He first gained fame in 1863 after the fall of Puebla, concentrating on raids against the French and their Mexican collaborators within a hundred-mile radius of Mexico City. The common people saw him as their champion, a leader who robbed foreigners, reactionary conservatives, and the wealthy to give to the poor. Although he had never served in an elected office or as part of the military under Juárez, he was hailed by middle-class liberals and the poor as a patriotic figure.

An informal underground network stole arms and ammunition for Nicolás Romero, raised money for him, and prayed for him. He didn't have to recruit helpers; young, able-bodied men showed up to join his organization all the time.

The *contre-guérillas* were busy in Tamaulipas, so General Bazaine sent a contingent of Belgians and Austrians to hunt for Romero. Bazaine had originally intended to use the Belgians and Austrians in the siege of Oaxaca, but when Oaxaca surrendered before they got there, he assigned them to capture the Mexican Robin Hood. They were placed under the command of Imperialista general LaMadrid.

After weeks of searching in all the states surrounding Mexico City, LaMadrid's troops received a tip that Romero's group was camped out near the village of Zitácuaro, Michoacán, about halfway between Mexico City and Querétaro. LaMadrid sent an Imperialista cavalry detachment to raid the village. The cavalry troop swooped down on Zitácuaro so quickly that the guerillas were surprised. Some of them were killed, and about twenty were captured. The rest—including Romero—got away.

Romero had just one problem: he couldn't find a horse. Running desperately to avoid being seen, he found a tree near the cottage where his group had been camped out and climbed up into it. He was able to catch his breath while hiding in the branches, but he knew LaMadrid's people down below him were hanging the guerillas they had managed to capture.

Finished with the hangings, the cavalry troop decided to have a picnic lunch in the garden next to the cottage. One of the cavalrymen was a trumpeter who, at some earlier time, had been a member of Romero's group, so he knew the guerilla leader by sight. While the trumpeter ate his lunch, he spotted a rooster strutting around the yard and decided he'd like to have it for dinner. As he chased the bird, it flew up into the very tree in which Romero was hiding.

As the trumpeter climbed into the tree to get the rooster, he came face-to-face with Romero. The Mexican Robin Hood, now captured, would probably have been hanged with all of the others if the trumpeter had not recognized him. The cavalry commander, understanding what a prize he had, was not going to hang Romero in the woods and lose a chance to become famous for the capture. No, he was going to take him back to Mexico City alive and show him off to all those he wanted to impress: generals, journalists, politicians, and most of all, his girl-friend.

They found a mule for Romero and seated him atop the animal, with his feet tied underneath. A Belgian detachment escorted Romero to Mexico City, where he was sent to Martinica Prison, a special facility for political prisoners. The mule was given to General LaMadrid as his prize for having dispatched the unit that successfully captured Romero.

It didn't take long for the news to spread throughout the capital that Romero was in custody. His court-martial was somewhat of a circus. The presiding officer was one of those "hanging judges" who had already sentenced many guerillas to death. At an earlier trial, he had been quoted as saying, "Every Mexican either is a guerilla or has been one or will be one, so it can do no harm if we shoot those we catch."

Romero's friends found a highly regarded lawyer from Brussels serving with the Belgian troops and asked him to represent Romero. When the counselor visited the Mexican Robin Hood in his cell, Romero told him that he would claim that the court had no jurisdiction to try him because it had not been appointed by President Juárez. He recognized no other authority. The attorney tried to talk him out of it, but Romero wouldn't change his position. Under the circumstances, said the lawyer, he could not accept the case.

Romero wound up conducting his own defense. He not only challenged the jurisdiction of the French court-martial, but he denounced the intervention, Maximilian's government, and all of the Mexicans who worked for it, whom he labeled as "traitors." To no one's surprise, that didn't win the sympathy of the court. Romero was found guilty and given the death sentence.

Romero had become a legend in his Robin Hood role, and thousands signed petitions to Maximilian for a pardon, but none was forthcoming. On March 20, 1865, Romero and two of his top men stood before a firing squad in the Plazuela de Mizcalco in Mexico City. Expecting trouble, General Bazaine had filled the plaza with soldiers. Even the fusillade from the firing squad didn't kill Romero, so a sergeant had to finish the grim task with his revolver. Even then, the cheap coffin broke apart as they were carrying the body away. The crowd departed in silence.

Did They Talk About Xalapa?

It was a quiet Sunday morning at the McLean house in Appomattox, Virginia. Confederate general Robert E. Lee arrived at the agreed-upon meeting place on his gray horse, handsomely dressed in a new uniform. He had come to surrender his eight thousand men to Union general Ulysses S. Grant. Lee had said that he "would rather die a thousand deaths" than give up the fight, but his starving, ragged troops were worn out. They had been retreating westward across Virginia for a week after a severe defeat. Lee had hoped that by some miracle he would be joined by General Johnston, who would be approaching from North Carolina. Unfortunately for the Confederates, General William T. Sherman's troops had decimated Johnston's forces farther south, and Grant had maneuvered his army to block Lee. The Confederates had run out of options. The enemy was closing in, so there was no other choice.

A short while later, General Grant arrived. He was about five inches shorter than the six-foot-tall Lee and was dressed only in a plain field uniform. He said later that he had not expected the surrender to come quite as quickly. He was notified while on horseback, without a sword and with only his shoulder straps to indicate his rank.

Extending a hand to Lee, Grant told him, "I met you once before, General Lee. I met you while we serving in Mexico." Grant later reported that the two of them got to talking in the parlor about "old army times," to the point where he almost forgot why they had come together that morning.

Historians have speculated about what the details of that conversation might have been. Grant had been a new second lieutenant in the Mexican War of 1847–1848, and Lee had been a captain. Maybe they said the Mexicans had fought bravely, but under poor leadership. Maybe they talked about the way Lee had lowered artillery down one wall of a canyon and hauled it back up the other by hand in the middle of the night, so that his troops could attack Santa Anna's forces from behind. It could be that they spoke fondly about Xalapa, and the beauty of the scenery and the women, of which Lee had once been quoted as saying, "I can conceive of nothing more beautiful!"

At any rate, Grant later reported that "after the conversation had run on in this style for some time, General Lee called my attention to the object of our meeting, and said that he had asked for this interview for the purpose of getting from me the terms I proposed to give his army." The aides for both men finally came into the room and the documents were signed.

General Lee responded mechanically to all the salutes as he left the front porch of the house. He had a distant gaze in his eyes as he patted his horse on the head, mounted, and rode away to convey the details of the surrender to his army.

As General Grant rode back to his camp he, too, had a distant look. His mind was obviously focused elsewhere. Finally, one of his aides reminded him that he had overlooked one important detail: notify the secretary of war in Washington about the surrender. He got off his horse, sat down by the side of the road, and quickly jotted the text of a brief telegram.

Telegrams from Washington

There was sensational celebration when the news reached the United States' capital that night. Princess Agnes Salm-Salm was in town, and later wrote that "the city resembled a madhouse...everybody embraced everybody on the streets." It had already been a good day for Agnes: she held in her hands the papers, signed by war secretary Stanton, promoting Felix Salm-Salm to the rank of general. She wasted no time in sending a telegram to "General Felix Salm-Salm."

Someone else was sending a telegram that night: Matías Romero couldn't wait to get a message off to Benito Juárez that the South had surrendered. The United States would not have to worry about France or Maximilian joining forces with the Confederacy. The attention would now shift in Mexico's favor, as Congress considered the problem of a European-backed monarchy south of the border.

There was one more telegram: the Marquis de Montholon, who had followed Pierre Saligny as France's minister to Mexico, had just been transferred to Washington, D.C. His message to Paris would not be exactly what Napoleon III might want to read.

Mexico City's Wedding of the Year

On June 26, 1865, who would ever have imagined that Archbishop Antonio Labastida, the man who had threatened to excommunicate all French soldiers, and General Achille Bazaine, the one who had threatened to blast church doors open with cannon fire, would be in the same room together, much less sharing the occasion of a wedding ceremony? The bride was none other than Doña Josefa de la Peña, the niece of a former president of Mexico. Emperor Maximilian and

Empress Charlotte not only acted as the godparents for the lovely señorita, but also sponsored a wedding breakfast for her and gave her a gorgeous palace at Buenavista as a wedding present.

All of the foreign diplomats posted to Mexico were present as Maximilian honored Bazaine with a speech at the old Palacio Nacional in a large, newly renovated room, which had been named *Salon des Ambassadeurs.* Charlotte even embraced the bride in public. As British author Joan Haslip writes in her book, *The Crown of Mexico: Maximilian and His Empress Carlota,* "Half the families in Mexico City claimed some kind of relationship [with the bride] and the Zócalo [main square] was crowded with carriages full of pretty young women, wearing their finest dresses and mantillas [shawls]."

The bridegroom was fifty-four-year-old General Achille Bazaine. His new wife, now Madame la Maréchale de Bazaine, was seventeen.

The archbishop was going along with it all, despite his disapproval of Maximilian's liberal policies, because he knew full well that the possible alternatives included an American invasion and the return to power of Benito Juárez. Even Maximilian, who had not been getting along with Bazaine that well himself, was charming and sociable for the occasion, but had written to his brother, "We have, alas, on Monday another great entertainment in the palace, the wedding between Marshal Bazaine and a charming seventeen-year-old Mexican, who will do us great credit in Europe with her beauty and amiability. The elderly Marshal is as much in love as a young subaltern. I only hope that his precarious conjugal bliss agrees with him."

Divided Camp: French Army versus Maximilian

It was becoming harder and harder to ignore the growing rift between Maximilian and General Bazaine. Some Zouaves who were trying to rescue people and property from the upper floor at a house fire in Mexico City were killed when the floor caved in. After the funeral for the Zouave commander who died with his men, a bystander shouted curses and insults at the Frenchmen and the passing cortége. A court-martial sentenced him to five years of hard labor, but Maximilian pardoned the man after just six weeks.

Bazaine and all his officers were outraged at the pardon, one of many by which Maximilian had freed convicted guerillas and bandidos. Sara Yorke, who later in her life wrote about her experiences during the French intervention, said that at a military ball, she had overheard General Bazaine complaining to friends that he was furious at having to order his men to risk their lives to capture guerillas, only to see Maximilian pardon them.

The French officers also began to suspect that Juárez was infiltrating Maximilian's Imperialista army and the crews of clerks who operated the newly installed French telegraph system. Juárez's guerillas were aware of Bazaine's plans before French officers knew about them.

Ex-Confederate Troops Head for Mexico

Confederate general Jo Shelby sat around the campfire with his troops from the Missouri Cavalry Division, pondering their options. They had learned of Lee's surrender to Grant a few days after it had taken place, and in the weeks that followed, there had been several attempts to get other Confederate units to surrender, with varying degrees of success.

Shelby had already informed his troops that their commanding general, Kirby Smith, wanted out, and that the governors and civilian leaders from Missouri, Arkansas, Louisiana, and Texas had all capitulated. What should the army do?

"'Surrender' is a word neither myself nor my division understand," said Shelby, adding that "we will march into Mexico and reinstate Juárez or espouse Maximilian. [We] should go at once to Marshal Bazaine, and learn from him whether it is peace or war." Shelby's troops considered themselves an elite force, well equipped and well trained. They were excited about the opportunities that awaited them in Maximilian's new empire, where Southerners who did not wish to live under Yankee oppression could start over again and build a new, stately, honorable society.

As the sun rose on the morning of June 3, 1865, Shelby's division began its march across the Red River and into Texas, headed for the Mexican border. There would be no trouble equipping the brigade, because weapons and ammunition had been stockpiled in Texas for battles that would never take place. Shelby's would be the last unit waving the Stars and Bars of the old Confederacy to obtain them.

For several days, they stopped at towns along the way, restoring law and order to places like Waco, Tyler, Bryan, and Houston, where deserters from both the Union and Confederate armies had become bandits, looting and terrorizing the local populations. Then Shelby's troops proceeded in a northwesterly direction along the Colorado River toward Austin.

Austin's ten-year-old capitol building, which sat at one end of Congress Avenue about a mile north of the river, overlooked what was still essentially a small shanty town, with a scattering of huts, cabins, and rickety, false-fronted stores. The governor's mansion, with its tall white columns, was across the street, to the southwest of the capitol. To the east, atop Robertson Hill, was the former French Legation, designed and built by none other than France's minister to Texas in the 1840s, Pierre Alphonse Dubois de Saligny.

Little did Shelby or his men suspect that a notorious gang that had been operating in the area for several months was planning to raid the state treasury at the capitol, which also had served as part of a subtreasury for the Confederate government. More than three hundred thousand dollars in gold and silver coins filled the five safes, and these were guarded by only a handful of soldiers. The bandits were led by an individual known as Captain Rabb, and as nightfall came over Austin, they quietly infiltrated the town and waited for a signal to begin the raid.

Suddenly, they charged the capitol building, shooting down the few guards and starting to hammer at the iron doors of the treasury section. Someone sounded an alarm. Church bells began to ring. The mayor sent an urgent message to Shelby.

From South Austin, across the river, came the sound of a bugle. Within moments, a cavalry charge—four men across—arrived near the capitol, where the mayor told them what was happening. Shelby's men quickly surrounded the building. As Captain Rabb's men came running out with their arms full of loot, they were greeted by whizzing bullets from about forty rifles. Shelby's men chased the raiders back into the building, where the now-darkened rooms were filled with shots, cries, gun smoke, and the sounds of shattering glass.

One of the bandits had taken off his pants and tied the bottoms of the legs. As he tried to run out of the building with his pants and his hat both filled with gold coins, he ignored shouts to stop and was shot dead at close range. Rabb and a few of his men, carrying some fifteen thousand dollars in gold and silver coins in a blanket, had escaped in the darkness as Shelby's troops arrived, Unfortunately for Rabb, a corner of the blanket became untied, and they left a trail of glittering gold and silver coins along the street. The robbers were not caught, but they had little more than a blanket to show for their efforts that night.

The captain in charge of the Confederate supply department and Governor Murrah of Texas both insisted that Shelby take the Confederate share of the treasury to pay his soldiers and to use for expenses, but Shelby and his officers declined. They had plenty of captured United States currency with which to pay for what they needed, and they believed that any Confederate money should be left to the state in which it was located. It was a matter of honor to them.

The very next morning, they left for San Marcos, Texas, and then went on to New Braunfels, San Antonio, and finally Eagle Pass. In San Antonio, Shelby and his officers made their headquarters at the Menger Hotel—next to the Alamo—for several days. Former Confederate soldiers kept arriving in town to join them, until the brigade numbered just over a thousand men. They hadn't decided whether they would fight for Juárez or Maximilian yet, but one way or another, they were going to reach Mexico.

28

Juárez and His American Friends

(Summer 1865)

Maximilian's New York Recruiting Office

Agnes Salm-Salm had been shopping in New York City. With her husband's new commission as a major general in hand, she ordered a brand new general's uniform for Felix, and all the accessories that would go with it. No matter that the Civil War was over and that the troops would all be demobilized within a few months. General Sherman had appointed the new General Salm-Salm as military governor of Atlanta, and Agnes was going to have Felix's picture taken with him in that role before it was too late.

As she walked up Tenth Avenue in Manhattan, she came upon an interesting storefront. It seemed that Emperor Maximilian of Mexico had opened up a recruiting office and was looking for a few good men—especially officers—to help him fight the Juaristas.

Agnes didn't have to think twice about it. She reasoned that both Maximilian and Felix were from Austria, spoke German, and would get along just fine. She went into the recruiting office and filled out an application on Felix's behalf.[1]

Grant to Sheridan: Pretend You're Going to Invade Mexico

With the American Civil War over, General Ulysses S. Grant had time to think about the situation south of the border in Mexico. Generals Grant and Sherman had been the Union's top two heroes during the war, but General Philip Sheridan had been a close third. The big victory parade for the Union troops was to be held in Washington on May 23, but Grant sent a telegram to Sheridan claiming that a division of Confederate Rebels was still holding out somewhere in Texas or

Louisiana. He said he needed Sheridan to pin them down and get them to surrender. Sheridan didn't want to leave Washington and miss the parade, so he went to Grant's office to see if he could delay the assignment.

It wasn't until the two generals were in the same room that Grant told Sheridan what was really happening. The "Rebels-on-the-loose" story was just a cover for something Grant had not told President Johnson or Secretary of State Seward. What he really wanted to do was scare the French into believing that the United States was about to invade Mexico on the side of Juárez. Sheridan thought it was a great idea, and the two of them decided that he should leave immediately, in case Seward were to find out about the plan and try to stop it.

It worked. President Johnson and General Grant stood in the reviewing stand to take the salutes as William T. Sherman and other top generals marched the troops by in a gala celebration. Sheridan, meanwhile, had set up forces in San Antonio, Houston, and Brownsville, the latter right across the border from General Mejía's Imperialista troops at Matamoros.

The reaction was panic in both Mexico City and Paris, as word spread that the United States was about to invade.

Napoleon III blinked. He didn't want a military encounter with the United States, and he ordered General Bazaine to pull all French and Imperialista troops back from the border immediately to avoid any incident that might touch off a war. In Paris, the French emperor drew up contingency plans for an American invasion. He would have the French retreat to just outside San Luis Potosí, about three hundred miles from the border, and try to hold the line there. He was hoping that a march across northern Mexico would wear out the U.S. troops, and that they would pick up some diseases, just as the French had done when they had traveled through the coastal lowlands around Veracruz. Unfortunately, he knew he couldn't count on it.

One thing Napoleon III had decided for sure: the Mexican expedition just wasn't worth it anymore. He'd have to start looking for a way out of it—the sooner, the better.

Shelby's Troops Cross the Border

It was the Fourth of July 1865, and a solemn ritual was about to take place on the United States-Mexican border at Eagle Pass, Texas, and Piedras Negras, Coahuila, Mexico. General Jo Shelby had his brigade lined up in "dress parade front," overlooking the Rio Grande from the American side. Before them fluttered the Stars and Bars of the Confederate flag. The banner had been hand sewn by the women of a small town in Arkansas and presented to the unit with great ceremony and speechmaking just two years earlier. Now, they were about to bury it in the river before they crossed into Mexico.

Shelby had chosen five colonels to perform the task. The group held the flag aloft for a few minutes, then hoisted it onto their shoulders and waded out into the river before lowering it gently into the water. Shelby himself was overcome with emotion and plucked a black plume from his hat, tossing it into the river. Tears could be seen running down the cheeks of many of the soldiers. The waters of the Rio Grande then closed over the last flag ever to be flown by an organized military unit of what had once been the Confederate States of America.

As they crossed the river, the men of the Iron Brigade already knew whose side they wanted to fight for. Shelby himself had used a small skiff to cross over to Piedras Negras the previous afternoon, and he had been offered the military command for the states of Tamaulipas, Nuevo Leon, and Coahuila if he and his troops would align themselves with Benito Juárez. After intense debate that night, Colonel Ben Elliott, speaking for the men, said they would prefer to offer their services to Maximilian.

"Is this your answer, men?" asked Shelby, to be absolutely sure.

"It is," repeated Elliott, as the men all nodded in agreement.

"Then it is mine, too," said Shelby. "Henceforth we will fight under Maximilian. Tomorrow, at four o'clock in the afternoon, the march shall commence for Monterrey."[2]

How to Smuggle Arms to Juárez

The French knew that not all the arms and ammunition obtained by the Juárez forces were coming across the border by land. Some was arriving at Mexican seaports on the Pacific. One individual who decided to track down this source was the French consul in San Francisco, a fellow by the name of Charles de Cazotte. The consul could pick up a lot of information by simply hanging around the waterfront and asking questions. Cazotte would chat informally with tourists arriving from Acapulco and with sailors from ships that had visited various Mexican ports.

Cazotte learned some amazing things during his conversations. For example, several of Juárez's former generals, who had supposedly surrendered to Maximilian in Mexico City, were actually passing vital information to a Juárez guerilla leader in Guerrero, the state where Acapulco was located. An *indígena* (Indian) reportedly made the trip to Guerrero from the capital twice a week, with a summary of the discussions from Maximilian's cabinet meetings. Cazotte also discovered that an agent by the name of Henry Kastan had come from Acapulco to San Francisco to arrange for the shipment of twenty-two cases of arms for the Juárez forces. The arms would be carried aboard a number of small ships, so as to avoid detection and possibly the capture of the entire shipment. Whenever he came across such leads, Cazotte forwarded them to Napoleon's admiral in charge of the Pacific coastline so that the French fleet would be on the lookout.

As some Juárez agents were preparing to make a major shipment from two ports in Southern California, Cazotte intervened by going to U.S. military commanders and getting them to order the shipments stopped. In going to the authorities, Cazotte blew his cover and allowed Juárez's agents to become aware of his snooping. Mexican ambassador Matías Romero heard of the California shipping ban and protested to Secretary of State Seward, saying that the U.S. military no longer needed weapons for the Civil War and so should rescind the ban. Hoping that U.S. policy would change, Romero himself placed an order for weapons to be shipped from New York. In Washington, Minister Montholon of France became aware of the order and protested to Seward. The secretary of state, still trying to avoid a war with France, got President Andrew Johnson to issue a general ban against all exports of weapons and ammunition.

Romero had worked hard at developing a network of influential contacts who could get around Seward. He was amazed that the secretary of state still felt it necessary to mollify Napoleon III now that the Civil War was over. Romero called on one of his contacts, Ulysses S. Grant. The general didn't think that President Johnson would rescind anything set forth by Seward, so he came up with something even more attractive for Romero: the army would secretly supply Juárez with everything he needed. Confidential orders went out to General Philip Sheridan to open up the army storehouses all along the border and just look the other way. Years later, Sheridan wrote that he had supplied the Juaristas with at least thirty thousand muskets from the Baton Rouge arsenal in Louisiana alone. All along the border, from El Paso to Matamoros, the Juárez forces were better armed than they had ever been.[3]

Shelby Threatens to Seize Monterrey

The citizens of Monterrey, Nuevo Leon, were fiercely loyal. Whenever the Juárez forces were in town, they were loyal to Juárez. Whenever the French or the Imperialistas were in town, they were loyal to Maximilian. As Edwin Adams Davis puts it in his 1995 book, *Fallen Guidon: The Saga of Confederate General Jo*

Shelby's March to Mexico, in late 1864 Juárez controlled most of northern Mexico, so the people of Monterrey shouted and made *fiestas*. Six months later the [states of] Nuevo Leon and Tamaulipas were in the hands of the Empire—and they shouted and made *fiestas*. Then Juárez returned, and the populace again shouted and made *fiestas*.

In early July, 1865, just as [General Jo] Shelby was entering the country, the Empire forces launched an offensive against Northern Mexico. Juárez lost Monterrey and the people of the town shouted and made *fiestas* in honor of Colonel Pierre Jean Joseph Jeanningros, the French officer who had been appointed military governor of the Monterrey district. Juárez retreated to El Paso.

This was the situation, then, as Shelby led his men southward from Piedras Negras toward the City of the Saddle [Monterrey].[4]

Shelby sent one of his scouts ahead to find out what Jeanningros was like. The scout reported back that there were ex-Confederates all over the place, including at least two former governors and six generals. About a hundred Confederate soldiers had already joined Colonel Francois DuPin's *contre-guérillas*, and others had been absorbed by French forces throughout the country.

The only major negative information was that Colonel Jeanningros was angry about Shelby's sale of artillery and ammunition to the Juarista mayor of Piedras Negras as he crossed into Mexico. Shelby was fairly confident that he could smooth things over with Jeanningros, but he had a backup plan that, if necessary, called for going back to the border to recruit more Confederates and then returning to attack and seize Monterrey.

Just outside of Monterrey, Shelby pulled his troops up into "battle front" and sent two messengers into town under a flag of truce. The message read,

> General:
> I have the honor to report that I am within one mile of your fortifications with my command. Preferring exile to surrender, I have left my own country to seek service in that held by His Imperial Majesty, the Emperor Maximilian. Shall it be peace or war between us? If the former, and with your permission, I shall enter your lines at once, claiming at your hands the courtesy due from one soldier to another. If the latter, I propose to attack you immediately.
> Very RespectfullyYours,
> J. O. Shelby

Jeanningros was impressed with Shelby's boldness, and he had also sympathized with the South during the American Civil War. He invited the brigade to enter the town and scheduled a banquet in Shelby's honor that evening. He turned on all the Old World charm he could muster and entertained not only Shelby, but also a large contingent of former Confederate generals, senators, and governors. He talked about European and Asian military campaigns and adventures that he had experienced over more than two decades, and displayed an extensive knowledge of the American Civil War.

Shelby asked about Maximilian.

Speaking more frankly than one would expect, Jeanningros pictured Maximilian as "more of a scholar than a king,..." and much too tender hearted to hang onto power for very long. "He can not kill as we Frenchmen do," said the colonel. "His faith is too strong in the liars who surround him...His days are numbered; nor can all the power of France keep his crown upon his head, if, indeed, it can keep that head upon his shoulders."

Then, Jeanningros probably realized that the wine was getting to him. The diplomatic façade returned. Asked about Bazaine, he replied, "Oh, the Marshal keeps his own secrets." He had not seen Bazaine since coming northward to take Monterrey.

It was almost dawn when Shelby and the other guests returned to their lodging.[5]

Napoleon to Bazaine: Try to Capture Juárez

June and July had now passed. In both Paris and Mexico City, the apprehension concerning a possible invasion of Mexico by the United States had subsided. Secretary of State William Seward had been busy reassuring the French that the United States really had no military plans involving Mexico.

In Paris, Napoleon III had just one long shot he wanted to try before starting to call his troops home to Europe. He knew that Benito Juárez was in the city of Chihuahua with a very small contingent of soldiers, and that he could easily be captured or driven across the border into the United States. Did General Bazaine think he could do either of those things quickly enough so that the United States would not have time to come to Juárez's rescue?

The answer was yes, but as Bazaine began stalking Juárez at the beginning of August 1865, Juárez climbed into his little black carriage and rode for nine days through rough terrain to the city known as El Paso del Norte on the Texas border. (Today, the American side is named El Paso and the Mexican side is named Ciudad Juárez.) Benito Juárez knew—and so did Bazaine—that if the French left

Chihuahua to follow him, the city would be occupied by guerillas, trapping the French in a no-man's-land near the United States border.

Besides, Juárez had a lot of friends on the American side. The officers from Fort Bliss, Texas, knowing that Juárez couldn't cross the river, staged dinners and parties for him in El Paso on the Mexican side, provided ten cannons to defend the central plaza, and helped set up defenses all around the town, in case the French dared to approach. Another three hundred Juarista soldiers arrived to strengthen the perimeter.

General Philip Sheridan saw another opportunity to intimidate the French. Sheridan blamed Secretary of State Seward for being "soft" on the French, and for allowing Napoleon III and Bazaine to send their troops northward to Chihuahua. He began communicating very openly with Juárez—fully intending the messages to leak. Pretty soon, Bazaine and Maximilian were being tipped off by various sources that Sheridan was only waiting for some reinforcements to arrive from San Antonio before launching an attack while Bazaine's forces were stranded out in the northern Mexico desert.

Bazaine was afraid to risk any confrontation with Sheridan. Avoiding war with the United States ranked as a higher priority than capturing Juárez. It was much easier to just spread the rumor that Juárez had left the country and then return to Mexico City. Those who were loyal to Maximilian would be left wondering, for many years afterward, why the French had pulled back and had never caught up with Juárez.

Shelby versus a French Colonel: Pistols at Ten Paces

There were French garrisons at Saltillo, some fifty miles to the southwest of Monterrey, and at Parras, about seventy-five miles west of Saltillo. General Jo Shelby and his troops had passed through Saltillo. They were approaching Parras on their way to Mazatlán, a Pacific coast seaport. Shelby planned to make his base in Mazatlán, as he built up his forces with more recruits, before setting out to deal with the Juaristas.

Shelby and Colonel Jeanningros had negotiated for about a week, with Shelby finally gaining permission for the project. Jeanningros was certain that every French soldier would be withdrawn from Mexican soil sooner or later, and he imagined that troops like Shelby's would take their place.

Several groups of ex-Confederates were already headed toward Parras, hoping to join Shelby's brigade on the march to Mazatlán. When Shelby arrived in Parras, he was told that the French garrison commander, a Colonel Marguerite

Jacques Vincent du Preuil, had an urgent message for him from General Bazaine in Mexico City. Bazaine apparently wanted to see Shelby face-to-face before approving any mission such as the one proposed for Mazatlán. The trouble was, as Shelby quickly discovered, that Colonel Preuil was not only rude and nasty but rather drunk. Preuil had interpreted Bazaine's message to mean that Americans like Shelby intended to overrun the entire country and had to be stopped at any cost.

When Shelby mentioned the agreement he had reached with Colonel Jeanni-gros back in Monterrey, Preuil flew into a rage and began shouting. Within seconds, they were trading insults and Preuil reached for his sword. Shelby left the colonel, screaming "you shall pay for this" as he walked out of the house. He sent a representative to challenge Preuil to a duel—pistols at ten paces—the next day at dawn.

By sheer coincidence, Colonel Jeannigros arrived from Monterrey a short while later, with four squads of cavalry on an inspection tour. As soon as he heard about the duel, he canceled it. Colonel Preuil was arrested and held until he could sober up and apologize. After sorting it all out with Shelby, Jeanningros decided that they'd better set the Mazatlán mission aside and head for Mexico City, where Bazaine would be the one to give the final orders.

Shelby's men were happy with the change in plans. It would have meant a march across nearly five hundred miles of desert to reach Mazatlán, and they had already seen enough cactus for a lifetime. The route through central Mexico would be very different, through historic colonial towns such as San Luis Potosí, Dolores Hidalgo, and San Miguel de Allende, where the journey would become one big fiesta after another. They looked forward to the floating gardens of Xochimilco, the massive Zócalo outside the Palacio Nacional, and beautiful señoritas on moonlit nights. They couldn't wait.

29

The Legend of Inez Walker

(Late August through Early September 1865)

A Midnight Rescue at the Hacienda

General Jo Shelby and his brigade had been riding through green, fertile valleys with flowing streams and abundant crops for several days, passing through frequent small villages. As two of the men sat by the still-glowing coals of their campfire one night, a stranger appeared out of the underbrush. It turned out that he was a goatherd. After determining that he was of no harm, they allowed him to sit with them. He wanted to tell them a story.

They were on guard duty, but the man persisted. He wanted to let them know about the nearby Hacienda de la Encarnación and the man who owned it, Luis Enrico Rodríguez. The stranger told the soldiers that Rodríguez was a very wealthy Spaniard who had bought the property a few years ago and had built a large mansion, surrounding it with high, thick walls. The man said everyone knew that the *hacendado* (wealthy landowner) was making a fortune by using shady and suspicious means, and that they were all curious about the fate of an American woman whom Rodríguez had been hiding behind those walls.

The woman's name was Inez Walker; she apparently was the daughter of an American who had found gold and married someone from the tribe that had helped him find it. The couple had moved to Guaymas and lived among the wealthy set there, and later they had sent their daughter to California to get an education. When the daughter returned to Guaymas, Luis Rodríguez fell in love with her at first sight and began courting her. When she refused him, he was furious and became totally obsessed with her. He showed up with a gang one night and kidnapped her, carrying her to his home, the Hacienda de la Encarnación. Inez Walker's father had followed the gang and caught up with them, but he was killed in the attempt to rescue her.

Despite all the servants, the finest clothing and food, and all of the luxuries that the *Doña* (Dame) of a magnificent estate could want, she still refused Don Luis. She saw him only as the murderer of her father and wanted nothing to do with him. She had been a prisoner ever since, her body turning frail and her hair turning gray. She was probably still there, awaiting rescue.

The two soldiers dared not tell Shelby the next day. Stealthily, they organized a posse of twenty men who would accompany them at midnight. Shelby had tightened security considerably since Parras, and he would not want any of his troops taking unnecessary risks.

Just after midnight, they crashed through the main gate of the Hacienda de la Encarnación, using a tree trunk as a battering ram. Dogs barked, horses neighed, and at least a dozen ranch hands shouted as the men ran toward the house. There was gunfire coming from the corral. They heard a bugle in the distance and knew that Shelby had been alerted and was on the way. If they didn't have the woman in about twenty minutes, they'd have a lot of explaining to do.

Breaking down the door of the house, they fought from room to room in total darkness, recognizing each other only by their Rebel yells from earlier Confederate battles. As the noise subsided and the invisible enemy had either died or fled, they managed to find some lanterns and light them. There—on the floor—lay the corpse of Don Luis Enrico Rodríguez.

At that very moment, Shelby appeared. He was seething with anger and demanded an explanation. It took great skill to tell the tale, but the men could see Shelby's expression soften as they related the tale of Inez Walker.

"And where is the woman?" asked Shelby.

A servant brought Inez from her room. Shelby's aide, Major John N. Edwards, told of her appearance in his book, *Shelby's Expedition to Mexico: An Unwritten Leaf of the War.*

"Grief-stricken, prematurely old, yet beautiful amid the loneliness of her situation, Inez Walker came into the presence of Shelby, a queen. Some strands of gray were in her glossy, golden hair. The liquid light of her large, dark eyes had long ago been quenched in tears. The form that had once been so full and perfect was now bent and fragile; but there was such a look of mournful tenderness in her eager, questioning face that the men drew back from her presence instinctively and left her alone with their general."

Shelby offered Inez Walker a safe journey to Mexico City, and promised to take care of all of her needs and wishes. The next morning, the rescued woman was riding in a closed carriage, flanked by an honor guard, as the brigade continued its trek toward San Luis Potosí.[1]

Napoleon III's Face-Saving Inspiration

In Paris, reality was beginning to set in for Napoleon III. He had counted on the South winning the American Civil War. That had not happened. He had assumed that Maximilian would somehow be able to keep his finances in order. They were out of hand. He had thought that Mexicans would be intimidated by floggings, hangings, and firing squads, but it turned out that this heavy-handed approach only strengthened their resistance. He had not counted on the overwhelming success with which Matías Romero had influenced public opinion and had lined up not only prominent but effective backers in the United States.

The last thing Napoleon wanted was a war with the United States, but the French emperor now realized that Seward and Johnson were just waiting him out. He also knew that the reasons for a withdrawal were piling up day by day, and that about the only rationale for keeping troops in Mexico was to avoid the humiliation of admitting he had made a costly mistake in sending them there.

But how was Napoleon III to withdraw his troops from Mexico without losing face? The answer to the emperor's dilemma came almost by accident when an old friend dropped by for a visit. James Watson Webb had been recalled to Washington after serving as United States ambassador to Brazil. On his way home, he visited Paris to see Napoleon, whom he had met in New York almost thirty years earlier. Over breakfast with the emperor, Webb said that there was no way the United States could recognize Maximilian, given the prevailing public opinion. In fact, he suggested, thousands of Americans might go to Mexico to fight for Juárez if Maximilian remained there much longer.

Webb had an idea. Had Napoleon III thought of withdrawing his troops in stages over the next year or two? It would give the clear impression that he was doing it at his own pace for his own reasons, and not just reacting to pressure. Napoleon hadn't thought of that. He called Webb's idea "an inspiration."[2]

Five Hundred Frenchmen and Two Thousand Juaristas: Shelby to the Rescue

Jo Shelby, now calling himself colonel instead of general, and his brigade had to pass through Matehuala in order to reach Mexico City, but as they approached the town, they heard gunfire and the sounds of artillery. After waiting for darkness, Shelby sent four scouting detachments to find out who was fighting whom. The scouts returned with a number of prisoners, who told them that a force of five hundred Frenchmen was surrounded by about two thousand Mexicans, and that the Mexicans under General Mariano Escobedo were planning an assault on the town first thing in the morning. Shelby didn't really have to ask his men; they were ready to rescue the French outpost, which was commanded by a Major Henri Pierron. Shelby sent two volunteers to tell Pierron that help was on the way.

The two soldiers dropped to the ground as the French forces fired a volley in their direction, but they managed to yell out who they were and the firing stopped. After they had briefed Major Pierron, they insisted that they had to report back to Shelby. After a quick huddle with his officers, Pierron assigned forty cavalrymen to escort them back through the lines.

As dawn broke, the Mexicans began their attack on the town, only to see Shelby and his brigade come riding out of the woods. The Mexicans didn't recognize the Confederate uniforms and assumed that Shelby's people were probably friends.

Wrong.

Too late, the Mexican forces realized that they were being attacked from two sides. The French cavalry came galloping out of the town and rode along their flanks, surrounding the Escobedo forces and killing most of them. Major Pierron rode up to Shelby as the smoke cleared, inviting him and his brigade into town for a victory celebration. Shelby's aide, John Edwards, wrote that "Pierron made Matehuala a paradise. There were days of feasting and mirth and minstrelsy, and in the balm of fragrant nights the men dallied with the women. So when the southward march was resumed, many a bronzed face was set in a look of sadness, and many a regretful heart pined long and tenderly for the dusky hair that would never be plaited again, for the tropical lips that for them would never sing again the songs of roses and the summer time."[3]

The next town of any major size would be San Luis Potosí, about a hundred thirty miles to the south.

Sick, Weakened French Forces Losing Ground by Default

Bazaine's invasion of northern Mexico and his last-ditch attempt to capture Juárez had left some weak spots in French coverage elsewhere. The Marquis de Montholon, who was passing through as he traveled to his new assignment in Washington, had discovered a serious troop shortage in Veracruz. The Sudanese troops, he reported, were being used as prison guards. They had neither the training nor the ability to handle such a task, and there had been incidents of prisoners being shot, and of escapes among those who had been taken to the hospital. Montholon urged the imperial commander in Veracruz to take advantage of a ship, which was standing by, to transport the prisoners to Yucatan.

To help speed the French withdrawal, the Juarista forces stepped up their raids on French supply lines between Mexico City and the coast. They staged renewed attacks on Medellín, La Tejería, Boca Ratón, and other communities surrounding Veracruz, including the alternate seaport of Tlacotalpan, ("t-lah-koh-TAHL´-pahn").

This caught Bazaine's attention. The only way he was going to get all of his troops, equipment, and supplies safely out of the country was through Veracruz. Sudanese troops were placed at four of the tower-like bastions surrounding the city, as well as at the main water supply for the town, La Noria, located along the west wall. They were also assigned to patrol the railroad right-of-way, escort the trains, and carry messages among French commanders by horseback.

That alternate seaport, which was under French control, was about to be lost to the Juaristas by default, as a result of widespread illness among the troops. The Imperialista commander at Tlacotalpan, Colonel Marino Camacho, told Marshal Bazaine that his sick list was up to one hundred eighty men, and that he could not hold on much longer. The cozy little town was located a few miles inland from the waters of the Gulf, just up the Papaloapan River, and was a strong competitor with Veracruz for shipping revenue. It was also surrounded by marshes infested by the enemy.

The Juarista forces had been bombarding the town more often lately. With all the sickness and the summer rains adding to the difficulties, Colonel Camacho decided to ask Bazaine for gunboats to evacuate Tlacotalpan. As the Juaristas were preparing another assault on the town—one that their commander was certain would result in reconquest—Camacho asked for a conference with the enemy under neutral conditions. He told the Juaristas that he wanted to avoid bloodshed during the withdrawal, but that if so much as one of his men were to be wounded in an attack, the gunboats would level the town.

To General Alejandro García, second in command to Porfirio Díaz, it was a really great offer. On one hand, Camacho could just have been bluffing and trying to negotiate an easy escape for his men, but it was also remotely possible that the gunboats could carry out the threat. In any case, General García got to retake Tlacotalpan without firing a shot. Marshal Bazaine's options for getting his French army safely out of Mexico had narrowed to little more than using the Port of Veracruz.[4]

30

Maximilian's "Black Decree"

(October 1865 through March 1866)

Maximilian Declares Victory

Autumn had arrived in Mexico City. As far as Maximilian was concerned, not only had Benito Juárez's term as president expired—in fact, his own Constitution said so—but also, as far as Maximilian's sources could determine, Juárez had left the country. So, on October 3, 1865, Maximilian decided it was time to issue his "Black Decree."

The decree effectively defined all Juárez supporters as bandits. Anyone who carried arms for Juárez or anyone who was a member of an armed group aligned with Juárez would be put to death within twenty-four hours of being caught. Even if such persons claimed to be acting out of patriotism or for political reasons, there would be no appeals and no pardons. Military commanders who captured anyone working for Juárez could simply execute the person without a court-martial. Maximilian ordered that the decree would become effective on November 15, and said that anyone to whom it might apply would be granted amnesty if he or she surrendered before that time.

In a proclamation explaining the decree, Maximilian said "the cause which has been maintained with so much courage and constancy by Don Benito Juárez" was no longer valid. "The time for indulgence," said Maximilian, "has passed…The government, strong and powerful, will henceforth impose inflexible punishment."

French army officers and conservatives in general were upset at the "courage and constancy" attributed to Juárez. They didn't think such language was appropriate to describe the guerillas and bandidos whom the French had been fighting for three years. Liberals, on the other hand, deplored the execution-without-trial provisions and were incensed over Maximilian's claim that Juárez had left the country, which they were certain was a lie.

Secretary of State Seward sent an official note of protest about the decree to Napoleon III, but was told to take it up with Maximilian. Seward knew such a move would imply recognition of Maximilian's government. He would have to find other ways to get his message across.

Maximilian had his answer from the Juarista guerillas on October 7, 1865, just four days after he issued the Black Decree. The guerillas had not really been active for many months along the route between Veracruz and the capital, but they chose a train guarded by French and Egyptian troops, running between Veracruz and Camarón, for a vicious attack in which everyone aboard the train was killed. French soldiers later found that most, if not all, of the corpses had been severely mutilated with machetes. That discovery sent a shock wave through the entire French army.[1]

The horrible atrocity aboard the train triggered a "take-no-prisoners" order from Bazaine, who told his commanders that "reprisals become a necessity and a duty. All these bandits, including their leaders, have been outlawed by the Imperial Decree of October 3, 1865,…Our soldiers must understand that they are not to return their arms to such adversaries; this is a war to the death, a war without quarter between barbarism and civilization. On both sides, it is necessary to kill or be killed."[2]

Bazaine didn't realize it, but he was sending a message to the enemy: the Juarista forces were apparently doing a great job of putting the invaders on the defensive, and the French were taking actions that revealed their desperation.

Maximilian didn't realize at the time that he, too, was sending an unintended message. The immediate, pitiless execution of many Mexicans without bothering to determine innocence or guilt would become a major factor in the decision as to whether or not to spare Maximilian's own life about eighteen months later.[3]

How to Get the French Emperor's Attention

Secretary of State Seward finally came up with a creative way to answer the suggestion that he make contact with Maximilian. He invited the new French ambassador, Montholon, who had just been transferred from Mexico City, to dinner. Seward told Montholon that President Andrew Johnson would be negligent if he were not to fill the American ambassador's post in Mexico promptly, replacing Thomas Corwin, since it was fully funded by Congress. Reassuring words were exchanged by both men as Montholon anticipated the news that the United States would recognize Maximilian by appointing a minister to the imperial government in Mexico City.

Instead, Seward dropped a verbal bombshell on the unsuspecting diplomat, telling him that Illinois Congressman John A. Logan, a former general in the Union army, would be nominated to become the new U.S. ambassador to the Juárez government. Logan already had a national reputation for his fiery speeches in Congress in favor of declaring war on France. Montholon was visibly shaken. As he fumbled to regain his composure, he called the appointment a provocation and an openly hostile act on the part of the United States. He told Seward that he thought the risk involved in such a move far outweighed the advantages.

"I hope you are wrong," said Seward.

Then, dinner was served.[4]

Matías Romero was thrilled with the announcement that Logan had been offered the appointment. He lost no time in relaying the information to Benito Juárez. Several weeks could go by before it would be known whether Logan accepted the appointment and before a Senate committee would hold hearings on the nomination. Just the suspense would cause some reactions.

Montholon was now afraid to tell Seward that he had been instructed by Napoleon III weeks earlier to offer French withdrawal from Mexico in exchange for recognition of Maximilian.

Among those suspected of putting Logan's name in nomination, regardless of whether he would accept or not, were General Ulysses S. Grant and the new president, Andrew Johnson. Grant may not have had any connection at all with the Logan nomination, but Confederate sympathizers who had assassinated President Abraham Lincoln as he attended a play in Washington, D.C., just five days after Lee's surrender to Grant, had also planned to kill Grant at the same time. Their scheme never materialized because the general had requested a leave of absence and was visiting his home in Illinois on the night that Lincoln was killed.

Johnson, who as Lincoln's vice president was sworn in to replace him, had already made it clear during the election campaign in 1864 that he was opposed to a monarchy south of the border. He wowed the crowds by saying, "An expedition into Mexico would be a sort of *recreation* for the brave soldiers of the Union, and the French concern would be quickly wiped out."[5]

Napoleon III: "Adiós, Maximilian!"

It was just a few weeks after Ambassador James Watson Webb's visit to Napoleon III, the one in which Webb had suggested removing the French troops in stages. Napoleon, still thinking the idea was brilliant, wrote to General Bazaine, preparing him for the possibility of leaving Maximilian and his Mexico to their fate.

"We cannot remain indefinitely in Mexico, and instead of building theatres and palaces, it is essential to introduce order into the finances and on the highways. Let him [Maximilian] know that it will be much easier to abandon a government that has done nothing to enable it to survive rather than to support it in spite of itself."

There would be more. The French emperor had not yet dropped the other shoe.

Just six weeks later, on January 15, 1866, Napoleon notified Maximilian that he had decided to pull the French troops out of Mexico. A week later, on January 22, Napoleon went before the Corps Législatif in Paris and publicly announced that France had performed her duty, and that Maximilian's government was strong enough to succeed on its own. The French troops would be withdrawn in three waves: nine thousand in October of 1866, another nine thousand in March of 1867, and all the remaining troops—just over eleven thousand—in October of 1867.[6]

An astonished Maximilian wrote back asking Napoleon to reconsider, but it was too late. Even Napoleon's wife, Eugénie, who had originally pushed for the French intervention in 1861, knew that it wasn't working out, and that a dignified withdrawal was the best option.

There was some confusion within the French army as the decision came down. A General Brincourt, who had occupied Chihuahua during Bazaine's northward push, left the town as he was ordered when Bazaine's priorities changed to avoid any conflict with the Americans. As soon as he did so, Juárez reoccupied the town. Fearing that local officials and civilians who had backed the French would be killed by the Juaristas, General Brincourt appealed to Maximilian. Maximilian asked Bazaine to recapture Chihuahua, and the general cooperated.

Once again Juárez found himself in the Mexican part of El Paso, just half a mile from the U.S. border. He had already learned of Napoleon III's decision to withdraw French troops altogether, so he knew it was only a matter of time before he would be free to fight Maximilian's Imperialistas without their foreign backing. He had no doubt about the outcome. Relaxing with some of his American friends, he opened a bottle of champagne to celebrate.

Shelby Meets with Maximilian

On September 3, 1865, after more than two thousand miles on horseback, Jo Shelby's troops arrived in Mexico City. Among the first items of business was to take care of Inez Walker, who had been with the brigade since her rescue at La

Encarnación. Among her first contacts, she was introduced to Princess Agnes Salm-Salm. Agnes and her husband, Felix, had recently arrived and had joined the emperor's forces. After their first meeting, Agnes and Inez would often be seen in the company of Empress Charlotte, walking through the *alameda* (arboretum) or in the Paseo de la Reforma.

Then, Shelby and his aide, Major John Edwards, visited the Palacio Nacional, where Maximilian, Marshal Bazaine, and their aides were waiting. Shelby had already been informed that Maximilian was a dreamer—not a military expert or politician—and that Bazaine was the soldier and administrator. Shelby's offer was to recruit an army of forty thousand men for immediate service in the emperor's imperial forces.

Shelby insisted that the United States government would not oppose ex-Confederates or former Union soldiers from joining the empire. He said he had heard that the French forces might soon be withdrawn. Besides, argued Shelby, Maximilian would need a corps of foreign soldiers that would be loyal only to him personally—and that he could count on in an emergency.

Bazaine was listening as Shelby made his case. The marshal knew that Maximilian could never survive without some kind of help once the last French soldiers left. It was obvious that this had not yet crossed Maximilian's mind. Bazaine was not sure that the emperor was in touch with reality at this point. Count de Noue, Maximilian's palace chief of staff, was also listening and acting as interpreter.

Maximilian stood and beckoned de Noue to one side for a few minutes, whispering to him at the far side of the room. Then, the emperor turned and left.

Shelby could tell that the answer was going to be no. As de Noue tried to explain to him, Maximilian still believed that he could bring good government to Mexico and prove to outsiders—particularly to the United States—that he was worthy of recognition. Shelby responded by saying that he could tell from the emperor's expression all along that he wasn't interested in building up his military forces.

Jo Shelby walked back down the stone stairs of the Palacio Nacional and outside into the great Zócalo, Mexico City's main plaza. He suspected that Maximilian's closest advisers had been telling him only what he wanted to hear, and that His Majesty was too busy collecting butterflies and writing poetry to grasp the real issues of running a country. He knew it was only a matter of time before Juárez gathered the strength to reclaim the country.

As he faced his assembled troops for the last time, Shelby asked, "How many of you know enough Spanish to get you a [Mexican] wife with an acre of breadfruit, twenty-five tobacco plants and a handful of corn?" The troops laughed, but they knew it was all over. They were not wanted.

Shelby told them about the "Carlota Colony"—named in honor of the empress—that was being built by a number of ex-Confederate generals outside of Orizaba, in a tropical portion of the state of Veracruz. A few of them went there to start farms. Others said they would seek their fortunes in California. About fifty of the men joined a regiment of Zouaves, and others marched northward to Sonora, where they signed up with the Juárez forces.

Shelby's aide, Major John Edwards, edited an English-language newspaper, the *Mexican Times,* for a while, and Shelby joined with a Major McMurty in starting up a freight-hauling business. The firm was based in Orizaba, and ran wagons from the end of the railroad line at Paso del Macho to Mexico City. Most of the men stayed in Mexico City for a short while, and then made their way back to Missouri, Arkansas, and other places from which they had come. One of them, a colonel, is said to have walked in on his surprised wife back home—after not having seen her for almost four years—and thrown his hat down in mock disgust, happily, calling out, "Good Lord, Sally. Dinner not ready yet?"[8]

31

Adiós, Mamá Carlota

(April 1866 through February 1867)

Napoleon to Maximilian: It's Not Negotiable

Napoleon III's letter to Maximilian of January 15, 1866, announcing the withdrawal of French troops, shook up the Empress Charlotte much more than it did Maximilian. The emperor was still dreaming that he could run things on his own, but Charlotte was certain that he would never survive without the French army on hand. What tainted her thinking, though, was the belief that she and Maximilian were doing the French a favor by accepting the Mexican throne. Her father, King Leopold, had convinced her that Napoleon III needed her and Maximilian more than they needed Napoleon.

The first attempt to turn things around came in the spring of 1866. Maximilian and Charlotte recalled Mexico's minister to France, José Hidalgo, and replaced him with General Almonte, who was certainly a traitor in the eyes of the Juaristas. Almonte accepted, probably realizing that his mission, and the empire, would fail. At least he would be out of Mexico.

Napoleon III and his Empress Eugénie laughed at the memorandum that Almonte brought to Paris with him. The memorandum proposed rewriting the Treaty of Miramar, and was simply out of touch with reality and beyond all rational presumption. Maximilian demanded that French troops be retained in Mexico indefinitely until the country was pacified, and he also wanted fleets from the French navy to protect both his Pacific and Gulf of Mexico coastlines. In addition, it was proposed that France could save money by appointing a general of lower rank to replace Bazaine, and that the general would report directly to Maximilian.

It would never happen.

Napoleon couldn't believe Maximilian's demands, and he wrote back curtly, "General Almonte has acquainted me with Your Majesty's ideas, and I was already aware from the memorandum of the considerable discrepancy between my judgment and yours. In order to clear up the outstanding issues once and for all, I have caused a note to be drawn up, which I recommend to Your Majesty's serious consideration."

The attached note was a cruel, take-it-or-leave-it memorandum that claimed Maximilian was to blame for everything that had gone wrong since his arrival in Mexico. It said that if the French army were to remain any longer, then France would have to take over all Mexican customs houses, and that half of their revenues would go toward financing the French effort and paying investors who had already underwritten the project. The French Foreign Legion would be under Maximilian for the next three years; Marshal Bazaine would remain in charge of the French army but would advance half a million francs per month toward equipping a new Mexican army. The French troops would be withdrawn gradually, so as to preserve law and order.

If Maximilian refused, however, all French troops—including the foreign legion—would be withdrawn immediately, and all financial aid from France would be suspended immediately as well. Twenty-four percent of the customs revenue was already going toward British debts. With another 50 percent going to France, Maximilian would become little more than a French government dependent.

The harsh terms were a rude awakening for Maximilian. He now knew that Napoleon III didn't care for him or for Mexico, but just for how much money he could recover before the last of his soldiers boarded their ships at Veracruz. With the customs revenues cut off and the French troops on their way out, there was no way the empire could survive. Thoughts of abdication were crossing Maximilian's mind, but he had not yet shared them with Charlotte.[1]

When Charlotte learned of Napoleon's ultimatum, she was in a fighting mood. No one was going to take away the throne of Mexico for which they had fought so hard. She had been through this before. Her own grandfather had fallen into disgrace by abdication, and so had Charles the Tenth of France. She put pen to paper: "Abdication is only excusable in old men and idiots. It is not permissible in a young man of thirty-four, full of life and hope for the future, for sovereignty is the most precious of all possessions." She added, "Emperors do not give themselves up. So long as there is an Emperor, there is still an empire, even if he has no more than six feet of earth belonging to him, for the Empire is nothing without the Emperor."

Charlotte would go to Paris and have a few words with Napoleon III about broken promises. She would let him know that emperors do not go back on their own words. Then, she would continue on to Rome and convince the Pope that she and

Maximilian were better Christians and stronger supporters of the faith than any of the bishops now backed by the Holy Father. Without an empire, she would argue, Mexico would sink into atheism and anarchy. She would warn of United States dominance in the Western Hemisphere, and urge bankers and statesmen to support a free and independent Mexico under Maximilian and herself.

An entourage was chosen and a date set for Charlotte's departure. She would leave on July 9, 1866. Letting her make the trip, Maximilian wrote to his brother, was the "heaviest sacrifice" he had made so far for his new country.[2]

Grant and Romero Feel They're Being Used

Back in the United States, the campaign for the Congressional election of 1866 was under way. President Andrew Johnson and Secretary of State William Seward were suddenly being very nice to the Mexican ambassador, Matías Romero. In fact, they took him on a campaign swing around the country, claiming that their approach had brought about Napoleon III's decision to withdraw his French troops from Mexico. Also along for the trip was General Grant. Romero later wrote that both he and Grant were being asked to generate support and elicit cheers from the crowds for the administration's Mexican policy. Since neither Romero nor Grant backed the approach that Johnson and Seward were actually using, both men were angry and resentful at being used in this way.

Grant had been thinking about a run for the presidency himself in 1868, and it was becoming very clear to those in contact with both Grant and President Johnson that a split was developing. Grant didn't want any part of the Seward-Johnson "mild" approach toward the Mexican situation, and he told General Sheridan, in a confidential letter, that he was not going to be forced to give up his goal of supporting the Juárez regime in any way that he could.

Romero was more or less caught in the middle. In 1865, Seward had issued an edict denying all foreign diplomats access to the president except through his office. At least Seward and Johnson were still maintaining the public position that they were opposed to the French intervention in Mexico and to Maximilian's so-called empire, which they refused to recognize as a sovereign government. Grant and Romero wanted a stronger, more confrontational stance, because they viewed earlier French sympathy toward the now-defeated Confederacy as a direct challenge to U.S. sovereignty itself.

During the campaign swing, both Romero and Grant were introduced at each stop as supporting the administration's policy. After Johnson dedicated a statue to Stephen Douglas in Chicago, Romero found an excuse not to accompany him on the return loop of the trip back to Washington. The Mexican ambassador continued his lobbying with business leaders and military figures, and with congressmen and senators. He also worked closely with newspaper reporters and editors.

Actually, Romero had a covert but rather significant role in the plot hatched by Radical Republicans to impeach President Andrew Johnson. The plan was to force Senator Foster of Connecticut to resign as president pro tem of the Senate and replace him with Senator Wade of Ohio. Then, a move would be launched to impeach Johnson, making Wade the president. The end result would be to get rid of Seward as secretary of state. Romero wrote to the Juárez minister of foreign relations, saying that secret meetings were under way, but that the Radicals wanted to be sure they would have a two-thirds impeachment majority in hand before making their move.

Also in Washington, Illinois Congressman John A. Logan announced that he would not accept the post of ambassador to Mexico's Juárez government, much to the relief of Napoleon III and Maximilian. Logan, who had spoken on the House floor in favor of declaring war on France, said he would rather run for the United States Senate.[3]

Charlotte's Strange Behavior en route to Veracruz

At four o'clock in the morning on July 9, 1866, Empress Charlotte and an entourage of fifty persons were escorted down the hill from Chapultepec Castle by several hundred members of the imperial cavalry. Maximilian had been ill, but he left his sickbed to accompany Charlotte for about twenty-five miles to the town of Ayutla. As they said their good-byes, the emperor broke down in tears and started to collapse. He had to be helped back to his carriage. He and Charlotte were never to see each other again.

Charlotte seemed at first to be in high spirits, but she wrote to Maximilian, during her first night in a very primitive setting at Río Frío, that the sight of his tears had made her so miserable that she herself had cried in front of the mule drivers. On the second night, she was the guest of honor at a banquet in Puebla, and those who saw her at the event said she looked charming and normal. It was later that night—at midnight—that she suddenly wanted to visit the home of a Señor Esteva, who sometime earlier had entertained her and Maximilian at a dinner in that same house.

Señor Esteva had been transferred to a government post in Veracruz, and the house was empty except for a caretaker and several servants.

The caretaker was awakened, candles were lit, and Charlotte wandered through the empty rooms. She was very excited, and when they reached the dining room she chatted on and on, recalling the dinner that had been given by Señor Esteva. By the next morning, she appeared to be back to normal. None of those accompanying her, not even her physician, dared send word to Maximilian about the previous night's bizarre behavior.

The journey became dangerous as they passed between the Cliffs of Acultzingo. Heavy rains had left the roadway in deep mud, and there were landslides, with large boulders, tumbling down the mountainside. The rains got worse as they made their way toward Orizaba; mules became stuck in the mud and carriages overturned. They dared not stop at any of the small villages along the route because the inhabitants in many of them would shoot first and ask questions later. These inhabitants had had all the guerilla and bandido raids they could endure.

As they reached Córdoba, a wheel on Charlotte's carriage broke and the party decided to seek lodging in a rustic *posada* (lodge), where a stagecoach full of other travelers had arrived earlier. The other guests had consumed quite a few drinks and were loudly singing dirty songs, laughing, and shouting obscenities. The colonel in charge of the cavalry escort decided that they'd better not let anyone know who Charlotte really was.

It was a good decision. Charlotte and her entourage were in adjacent rooms as the crowd in the bar sang "*Adiós Mamá Carlota*" to the tune of "*La Paloma*":

Adiós, Mamá Carlota (Good-bye, Mama Carlota)
Adiós, mi tierno amor (Good-bye, my tender love)
Si se van los Franceses (If the French go)
Se va el Emperador (The emperor goes too)

What to do? Charlotte's ladies pretended not to hear, and the officers escorting them wanted to avoid a fight with any of the drunken travelers, but Charlotte just couldn't take it any more.

In her mind, it was all a plot. The carriage wheel had been broken on purpose to prevent her from reaching Veracruz in time to catch the ship. She was surrounded by enemies, and she feared for her life.

Charlotte ordered the horses saddled immediately; there was no time to wait for another carriage. She would ride through the night to the village of Paso del Macho, where she could take a train to Veracruz. Just as she was about to leave, a spare carriage arrived. She climbed aboard and departed for Paso del Macho, connecting with a train at one o'clock in the morning.

It was Friday, July 13, at two o'clock in the afternoon, when she pulled into Veracruz. There was no welcoming committee; there were no flowers, fireworks, or adoring crowds. There were just a few locals with surly expressions wandering in the streets, and of course the ever-present buzzards, staring coldly down from the rooftops. Rumors had already spread that Charlotte would never return from Europe, and that Maximilian would be following her shortly.

There was quite a scene as the empress discovered that the packet steamer awaiting her at the dock was flying neither a royal banner nor a Mexican flag. Furious, she told the head of the port authority to inform the ship's captain that she refused to board until the outrageous situation was rectified. Commander Cloué quickly realized that there was no point in making any excuses.

Charlotte appeared to be acting hysterically, and trying to reason with her would be out of the question. Not only that, but he was already behind schedule. There was a scramble as officials obtained and hoisted the appropriate flags. Cloué escorted Charlotte aboard, and the engines went into gear as the steamer pulled out of Veracruz harbor and into the Gulf of Mexico. Next stop: Havana.

United States Still Backs Juárez; Frenchmen Close Shops in Mexico

One week later, on July 20, 1866, the U.S. Congress reaffirmed its recognition of the Juárez government. Juárez began to reoccupy towns as Bazaine withdrew his French forces.

Throughout the fall of 1866, French-owned businesses began to wind down their affairs and the owners prepared to return to Europe. Foreign civilians were making travel arrangements to go back to their home countries. The Church turned its back on Maximilian's empire, there was little or nothing left in the treasury, and corruption was running rampant among the remaining imperial government bureaucrats. Those who had been influential under Maximilian just a year earlier were now fleeing, before the entire regime collapsed.

Sensing that the French grip was loosening in the tropical lowlands around Veracruz, all kinds of bandidos and criminals began to cause trouble near the coast. The task of patrolling the highways and the railroad now fell to the Sudanese troops. These troops were attacked at two o'clock in the morning on July 25 in their garrison at Medellín, with each side losing two men. Sudanese troops stumbled onto a group of guerillas trying to vandalize the railroad near La

Soledad the next day, killing two, and wounding fourteen before driving them away. The Mexican groups were led by a Lieutenant Colonel Prieto, who had escaped from French custody earlier in the summer.

Earlier, there were so few French troops available as Charlotte pulled into Veracruz on July 13 that her honor guard was made up entirely of twenty-five Sudanese, who fired off a 101-gun salute as the empress drove from the railroad station to the ship.

Charlotte had hardly left for Europe when Maximilian openly resumed his affair with the gardener's daughter in Cuernavaca. As one French officer wrote home, "The Emperor and the Empire remain as unpopular here as ever. Everyone awaits their collapse. But Maximilian's great occupation is his continual trips to Cuernavaca to visit the young Mexican by whom he is to have a child; proud in this proof of his capacity for parenthood. Meanwhile, the country is without direction, without confidence, and without a *sou* [penny]!"[4]

Ortega Claims He Should Be Mexico's President

What Benito Juárez didn't need right now was a challenge to his presidency from a fellow liberal Mexican. General Jesús González-Ortega, who had been living in New York, issued a proclamation that stated the obvious: since Juárez's term in office as president had expired, and since no election could be held, Ortega, as chief justice of the Supreme Court, should become president. Technically, he was right according to the Constitution, but this was the worst possible time for something like this to happen. Ortega claimed that he was going to lead a force of volunteers into Mexico to take on both Maximilian's Imperialistas and the gradually withdrawing French forces.

What was Juárez to do? Matías Romero had the answer. He had been more or less monitoring Ortega's activities while the general was in the United States. Romero got in touch with General Grant, who got in touch with General Sheridan. Sheridan had Ortega arrested just outside of Brownsville, Texas. American troops briefly occupied Matamoros, just across the border from Brownsville, but were replaced by Mexican troops under the command of General Mariano Escobedo. Ortega was certain that Escobedo, a Juárez supporter, was coordinating his moves with the Americans.

After about a month, General Sheridan contacted Escobedo, and the two of them agreed that since Ortega's followers had drifted away, it was safe to let him back into Mexico. Ortega went to his former stronghold in Zacatecas, where he had been the governor, and proclaimed to the local army commander that he was now the president of Mexico. The commander turned out to be a Juárez supporter and arrested Ortega all over again. Meanwhile, Juárez had gathered declarations of support from almost all his generals. No one was about to back Ortega. He was sent to a prison in Saltillo until things settled down.

Charlotte Hospitalized—But Where?

Back at Chapultepec Castle, Maximilian had recovered sufficiently from an illness and fever that he was getting ready to entertain again. It was mid-October of 1866, and there would be a dinner on October 18, followed by a smaller affair on October 23.

The only guests scheduled for the event on October 23 were Prince Felix Salm-Salm and his wife, Agnes. Maximilian had learned that the couple had met President Andrew Johnson while they were in Tennessee. Agnes had a knack for politicking, and later she had dropped by the White House to say good-bye to Johnson before leaving Washington. What Maximilian wanted the couple to do was to pay another visit to Johnson and persuade him to recognize the Mexican Empire. It was just the kind of thing that Agnes thoroughly enjoyed doing.

The dinners never took place. The trans-Atlantic cable had been inaugurated just two months earlier in August, and two messages arrived for Maximilian that would change everything. One was from Rome, the other from Miramar, but they both concerned Charlotte. A young naval officer by the name of Stefan Herzfeld, one of Maximilian's aides, was supposed to give the telegrams to the emperor. Herzfeld stalled, but Maximilian finally got him to disclose that Charlotte had been hospitalized under the care of a Dr. Reidel. Herzfeld left the emperor alone with the telegrams.

After a few moments of thought, Maximilian called for his personal physician, Dr. Samuel Basch.

"Do you know a Dr. Reidel?" asked the emperor.

"Why, yes," answered Basch, without hesitating. "Dr. Reidel is one of Europe's leading authorities on nervous diseases. He is the director of the Vienna Lunatic Asylum."[5]

Maximilian was shaken. Thoughts of abdicating and leaving for Europe filled his mind.

Is Maximilian about to Flee—or Not?

It was four o'clock in the morning on October 21 when Maximilian left Chapultepec Castle and headed for Orizaba. He had not even notified General Bazaine. The silent procession, taking a route that avoided the populated areas of town, was guarded by three hundred armed men on horseback. As the sun came up on Mexico City, word quickly spread that the emperor had fled. The French army was already preparing to leave the country, and foreign residents, especially those who had been involved with Maximilian's government, started lining up transportation to Veracruz.

Sarah Yorke's family members were among those booking passage to France, since they had become closely associated with the French as soon as the American ambassador, Thomas Corwin, had left town. The parties and the balls had all but ceased after Empress Charlotte departed. Now there were fears that those who had enjoyed a privileged social life under Maximilian might suffer terrible consequences if they were still there when Juárez returned. They didn't want to wait around to find out. Servants at Chapultepec Castle, certain that Maximilian would never return, ransacked the place and carried away whatever they could.

Upon his arrival in Orizaba, Maximilian was greeted by the sounds of church bells and firecrackers, as well as the chanting of thousands of *indígenas* (Indians), who had been rounded up by conservatives to provide a royal welcome. Led by Father Fischer, a Jesuit priest, the conservatives were going to mount a last-ditch effort to save the empire and their jobs. Father Fischer's main concern was to get rid of those aides who might advise Maximilian to abdicate.

Among the first to go was Stefan Herzfeld, the young naval officer who had delivered the telegrams about Charlotte's illness. Maximilian was already sitting down with Herzfeld to write the first draft of the proclamation announcing that he was stepping down. Father Fischer told Herzfeld that he had been assigned to help with Maximilian's departure by supervising the transport of the emperor's belongings aboard an Austrian ship, the *Dandalo,* which was waiting at Veracruz.

Maximilian, with or without Herzfeld's influence, was still consumed by thoughts of abdication. He was writing letters and telegrams of farewell to his friends and relatives. Servants at his country estate outside of Orizaba, known as Jalapilla, told friends that the emperor was wandering around in a sort of stupor, wearing bedroom slippers and an old, ragged robe, and that he was drinking as many as twenty glasses of champagne a day, in addition to the wine and brandy that he normally consumed every evening. Father Fischer was going to have a real challenge to turn the situation around.

General Grant Refuses a Trip to Mexico

In Washington, D.C., elections were approaching and President Andrew Johnson wanted to get General Ulysses Grant out of the country. Grant, along with Secretary of War Edwin Stanton, had opposed the "soft" policy of Johnson and Secretary of State Seward toward France. Johnson dreamed up a plan that would have Grant accompany the new U.S. ambassador to Mexico, a Lewis D. Campbell, on a mission to renew ties with the Juárez government. They would arrive at Veracruz just as Maximilian would be leaving. Grant's presence would imply that the general supported the Johnson-Seward policy.

Grant would have none of it. He politely declined in writing on October 21, 1866, but when Johnson persisted, he got into a shouting match with the president and stormed out of a cabinet meeting. About a week later, Johnson replaced Grant with General William T. Sherman asked him to take on the Mexico assignment. Sherman and Campbell embarked from New York aboard the U.S. frigate *Susquehanna,* headed for Veracruz.

Márquez and Miramón Pressure Maximilian into Staying

Back in Orizaba, two widely recognized conservative generals arrived to bolster Father Fischer's efforts to save Maximilian and his empire. Generals Leonardo Márquez and Miguel Miramón had no trouble rallying the imperial ministers, but Maximilian was yet to be persuaded. Things came to a head-on November 21, when the emperor convened an eighteen-member council of state to decide the question. Three of the council's members were known to be moderates, but the rest were zealous conservatives.

Maximilian was wavering. Council members reminded him of the pledge he had made on Mexico's Independence Day two months earlier never to abandon his post in times of peril. Also, Maximilian was in anguish over the thought of returning to the humiliation of failure and the screams of an insane wife that awaited him in Europe. There wasn't much to look forward to. He would leave the decision in the hands of the council, while he went butterfly hunting with his physician, Dr. Basch.

At the council meeting, each of the four imperial ministers—whose jobs were at stake—had two votes. Although there were eight votes for abdication, they were cancelled out by the eight votes of these imperial ministers. The six remaining members, all of whom voted against abdication, made it fourteen to eight in

favor of the emperor returning to Mexico City. As he returned to hear the outcome, Maximilian declared, "I am deeply moved by the evidences of love and
loyalty I have met with from the ministers and councillors of state."[6]

Crowds were gathered by torchlight in the town squares at Orizaba, Puebla,
Veracruz, and other cities where, thanks to the newly installed telegraph lines,
they waited to hear the news.

In Veracruz Harbor, as the word spread of the emperor's decision to remain,
the U.S. frigate *Susquehanna* pulled up anchor. General Sherman and Lewis D.
Campbell, the man who would have been the new ambassador to the Juárez government, headed for New Orleans.

32

Maximilian Heads for Querétaro

January through March, 1867

Sighs of Relief as the French Army Departs

General Achille Bazaine was riding at the head of his corps of officers as they marched from what had been the French headquarters through Mexico City's *Alameda* (in the Mexican capital, a major tree-lined boulevard). It was now February 5, 1867. As they traveled down the Calle San Francisco, along the Calle Plateros, and across the Zócalo, Princess Agnes Salm-Salm and her husband, Felix, now an Imperialista colonel, waved from their balcony at the Hotel Iturbide.

Not everybody was waving. In fact, the large crowd that had gathered along the route of departure talked quietly among themselves, most expressing relief that the French were on their way out. Even Maximilian didn't want to look out the shuttered windows of his apartment on the Calle de Moneda. As the footsteps faded, he turned to an aide and said, "At last we are free!"[1]

Outside Maximilian's apartment stood a cadre of armed Imperialista security guards. The emperor's castle at Chapultepec had been pillaged by the servants when he had left for Orizaba the previous fall. The same thing had happened to his estate at Cuernavaca. No matter. Maximilian had just received word that General Miramón had seized Zacatecas. He hoped they would capture Juárez.

Juárez Eludes an Attempt to Capture Him

As French forces gradually withdrew from northern Mexico, the Juaristas peacefully reoccupied town after town. Benito Juárez followed his troops at a prudent distance. He had left Chihuahua on December 10, 1866, had stopped for a while in Durango, and had reached Zacatecas on January 22, 1867. He was greeted by the locals with fireworks, balls, and other celebrations, and had been presented with a two-thousand-peso ceremonial walking stick, made possible by donations from a grateful public.

On February 5, the same day the French were leaving Mexico City, General Miguel Miramón staged what he had planned to be a lightning raid on Zacatecas, hoping to capture Juárez. Zacatecas was in a remote, sparsely settled region, far behind the front line, and was lightly guarded by just a handful of Juaristas. It might have worked, but the element of surprise was missing. For one thing, Miramón had already used this tactic before. For another, one does not achieve "lightning" raid status with four thousand men.

Miramón's people had never seen Benito Juárez riding a horse. They were betting that they only would have to spot his little black carriage and then capture him, and the game would be over. There was no resistance as most of them raided the town and broke into Government House, while a small detachment chased down the fleeing presidential carriage northward on the road toward Fresnillo. To their great surprise, the carriage was only a decoy. It was empty. Juárez and his government ministers had been tipped off about fifteen minutes before the raiders reached the town; they had mounted horses and had galloped off to the west toward Jerez. The Miramón people didn't discover which way the Juárez group had fled until it was too late, so the raid fizzled.

General Escobedo had been rehearsing Juárez and the ministers on that kind of maneuver for several months. The strategy had been adapted from one the Mexicans had learned many years earlier, during the war with the Americans. It had been used against them by a young captain named Robert E. Lee. Basically, it was this: flee for the hills, hide there overnight, and then surround the town and counterattack the enemy while they're settling in. Escobedo would be back.

Bloodiest Battle Since the French First Arrived

General Escobedo got even a week later. Miramón's objective had been to capture Juárez, not to tie up his troops by occupying the town, so he had them bivouacked at the Hacienda San Jacinto just south of Zacatecas. He should have left the area while he had the chance, because Benito Juárez, after almost being caught, decided that he'd been on the run for too long. He would now go on the offensive. He told Escobedo to take no prisoners and show no mercy. The French were on their way out, and it was time to take Mexico back.

As the sun came up on the *hacienda* (plantation/estate), Miramón's people found that they were already surrounded and vastly outnumbered. Some of them tried to break free, but they were slaughtered on the spot in the bloodiest, most vicious battle in the five years since the French first landed. Miramón lost more than three thousand men, including more than a hundred French foreign legionnaires, who had volunteered to remain in Mexico to support Maximilian and the Imperialistas.

As the smoke cleared and darkness fell upon the screams of the wounded and the dying, a courier rode up and handed an envelope to General Miramón. It was a message from Maximilian, congratulating him on having successfully captured Zacatecas a few days earlier.

Mint Juleps under the Mango Trees

For American newspaper reporters covering Mexico, the journey to the capital usually began aboard a ship bound for Veracruz; continued with a bumpy, winding ride by railroad to Paso del Macho; and concluded with a stagecoach journey from there to Mexico City. Most reporters knew that their readers were curious about the colony set up by Confederates just outside of Córdoba. The founders, including General Sterling Price, claimed that, before long, the settlement would be as large as Richmond or New Orleans. That was enough to attract attention, and many of the reporters made it a point to stop overnight in Córdoba and ride out to take a look for themselves.

Very few were impressed, judging from headlines that appeared back in the United States, which included "…Utter Failure,…" "Seedy Southern Exiles,…" "Miserable Conditions," and so on. One such account describes a number of scattered tents among some unfinished houses along the banks of a tree-shaded brook. General Price emerged from one of the tents to show a reporter around his farm, with coffee, tobacco, and sweet potatoes growing in the fields, orchards of fruit trees, and cattle in the pastures. His neighbors, he said, were generals Shelby and Ewell, who had both sent for their families. Price said he would do the same when his house was finished, and indicated that the French and Maximilian would protect the colony.

Another general, Isham Harris, had written to a friend in Atlanta, bragging that the part of Mexico around Córdoba was not only the most beautiful, but was the best land for agriculture that he had ever laid eyes upon. When he turned his eyes to the northwest, he told his friend, he could always see the snow-capped volcano known as the Pico de Orizaba. All he needed to do to chill his drinks was to send an *indígena* (Indian) runner there—forty miles each way—to "draw my ice at all seasons of the year." Then he could sit back, "constantly inhaling the odors of the rich tropical fruits," and enjoy his mint juleps under the shade of the mango trees, "in an atmosphere of perpetual spring."

Several generals had gone into business for themselves. Jo Shelby had started a freight service to transport goods from Paso del Macho, where the railroad ended, to Mexico City. General Slaughter had opened up a sawmill in Orizaba, just a few miles to the west. The former Texas chief justice, General Oldman, had become a photographer, and General Hindman had established a law office, both in Córdoba. Life was good.[2]

The Violent Demise of Carlota Colony

That was in 1865 and 1866. Now, with Charlotte gone to Europe and all the French troops gravitating toward Veracruz for the final trip home, Jo Shelby found that the freight business wasn't that rewarding any more, and that he wasn't making any money. He and his business partner, Major McMurty, sold what was left of their rolling stock and moved on to other things.

Shelby caught a schooner to Havana and bought a large sailboat there, loading it up with American farming and railroad tools. He returned to Veracruz, where he bought another schooner, one the French had been using to patrol the harbor. He learned that Marshal Bazaine just happened to be in town, so he went straight to his hotel. He told Bazaine about his farming implements and his plans for the colony, but he asked the marshal to give him weapons and enough ammunition to withstand a six-month siege. Before the day was over, Shelby's new schooner was sailing past Fort San Juan de Ulúa in Veracruz Harbor, with five hundred guns, plenty of ammunition, and great hopes for the success of Carlota Colony.

Shelby's optimism lasted for many months. He threw himself into the Carlota project, playing the roles of mayor, judge, mediator, interpreter, physician, surveyor, contractor, and a whole lot more. The two schooners were filled with the colony's tropical fruit and sent to New Orleans, returning with settlers who were given land. Shelby's wife Betsy arrived from Missouri with their two sons, Joe and Orville. Soon she was expecting another child, the third of eight the couple would eventually have. The future looked bright.

Then suddenly—in a single night—everything was destroyed. The nearest French garrison had already been evacuated, and there was nothing to protect the settlement from whoever might decide to attack. A few of the ex-Confederates had arrogantly thrown an Indian family off some land that they were claiming for themselves, and the Indians had taken their case to a Juarista commander—Colonel Figueroa—who was looking for an excuse to stage an assault. Some two thousand Juarista guerillas, bandidos, and other freebooters stormed through a mountain pass and swooped down on Carlota Colony, burning and pillaging everything in sight. A hundred colonists—all male—were captured and marched off into the darkness. Major John Edwards wrote,

> Their sufferings were terrible. Barefooted, days without food, beaten with sabres and pricked with lances, some few died and the rest, after a month of barbarous captivity, made their way back to the French lines, scarcely more than alive. All had been robbed, many had been stripped. Those who survived the blow and the thrust were but few—those who were naked were the most numerous. The blow finished the colony. The farming implements were destroyed, the stock was slaughtered in the fields, the cabins were burnt, the growing crops beaten down under the feet of the horses, and what the hurrying cavalry spared the winds and the torches finished.[3]

Maximilian Rejects Bazaine and Sends for Shelby

Elsewhere throughout Mexico, General Miramón's loss of three thousand men in the battle at Hacienda San Jacinto simply could not go unnoticed. The shocking news reached Marshal Bazaine as he stopped off at Puebla on one of his trips to Veracruz. He took the time to send a telegram to Maximilian, telling the emperor that he would wait for him there in Puebla if he had changed his mind about abdication. Bazaine offered to escort Maximilian to a French ship waiting at Veracruz, but the emperor declined. Instead, Maximilian sent for Jo Shelby.

Shelby was in Córdoba, still trying to sort things out after the Carlota Colony disaster, when the emperor's summons arrived. The former Confederate general doubted that he'd be able to help Maximilian at this point, but he showed up in Mexico City anyway.

"How many Americans are still in the country?" asked Maximilian.

"Not enough for even a corporal's guard," answered Shelby, "and the few who are left cannot be utilized." As diplomatically as he could, he told the emperor that he had waited too long.

Had Maximilian adopted the plan Shelby had first presented to him more than a year earlier, he probably could not have matched the number of soldiers that France had maintained in the country. However, he would at least have had a force to be reckoned with—one that would have stayed the tide of reverses that even Maximilian could see was rising all over Mexico. Said Shelby, "I don't know of two hundred effective soldiers among my countrymen who could be gathered together before the French evacuation is complete."

"I need twenty thousand," sighed the emperor.

"No, you need forty thousand, Your Majesty. Of all the Imperial regiments in your service, you cannot count upon one that will stand fast to the end." Shelby had been keeping score. "What are the tidings?" he asked. "In Guadalajara—desertion. In Colima—desertion. In Durango, Zacatecas, San Luis Potosí, Matehuala—it is nothing but desertion, desertion, desertion. I'm only one man, but I'll do what I can."

Maximilian pondered silently for a few seconds. "It's so refreshing to hear the truth," he finally told Shelby. "Take this in parting," he said, "and remember that circumstances never render impossible the right to die for a great principle." As he spoke, Maximilian removed the golden cross of the Order of Guadalupe from his chest and put it into Shelby's hands.

Shelby thanked the emperor and left. He would guard Maximilian's precious souvenir for the rest of his life.[4]

The Kindly Old Gentleman with the White Beard

Sara Yorke had been schooled in Paris. Her family was more comfortable with the French, especially since the Confederate loss in the U.S. Civil War, so they were in Veracruz, waiting to leave with all of the others who were seeking transportation to France. Along with them were other expatriates, who had been wealthy landowners, mine owners, business people, and members of elite society in Mexico City.

Sara sat with friends and relatives out on the patio of their hotel. There was Captain Charles Blanchot, who had married Sara's sister, Ellen. Their son was now two years old. Where had the time gone?

Then, there was that soft-spoken, good-natured gentleman with the blue eyes and the white hair and beard. He had been quite entertaining, relating to Sara and the other young ladies somewhat like a kindly old uncle. If they were to remain in Veracruz for another day or two, he warned, they had better be careful to stay indoors as much as possible at midday to avoid sunstroke. They enjoyed hearing the colonel's stories and laughing at his jokes. His name was DuPin: Colonel Francois DuPin.

Yes, Maximilian had asked Bazaine to send DuPin back to France, but the wily colonel went straight to his old friend, Napoleon III, and managed to stay on the payroll. He was back in Mexico at an obscure desk job, still with the rank and pay of a colonel, until the final French withdrawal.[5]

The Lieutenants Were Fourteen and Fifteen Years Old

It was February 13, 1867, and the ragged line of Imperialista troops stretched along the road to Tepozotlán for miles, flanked by women, children, and stray dogs. Occasionally a small group of Maximilian's new Imperialista force, half of them grabbed off the streets of Mexico City a day or two earlier, would stoop down by the roadside to fry tortillas on small fires made from dry cacti.

Emperor Maximilian led the procession on a spotted horse with a high-backed Mexican saddle. He was wearing the uniform of a Mexican general, with a giant sombrero, a saber at his side, and a pistol on each hip. Riding with him were generals Márquez and Miramón, along with colonels Miguel Lopez and Felix Salm-Salm. Leading the troops behind them were fourteen- and fifteen-year-old lieutenants, in their bright, new red uniforms embroidered with gold lace.

Maximilian didn't feel safe in Mexico City, so Márquez and Miramón had sold him on Querétaro. They told him that it was strategically located along the main highway to all of northern Mexico, which would make it a good headquarters from which to launch several campaigns. In addition, they persuaded him, the people and the clergy were very conservative. They said they doubted that His Majesty would find a single monk in a monastery or a nun in a convent in Querétaro who wouldn't become martyrs for the cause.

Of course, they had said things like that to all the French generals about Puebla.

Six days later, on February 19, at about two o'clock in the afternoon, the emperor and his top aides found themselves at a clearing in the woods atop the hill known as Cuesta China, about a mile and a half from Querétaro. It had been a rough morning, and there would be a whole evening of welcoming festivities ahead. Maximilian wanted to change to his best uniform here, and to switch from his favorite burro to the white stallion that would carry him into town.

They had been attacked by a Juarista reconnaissance patrol about two hours earlier, and for some unknown reason, Maximilian had decided to assume command. None of his officers had expected him to just throw himself into the middle of it all, shouting orders and riding through the gun smoke and battle cries. His eyes were glazed with some sort of exhilaration that none of them had ever seen before. As some of them confided to each other, "It's a wonder that he wasn't killed!"

Now, here they were, looking down on the colonial city, with its churches, fountains, and monuments. The emperor was changing from his civilian clothes to an Imperialista general's uniform. Maximilian seemed inspired from his earlier "victory." Aides placed the Grand Cross of the Mexican Eagle across his chest. Now, he was ready for the grand entrance. Appearances were everything.

No Detail Spared for the Emperor's Arrival

Generals Miramón and Mejía had gone ahead of the emperor's party to be sure that a gala welcoming ceremony had been organized. Some of the most beautiful women the troops had seen in a long time were rounded up from many of the elite local families. They were waiting with most of the population as Maximilian rode in on his impressive white horse. He waved and acknowledged the cheers.

It had been an arduous week's ride from Mexico City, and the emperor was in poor health. He had survived the attack on his entourage by the Juaristas earlier in the day, and had used the last ounce of his energy to make his grand entrance. That night, at a banquet thrown to honor him, generals Miramón and Mejía sat at the head table on either side of an empty chair. Maximilian was too exhausted to attend. He had gone to bed.

After the banquet, Colonel Felix Salm-Salm stood atop the small, rocky hill that rose in the center of town. It was known as Cerro de las Campanas, or Hill of the Bells, and as Salm-Salm looked down at the city, a knot formed in his stomach. *"Anyone who has the least bit of experience in military strategy,"* he thought, *"would only have to stand right here to assume that Querétaro is probably the worst place in the world to defend."*

Looking up at the Sierra Corda mountain range to the northeast, and at the ring of low knolls and uplands surrounding the rest of the city, he realized that every house in town could be reached by gunfire from those hills.

"This is not good," he muttered to himself. "Not good at all. It is a mouse-trap!"[6]

33

Díaz Retakes Puebla, Querétaro Is Surrounded

April 1 through May 14, 1867

French Withdrawal Affects American Politics

Matías Romero was pretty sure the Radicals in the U.S. Republican Party were about to make their move to impeach President Andrew Johnson, but he couldn't determine exactly when. He knew that they were carefully counting heads, and that nothing would happen unless they were sure they'd get two-thirds of the Senate vote. There was nervousness among several of the president's cabinet members, along with rumors of "secret meetings" and "a conspiracy."

The divisive quarrels in Congress between pro-administration and anti-administration forces over whether to give the French a military "nudge" raged on during the spring of 1867. Senator Jacob M. Howard had already made a speech in January, harshly criticizing the Johnson administration's Mexico policy and claiming that Johnson was planning to negotiate some kind of agreement with the French invaders to recognize Maximilian. It was common wisdom in Washington political circles that the real target was Secretary of State Seward, but that the only way to get rid of Seward was to get rid of Johnson.

If the Radical plan succeeded and Senator Benjamin Wade of Ohio became president, Romero would have closer ties than any foreign diplomat could ever dream of. Romero had been following Wade's career for four years and had maintained frequent contact all along.

Then things began to change. It wasn't just the vote counting that slowed the Radicals. It was the fact that Napoleon III changed his withdrawal timetable. Initially, Napoleon had planned to withdraw nine thousand French troops in October of 1866, another nine thousand in March of 1867, and the remaining eleven thousand or so in October of 1867.

221

By the summer of 1866, it had dawned on Napoleon that withdrawing his forces in stages would leave the remaining troops weakened and vulnerable to a possible American attack. Therefore, he cancelled the first stage of withdrawal and said that he'd take his troops out all at once in March of 1867. Radicals in the United States Congress saw Napoleon's change in timetable as foot-dragging and going back on his word. There was anger in both the American public and the Congress, showing that the Mexican situation was having a major impact on U.S. domestic politics.

Despite the anger, Johnson and Seward continued to insist that their approach was working, and pointed to the fact that French units and supplies were already on their way to Veracruz. From their view, the problem was headed toward a peaceful solution, or at least one that would not involve U.S. troops.

American capitalists and speculators were eagerly awaiting opportunities for trade and investment with Mexico. As more and more French troops abandoned their garrisons and marched toward Veracruz, the impeachment issue began to subside. The Radicals couldn't topple Andrew Johnson this time—but they would be back. Meanwhile, Secretary of State Seward had begun to reward investors who had backed his position by appointing them to influential diplomatic posts. A businessman who had been involved in railroad building and development of mines in Mexico for many years was named the new U.S. chargé d'affaires: Edward L. Plumb.

What Díaz Had Waited for: The French Are Gone

Late in the afternoon of March 16, 1867, a ship named the *Magellan* left the Port of Veracruz with the last French soldiers aboard. Marshal Bazaine had already departed on the *Souverain,* leaving the military authority in the hands of Maximilian's Imperialista commander, General Taboada, and civilian control under Maximilian's prefect, a man by the name of Bureau.

It was just over two weeks later, on April 2, that General Porfirio Díaz decided that the city of Puebla was ready for recapture. The Imperialistas occupying the town were led by General Noriega. Within a few hours, the Díaz forces had taken over all seven forts surrounding the town. They were breaking through the remaining barricades and bulwarks when Noriega, seeing that the situation was beyond recall, surrendered unconditionally.

It was all over by 5:00 PM.

General Díaz moved quickly. He collected all the weapons and dismissed the forlorn rank-and-file soldiers, telling them that they were invited to join his army first thing the next morning. Then he lined up the Imperialista general and his seventy-four officers in the main plaza opposite the cathedral.

"Although you may not have lived like men," he told them, "the least you can do for your country is die like men."

He ordered them all to be executed on the spot.[1]

Later, Díaz gathered his troops together and praised them for their swift capture of Puebla. "The world's greatest army," he said, referring to the French, "needed nine weeks to do what you have just done in seven hours!" Cheers went up. Now they were ready for Mexico City. Díaz told one of his aides that he hoped he would not have to repeat the harsh lesson of Puebla elsewhere.[2]

Meanwhile, Back in Querétaro...

Roast mule was on the menu—again.

It was late April, now, as Maximilian's entourage sat down to afternoon *comida* (dinner; served in Mexico at midday) at the Hotel Diligencias in Querétaro. What was becoming painfully obvious to everyone was that this could not go on indefinitely. The emperor was not only very sick, he was in deep depression. Maximilian had moved his headquarters from atop the Cerro de las Campanas down to the Convento de la Cruz (Convent of the Cross). It was not only more comfortable, but also it was less exposed to the constant artillery fire.

The forces protecting the emperor had dwindled to just seven thousand men, with more desertions occurring every day. In the hills overlooking the town from all sides, the Juarista forces under General Escobedo had swelled to forty-one thousand. The Juaristas had cut off the aqueduct, so the only potable water was from Querétaro's few wells. Even the river running downhill into the town was filled with the amputated corpses of Imperialista soldiers, which Escobedo's troops kept dumping into the water.[3]

Prince Salm-Salm, among other officers, kept referring to Querétaro as a mousetrap, but apparently he remained very loyal to the emperor. He told others of the night he had fallen asleep in the trenches, awakening to find Maximilian standing right next to him. "He just smiled," said the prince, "as though he understood perfectly what we were going through. He always had his little telescope with him as he made the rounds at night, checking to be sure that we officers were treating our soldiers humanely."[4]

The siege had gone on for more than six weeks. It was too dangerous to send any patrols out to scout the Juarista lines. The Juaristas would immediately butcher any Imperialista prisoners up in the hills and send their body parts floating down the aqueduct back into town.

One strange way in which the defenders of Querétaro could tell that General Escobedo's forces were probably going to launch an attack was that the Juaristas would all stand on the hillside totally naked. Looking through binoculars at this frequent phenomenon, Maximilian's people finally deduced that this was "laundry day." The Juaristas would take off their dirty uniforms and lay them on the ground. Then they would all stand there in the nude while those were collected and clean, newly washed outfits were placed at their feet. When the order was given, they would all get dressed again. After a formal inspection, they might or might not launch an attack, but they always went into battle in clean uniforms.[5]

By the second week in May, the situation had become surreal. Maximilian would walk about among the population downtown, tipping his hat to ladies and smoking his cigar as though he had not a care in the world. Sometimes he would stop and light another gentleman's cigar from his own. He chose to ignore the occasional artillery shells landing in the plaza nearby.

What few Imperialista generals were left had become irritable and arbitrary. General Ramón Méndez stopped by a local tailor shop where he had left some clothing several days earlier. The tailor, a hunchback, produced the clothing as requested, but something was not to General Méndez' satisfaction.

A heated argument ensued, with the tailor hurling a verbal insult at the general.

General Méndez took out his whip and lashed the tailor across the face, grabbed his clothing, and stalked out of the shop without paying.

"You will pay for this—dearly!" shouted the tailor, as he shook his fist at the departing general. He had only to wait until the Juaristas took over the town, and then he planned to have his revenge.[6]

A Midnight Escape Plan: *Indígenas* (Indians) as Decoys

It was the afternoon of May 14. During a meeting at the Convento de la Cruz, all of Maximilian's generals agreed that Querétaro could not be defended for more than another day or two. A plan was developed for a mass escape at midnight. The scheme would involve recruiting several hundred members of General Mejía's tribe of *indígenas* (Indians), who lived in the city, to act as decoys. They would take up positions now occupied by the departing troops and create a distraction by firing weapons. As the sun came up, they would all go back to their homes.

Led by Maximilian and the cavalry, the Imperialistas would break through the Juarista lines and flee to the Sierra Corda mountains. The foot soldiers would scatter, while Maximilian and those on horseback would head for Veracruz and a ship that was waiting in the harbor.

There was just one hitch.

General Mejía had no idea how he would be able to gather enough of his people to act as decoys by midnight. He insisted that he would need twenty-four hours to round them all up and get them organized. One other thing: the emperor's own soldiers had not been told about the plan, and if something like that were tried during the next few hours, there would be nothing but confusion.

Maximilian agreed. Mejía would get his twenty-four hours.

As the meeting broke up, one of the officers cast a glance at Felix Salm-Salm. The colonel looked angry. "Are you all right, Colonel?" the officer asked.

"Am I all right?" Salm-Salm echoed. "No, I'm not all right. The whole plan is insane. It would have been dangerous enough to try it tonight, but waiting another twenty-four hours will make it not just dangerous but totally reckless! But then again," he added, "they didn't ask me."

Colonel Lopez: Negotiator or Traitor?

Historians disagree on the role played by Colonel Miguel Lopez, the man who, in the final days, was the commander of Maximilian's household cavalry. Die-hard supporters of Maximilian claimed that he betrayed the emperor, but Lopez insisted that Maximilian himself had sent him to negotiate surrender terms with General Escobedo. At any rate, most agree that Lopez was followed after meeting with Escobedo, which enabled the Juaristas to locate Maximilian.

Lopez was an uncle to the señorita who had married Marshal Bazaine. He was one of only four Imperialista officers who had been awarded the French Legion of Honor. He had been in charge of the Mexican troops that had escorted Maximilian and Charlotte from Veracruz to Mexico City when they arrived in 1864. For a while, he had headed the Empress's Regiment, and then he became commander of the Imperial Guard that provided security for Maximilian himself.

A typical account of Lopez's activities is provided by Gene Smith in his book, *Maximilian and Carlota: A Tale of Romance and Tragedy*. Smith indicates that several days before May 14, Lopez had gone behind enemy lines to meet with General Escobedo about the terms of surrender. Could Escobedo promise the emperor safe passage to Veracruz, where he would sign an abdication and recognize Juárez as ruler of Mexico as he boarded a ship bound for Europe? General

Escobedo replied that he'd have to get Juárez to agree. He'd send a courier to find out.

Several nights later, Lopez got his answer: there would be no conditions. Lopez denounced the decision as murder.

"No, this is justice, Colonel," replied Escobedo. "If he [the emperor] wants to spare Mexican blood, if he does not wish to increase the number of victims which is already so enormous, he should not delay his surrender." Twenty-four hours later, on the night of May 14, Lopez again told Escobedo the emperor would abdicate and support Juárez if his life were spared.

Escobedo said he should have done that three months earlier. Now, it was too late.[7]

Juaristas in the Convent: It's All Over

At four o'clock in the morning on May 15, Maximilian was awakened and told that the enemy had breached the walls of the convent. The courtyard was filled with the grey uniforms of the *Supremos Poderes,* the most elite unit in the Juarista army. Maximilian came down the twisting stone stairway to come face-to-face with Juarista lieutenant colonel José Rincon Gallardo. Standing next to him was Maximilian's own Colonel Miguel Lopez.

Several of Maximilian's officers offered him a saddled horse, but the emperor declined. Instead, he walked with General Mejía and Colonel Salm-Salm to the base of Cerro de las Campanas. Maximilian hoisted some white material on a stick as he approached one of Escobedo's officers, who turned out to be an American citizen, Colonel George M. Green, who commanded a unit known as the Legion of Honor from San Francisco, which had come to fight for Juárez. Green took off his hat and said, "Your Majesty is my prisoner."

Maximilian nodded. Colonel Green led the three men to the top of the hill, where Maximilian unbuckled his sword and surrendered it to General Escobedo. Escobedo ordered that he no longer be referred to as "Emperor" or "Your Majesty," but simply as "Archduke Ferdinand Maximilian," and that he should be held in custody at his former headquarters, the Convento de la Cruz. Maximilian asked that he be taken there through the outskirts of Querétaro rather than through the main streets of the city, and Escobedo granted the request.[8]

34

Maximilian Is Executed

June 1-19, 1867

Princess Salm-Salm Has All the Answers

General Escobedo was in a bind.

Here he had Maximilian under guard in the very same convent that the emperor had used as his headquarters, but he wasn't really sure what to do next. Colonel Felix Salm-Salm was also in captivity, and was pacing up and down in his room at the convent like a caged animal, planning an escape. If Maximilian were treated harshly, there would be outraged headlines in both the American and European newspapers. If Escobedo were to be too soft and tolerant, he would lose the backing of the rest of the Mexican army. There was only one thing to do: wait for orders from President Juárez in San Luis Potosí.

That's when Agnes Salm-Salm arrived.

Agnes and the general got into an argument over whether she could visit Maximilian and her husband, and whether or not he had the authority to carry out executions. He didn't really want to talk about it, insisting that he could execute both men immediately without a trial. She warned him that the international community would see the Mexicans as barbarians, and that the United States might even invade again. If he were to execute them on his own, he would be to blame for all the consequences that followed. Why not get specific orders from President Juárez, she argued, and let him be accountable for the outcome. Agnes offered to go to San Luis Potosí and get the appropriate documents from Juárez.

That sounded pretty good to Escobedo. He would not be granting a stay; rather, he'd only be waiting for clarification from the president. While Agnes made the trip to San Luis Potosí, Felix and Maximilian would be treated by international standards as prisoners of war. The general allowed Agnes to tell her husband and the emperor what she was trying to do.[1]

The Hunchbacked Tailor Settles an Account

As of May 25, weapons had been collected, Imperialista soldiers had been processed and released, and the wounded were being cared for in hospitals. General Escobedo had given Maximilian's officers twenty-four hours to turn themselves in or be shot on sight, and most of them had surrendered. Among those still missing was General Ramón Méndez.

At General Escobedo's headquarters, an elderly-looking, hunchbacked man came in. He said he was a tailor in Querétaro, and that two weeks earlier the Imperialista general Méndez had whipped him in the face. He showed the officers his whiplash burns. He told them that he knew where General Méndez was probably hiding.

Within moments, they had followed him to a back street in Querétaro, where the tailor pointed out the house. He claimed that he had seen Méndez entering the house, and said that others might also be inside.

As they opened the door, it was deadly silent. The soldiers proceeded to search all of the rooms, looking behind and under furniture. They were just about to leave when a floorboard creaked under one soldier's footsteps. Running his fingers around the edges of the board, the soldier discovered a slightly hollowed-out spot. He leaned down, gripped the edge of the board, and yanked upward.

Huddled in a pit beneath the floor were General Méndez and three fellow officers. They looked at the weapons pointed at them from above and decided not to resist. Méndez glared contemptuously at the hunchbacked tailor as he climbed out of the hole.

Back at the Convento de la Cruz, Méndez was allowed just a few minutes to say farewell to Maximilian. Then—without any sort of trial—he was executed in the courtyard.[2]

The Brand-New Yellow Sports Carriage

It was very late at night, but Agnes Salm-Salm was not about to give up. She had managed to persuade the Prussian vice-consul, Franz Bahsen, to accompany her as she visited her husband, Felix, and Maximilian in their cells at the Convento de la Cruz. They came away with a written request from Maximilian, endorsed by Bahsen, which asked Benito Juárez for time to get defense lawyers from Mexico City.

Now, the challenge was to get the document to San Luis Potosí.

Bahsen said he was sorry, but his old, tired horse would never make it to San Luis Potosí. His driver could barely manage to get the horse to pull the carriage around town. She would have to make other arrangements.

"*Driver? Carriage?*" thought Princess Salm-Salm. "*At least they would be a good start!*"

It may have been after midnight at General Escobedo's headquarters, but the place was very much alive. There were wagon wheels rumbling across the ground, whips cracking, sergeants shouting orders, pigs grunting, and cattle mooing in temporary slaughter corrals.

General Escobedo was still trying to convince Agnes Salm-Salm that there was no way he could order a stay for the man she was calling "the emperor." When she told him that Vice-Consul Bahsen was willing to let her use his new carriage, but that his horse would never make it to San Luis Potosí, Escobedo saw his chance to get her out of town. He told her that he had not only two drivers, but four—no, five—mules to pull the carriage.

Vice-Consul Bahsen looked very nervous. It had taken him many months and a lot of money to acquire the carriage, and he wouldn't want anything to happen to it.

General Escobedo assured Herr Bahsen that the drivers were highly trained. He said they knew the mules well, and that they could take turns all night to get Princess Salm-Salm to San Luis Potosí in half the normal time.

Outside the general's headquarters stood a bright yellow, highly-decorated fiacre. It was a very light, sporty vehicle with trim wheels. Two army mule-skinners were awakened and told of their assignment. Agnes profusely thanked both Bahsen and a very relieved General Escobedo and climbed up into the carriage.

As they sped toward San Luis Potosí, it was approaching six o'clock in the morning, and they had been driving all night. Agnes was getting no sleep at all. She was rehearsing her speech for President Benito Juárez—the one she would deliver as soon as she arrived in San Luis Potosí. That was still many hours ahead. There was a strong wind, and it was still dark outside.

She would remind *El Presidente* that the world was watching. Newspapers and governments throughout Europe and the Americas would react harshly if the Mexicans simply executed Maximilian without a trial. The United States, no longer tied up with its Civil War, might invade once again and make things even worse. She would ask for time: time for Maximilian and for her husband, Felix, to arrange for lawyers, and time for the lawyers to prepare for an adequate defense.

The little yellow fiacre was very light, and it was making good time. The road did not seem nearly as bumpy as it had when riding in a heavy, fully-packed stagecoach. The sporty little carriage really needed only one horse, but General Escobedo had been kind enough to provide not one, but five strong mules. The mules were running along furiously, and trees whizzed by in the darkness at the side of the road as they went down a long hill. At the bottom of the hill, the road turned sharply to the left.

The mules and the carriage did not.

Maybe the drivers had fallen asleep. Maybe hitching five mules to a one-horse carriage was not such a good idea, after all. The mules were accustomed to pulling heavy freight wagons and stagecoaches, but nothing like this. The fiacre smashed into a stone wall.

As they picked themselves out of the wreckage, all four of them stood by the roadside, hoping to flag down a passing carriage. Agnes was worried about getting to Benito Juárez, the two soldiers feared facing General Escobedo, and the Prussian driver wondered what to tell Herr Bahsen.

Agnes Won a Delay from Juárez

Prince Felix Salm-Salm and Emperor Maximilian were glad to see Agnes, even though she looked quite beaten, as though she had been in a fight.

It was now June 2, 1867. The bedraggled princess stepped out of the carriage directly from San Luis Potosí, and went immediately to see the two prisoners. Her shoes were all torn up from the hitchhiking experience of a week earlier, and she badly needed a bath and clean clothes. Both men overlooked that. They were eager to hear what she had to say.

Prince Felix asked her if she had been successful with Juárez. What had he told her?

She said that they had won a delay, but that there would not be a trial. Rather, there would be a court-martial. That meant the death penalty would be unavoidable. Suddenly they were to be considered not only as common criminals, but also as prisoners of war. They would need the best lawyers they could get—but who?

Maximilian had an idea. Most other countries had withheld recognition of the emperor's regime, but not Prussia. He would call on his old friend, Baron Magnus, the Prussian minister in Mexico City, to recruit the finest legal minds in the capital and bring them to Querétaro. He asked Agnes to have Vice-Consul Franz Bahsen get in touch with Magnus immediately.

Agnes had to tell them the story of the wrecked yellow fiacre. She doubted if Bahsen would ever speak to her again, but she offered to send a telegram to Baron Magnus in Maximilian's name. The emperor thought that was a splendid idea.

Prince Salm-Salm's Escape Plan Is Overheard

After Agnes left, Felix Salm-Salm had some surprising news for the emperor. Salm-Salm had collected some money from among the emperor's staff and had bought some horses and pistols through an Italian officer in the Juarista army by the name of Signor Borgo. The horses would be standing by, guards had been bribed to look the other way, and everything was ready for an escape that very night. Even the chief officer on duty had pledged his support.

Why hadn't Salm-Salm told him this before, asked Maximilian. The prince said the authorities had kept them separated until Agnes had arrived a short while earlier, and that he had been waiting until she left before saying anything. Maximilian claimed that it would be embarrassing if the Prussian minister and the best lawyers in Mexico City were to arrive and find him gone. He simply would not go along with the prince's plan.

Felix Salm-Salm got down on his knees, imploring Maximilian to take advantage of what was most likely his last chance to escape. He warned that if the opportunity passed, they might both be sentenced to die. Maximilian would hear none of it. He felt sick, he said. It might be a trap, the Prussian minister's trust would have been violated—and on and on. He just wasn't going to do it.

In the hallway, several guards had been eavesdropping. Felix Salm-Salm was immediately transferred to another convent, La Teresita, so that he and the emperor would no longer be able to communicate. The prince was warned: one more wrong move and he would be shot immediately.

Outside, Signor Borgo waited until late at night. After realizing that the plot had fallen through, he disappeared with the horses and the money.

A Bribe and a Striptease Won't Persuade the Warden

With Felix grounded, Agnes Salm-Salm once more swung into action. She visited Maximilian in his cell and came up with yet another escape plan. This one would be accomplished through bribery. She arranged for the emperor to give her two signed checks.

Each one was for one hundred thousand United States dollars' worth of gold, and both were drawn on Maximilian's account with the royal family of Austria.

She had been working the commanding officer of the guards, a Colonel Villanueva. Villanueva had told Agnes that he could go along for one hundred thousand dollars, but the assistant provost marshal, a Colonel Palacios, who was in charge of the prison, would have to be won over. Villanueva had said he was fairly sure that another one hundred thousand dollars would do it.

Agnes found Palacios, but finding him and persuading him were two different matters entirely. He was just leaving for the evening, so Agnes asked him if he could give her a ride home. "*Good so far,*" thought Agnes, as they rode along toward the house where she had been renting some rooms. She had worked hard at making acquaintances with both Villanueva and Palacios, and now it looked as though it might pay off.

As the carriage pulled up in front of the house, Colonel Palacios helped Agnes out onto the curb and began to escort her toward the front steps. Timing was everything for Agnes now. She asked the colonel to come inside, because she had an urgent matter to discuss with him.

Palacios hesitated, looking up and down the street, but agreed to go in for just a moment. Once inside, she asked him to pledge his word of honor that he would not reveal to anyone what she was about to say, whether he agreed with her or not. He consented.

Then Agnes spelled it out. She told him that the arrangements had all been made for an escape, if only he would look the other way for ten minutes at the appropriate time. She handed him the one-hundred-thousand-dollar check, saying that she knew he had a wife and child to support. He looked at the check briefly, but handed it back to her. He said he would have to think about it.

"Isn't a hundred thousand dollars enough, Colonel?" asked Agnes.

Palacios began to mumble, somewhat incoherently, about his honor and his family.

"Well, then here I am!" Agnes began to undress, scattering clothing about the room as she taunted the colonel and wiggled her hips.

Palacios ran to a window overlooking the street and opened it, shouting about his honor, his wife, his child.

Agnes backed off.

"Remember, Colonel," she said as he stalked across the room and started down the hallway, "you promised me that this would be in the strictest confidence. I'm counting on you not to tell anyone about this at all!"

Palacios didn't say a word to anyone—until midnight. Then, he went to Escobedo and unloaded the whole incident to the astonished general.

At daybreak, Agnes was arrested. Later that afternoon, she was escorted out of town.[3]

The Trial Begins

The Iturbide Theater in Querétaro was colorfully decorated with flags and streamers as though a show—not a court-martial—was to take place. General Escobedo had not only chosen the venue for the trial, but he also had handpicked a panel of officers so young that they appeared to be barely out of their teens. Prince Salm-Salm said he was pretty sure that not all of them could read. The judges, lawyers, and the prisoners were to sit on the stage, while the auditorium was spacious enough to accommodate fifteen hundred onlookers. Proceedings got under way at eight o'clock on the morning of June 13.[4]

Generals Miramón and Mejía were led in, but Maximilian's physician had sent a certificate stating that the ex-emperor was too sick to attend. The panel of judges decided to go ahead anyway, and the prosecutor, or *fiscal* in Mexican terms, began to read a thirteen-count indictment.

Basically, Maximilian was charged with offering himself as an instrument of the French intervention, meaning that he voluntarily accepted any liabilities that arose from it. He was accused of disposing of the lives and interests of the Mexican people with armed forces, and of authorizing "molestations and atrocities of all kinds" in order to oppress the inhabitants of Mexico. He was not entitled to treatment as a sovereign, since he had assumed the title of emperor illegally, and his refusal to recognize the jurisdiction of the court would be considered an admission that all of the other charges were true.

The trial concluded at one o'clock on the afternoon of the second day, June 14. The panel of judges then retired to consider their verdict and the penalty. After nine hours of debate, there was a three to three tie vote between the death penalty and banishment for life. The young president of the panel cast the deciding vote, and at ten o'clock at night the court notary announced that the verdicts and sentences were the same for all three defendants: guilty—death by firing squad.[5]

Agnes Kneels Before Juárez—Grabbing Him by the Legs

President Benito Juárez was Agnes Salm-Salm's only hope now.

General Escobedo had provided the carriage, the horses, and the armed guards to see that Agnes left Querétaro. He didn't care where she went, as long as she didn't return. If she were somehow to be successful in getting a stay of execution from Juárez, she was not to be the messenger. He had also warned her that unless he heard from Juárez through official channels, the execution of Maximilian and General Miramón and Mejía would take place on Sunday, June 16, 1867—at 3:00 PM.

There was not a moment to lose as Agnes raced up the stairs to Juárez's residence on the upper floor of the Palacio del Gobierno (Government Palace) in San Luis Potosí. She had to make one last, desperate plea for Maximilian's life.

At first, Agnes attempted to reason with Juárez, trying all the arguments about international implications, justice, and whatever else she could think of. *El Presidente* told her that he had been hearing the same arguments all day. Was she not aware that Maximilian's lawyers, plus diplomats from various European countries, had ridden through the previous night and made their pleas earlier in the day?

Princess Salm-Salm fell to her knees. She wrapped her arms around Benito Juárez's legs, sobbing uncontrollably. "Please, please!" she groaned.[6]

"Madam, I am grieved to see you on your knees before me," said Juárez. "If all the kings and queens of Europe were kneeling beside you, I would still not be able to spare his life. It is not I who take it, it is the people and the law; and if I should not do their will, the people would take it and mine also." One thing he did promise her: he would spare Prince Salm-Salm's life.[7]

As for the emperor and the two generals, said Juárez, their executions would be postponed until early Wednesday morning, June 19, so that their lawyers might visit with them and have them sign whatever documents were necessary to wrap up their personal affairs. He had sent a telegram to Escobedo with that order, but he had reassured the general that the executions would still take place.

On the Hill of the Bells—June 19, 1867

On a parade ground atop Cerro de las Campanas, there was a clear view of the church steeples, tiled roofs, and gardens of Querétaro. The rectangular area was surrounded by soldiers who were on the lookout for any intruder who might yet attempt a rescue of the prisoners.

Three black carriages made their way slowly to a point just below the summit. Then Maximilian and the generals each stepped out of his own carriage, accompanied by priests who walked with them the rest of the way to the area where the firing squad was assembled. Three simple coffins, made of pine boards, were on the ground nearby.

The prisoners were made to stand against the wall at one end of the yard. None of the three was blindfolded. There were twenty-one soldiers on the firing squad, seven for each of the condemned men. Maximilian would go first.

"*¡Listos!*" ("Ready!"), shouted the captain of the firing squad, as he raised his sword.

"*¡Apunten!*" ("Aim!")

"*¡Fuego!*" ("Fire!"), he ordered, as the sword slashed downward.[8]

35

Mexicans Take Back Their Country

(June 20 through July 15, 1867)

Unfinished Business

Mexico City was still in enemy hands.

General Leonardo Márquez had been sent by Maximilian back in late March to raise some much-needed money and to recruit an army that would come to the rescue of Querétaro. Márquez managed to get some money through forced loans, and he had gangs roaming the streets of the capital to grab young men and enlist them in the Imperialista army. The mission was proceeding smoothly until Porfirio Díaz showed up.

General Díaz had retaken Puebla on April 2, and his troops had surrounded Mexico City a few days later. Márquez was blocked from returning to Querétaro, and he was well aware of what would happen if Mexico City fell to the Juaristas. He issued a proclamation to the public: "I have undertaken the command of this beautiful city, and as you know me I think it unnecessary to say more. I am ready to sacrifice myself and would rather die than to allow the slightest disorder."[1]

Indeed they did know him—all too well. Márquez was the one who had carried out a bloody massacre during the War of the Reform in 1859, killing all of the doctors, interns, patients, and workers in the hospital at Tacubaya, a section of Mexico City. He was known as the "Tiger of Tacubaya." Now he was cornered, but he was not about to yield the capital without a fight.

When June began, the Díaz siege already had lasted for seven weeks. Just as when the French had laid siege to Puebla in 1863, food was running out. Food was kept in warehouses and was rationed to the public every day, but before long, there were riots. Only women dared to leave their homes to fetch meals for their families, because any able-bodied men would be seized for the army.

Former British Captain J. J. Kendall had joined the Imperialistas to help Maximilian's cause, and in his 1871 book, *Mexico Under Maximilian,* he provides an

236

eyewitness account of some of the desperation as food supplies dwindled. As one starving woman tried to push her way to the front of the line at a warehouse, a soldier who punched her in the face was immediately trampled to death by the crowd. At another warehouse, a soldier drew his sword and slashed a woman and her baby, killing the infant. He was stabbed to death by the mob at the scene. A man who ventured out in search of food after his wife had died of starvation was grabbed by the army. He begged for three days to be allowed to attend to his children, but when he finally managed to return to his home, he discovered that all three of his children had also died.[2]

When a rumor spread throughout the capital that General Díaz was going to let civilians leave, about three thousand people headed toward Díaz's headquarters at Chapultepec, which at the time was outside of Mexico City. General Díaz, who had not agreed to any such thing, forced them back with gunfire. He was not going to allow Márquez to shift the responsibility of feeding the population to the Juarista forces.

The Díaz strategy was simple: he was not going to risk the lives of his own men by launching a direct assault on the city, because he knew that starvation—punctuated by some occasional bombardment—would eventually wear the Márquez forces down. Díaz's soldiers taunted the Márquez sentinels by hanging up a dead mule with a sign that read, "Meat for the traitors." The Márquez people responded by hanging up the body of an elderly woman who had died of starvation. Their sign read, "Meat for the cowards." They were daring the Díaz forces to launch an attack, but to no avail.[3]

Márquez Resigns and Flees

The situation dragged on for almost three more weeks, with some of Márquez's officers becoming fatigued and hinting at possible surrender. General Márquez quickly shut off any such talk by threatening to shoot anyone uttering a word about the topic.

All that changed on a Wednesday afternoon, June 19, 1867, when Porfirio Díaz' troops heard the news about Maximilian's execution that morning in Querétaro. They shouted the information to Márquez' sentries, who quickly spread the word to the rest of his four thousand men in the capital. Almost immediately, an Austrian unit among the Márquez forces declared that their allegiance had been to the emperor—not to Márquez—and they refused to fight any longer.

For civilians in Mexico City, it was time to call Márquez' hand. Early the next day, a delegation of civic leaders insisted that Márquez' military situation was untenable, with no alternatives in sight except to hand over the city. They demanded negotiations with General Díaz for terms of surrender. Instead of stubbornly hanging on, Márquez surprised everyone by simply resigning and handing over the control to General Ramón Tabera. Márquez knew that he would certainly be executed—just as generals Miramón and Mejía, along with Maximilian, had been—if he were caught. The only thing on his mind was his own escape.

General Tabera immediately dispatched messengers to General Díaz, asking for a meeting to discuss the surrender. Díaz was in no mood to negotiate after the exhausting ten-week siege, and sent word that the surrender would be unconditional. The only concession he would offer was to guard the safety of the civilian population once he occupied the city. Tabera would have only until 5:00 PM that afternoon—Thursday, June 20—to accept the offer.

Tabera's officers didn't like the Díaz ultimatum. They were still arguing over it when the hour of five o'clock arrived, and the heaviest bombardment so far erupted from the Díaz forces. After several hours, there was no longer any argument. A delegation was sent under a flag of truce to General Díaz' headquarters, just outside of town at Maximilian's former castle. Tabera's representative and Porfirio Díaz signed the surrender document at Chapultepec late that night.

It was six o'clock in the morning on Friday, June 21, as General Díaz rode into the capital at the head of six thousand troops, pledging not to harm any civilians. All he wanted was for Márquez's officers and soldiers to surrender peacefully. He announced in a proclamation that any of them who did not comply would be shot as soon as they were captured. Almost all of the Márquez troops and officers surrendered, were processed, and set free. There were just three major figures still missing: generals Márquez, O'Horan, and Vidaurri.

The Díaz troops immediately began a house-to-house search. General Díaz announced a ten-thousand-dollar reward for the capture of Márquez.

Vidaurri was found at midnight, hiding in the bed of a friend, who happened to be an American citizen. The Díaz soldiers beat him with their rifle butts and tied his wrists so tightly that he was bleeding as they hauled him off to an army barracks. At four o'clock on the morning of Saturday, June 22, they had him on his knees—blindfolded—and were about to shoot him at the city garbage dump when one of the soldiers said the spot they had chosen was "too clean." They moved him to a place that was covered with horse manure and shot him there.

That left generals Márquez and O'Horan still at large. Márquez had stolen a million dollars from the imperial treasury and met O'Horan at a mill just outside Mexico City. After a while, Márquez said he felt uncomfortable with the location. He had a hunch that the Díaz people would search the mill sooner or later, and he wanted to move on. O'Horan disagreed, saying that they were more likely to be caught as they fled. Three hours after Márquez had bidden him good-bye and left, O'Horan was captured and executed.

The wily Leonardo Márquez would not be caught. He hid for two days in a freshly dug grave at a local cemetery before making his way successfully to Veracruz. From there, he sailed to Havana, where he ran a pawn shop—incognito—for many years.[4]

Lackluster Homecoming Parade

On July 15, 1867, the crowds in Mexico City were not nearly as large or enthusiastic as they had been in January 1861, after the War of the Reform.

Maybe it was because some of the citizens thought that Juárez should not have extended his term as president, and that General Jesús González-Ortega should have held the office as called for in the Constitution. Maybe it was because they were tired and worn out after General Díaz' ten-week siege of the capital.

It was now seven and one-half years later, and a relatively small crowd of well-wishers lined the curbs to applaud as a lonely figure entered the town in a black *diligencia* (stagecoach). President Benito Juárez had come home.

The Mexicans had their country back.

Epilogue

Mexico's Isolation

For the next few years after Juárez returned to the capital, practically all of Mexico's diplomatic ties with Europe were cut off. Most European governments expressed indignation over Maximilian's death and refused diplomatic recognition for any government headed by Benito Juárez, whom they called a "blood-stained assassin."

In the United States, initial reaction to the news of Maximilian's execution was mixed. The *New York Times* ran an editorial on July 4, 1867, deploring "the bloody tragedy enacted at Querétaro" under a bold headline, "The Mexican Savages and Their Crime." On the other hand, the House of Representatives passed a resolution congratulating Juárez for everything he had done to reclaim his country—including the execution—which congressmen called "eminently right and proper."

Actually, Juárez's relations with the United States were quite good. He invited William Seward on a tour of Mexico when Seward's time in office ended in 1869. The former secretary of state was welcomed cordially all over the country in a series of banquets and speeches, where the theme was that the Americas should be free of all foreign control and Old World monarchies and aristocratic systems.

Predictions by the press in Europe and by some newspapers in the United States that Juárez and his liberals would take revenge on their opponents with thousands of massacres proved to be untrue. Besides Díaz' execution of officers after he reclaimed Puebla, just a handful of others received the death penalty: Maximilian and generals Miramón and Mejía atop the Cerro de las Campanas, General Méndez (the one who had whipped the tailor) in Querétaro, and generals Vidaurri and O'Horan in Mexico City.

Trade relations were resumed with Prussia in 1869, as well as diplomatic ties with Spain and France in 1871 (after the collapse of Napoleon III's Second Empire) and with Britain in 1884. Juárez held fast to his belief that clemency constituted weakness, so Maximilian's execution served as a harsh warning to the monarchies of Europe that their form of government would not be tolerated in the Western Hemisphere.

241

Thus, the American Civil War and the French intervention in Mexico together were seen as a turning point. After the domestic situations in each country settled down, both the United States and Mexico looked forward to building a new relationship, based not only on material prosperity but also on future political maturity and social progress.

The following is where many of the major players ended up after Mexico's seven-year struggle to regain its own sovereignty.[1]

Napoleon III and Eugénie

The news of Maximilian's demise could not have reached Paris at a more embarrassing time for the French emperor and empress. It was received ten days after the execution, just as Napoleon and Eugénie were about to hand out prizes at the Great Exhibition of 1867, which was being held at the place where the Eiffel Tower stands today. As the news spread throughout the crowd, several diplomats and heads of state from other countries got up and left. The couple continued to award prizes, smiling as an orchestra played in the background. As they arrived home afterward, Eugénie collapsed and was carried to her bed.

Poor health and troubles with European neighbors dogged Napoleon until his Second Empire finally collapsed in 1870. Empress Eugénie felt somewhat guilty for the failure of her husband's adventure in Mexico, since she had persuaded him to undertake it. The Mexican expatriates who had influenced her and pushed for Admiral Jurien's original expedition in 1861 lost everything in the gamble. Their success depended entirely on the French military, and General Juan Almonte and the others lost everything when the army failed to pacify the country.

Napoleon III and Eugénie later lived as exiles in London. He died in 1873, but she outlived him by forty-seven years, finally expiring during a visit to Madrid in 1920.[2]

Maximilian's Corpse

After a dispute with Mexico's Benito Juárez over who was authorized to claim Maximilian's body, family members finally retrieved the coffin and placed it aboard the ship *Novara,* the same one that had carried Maximilian and Charlotte to Mexico in 1864. The coffin crossed the Atlantic in a special room, which had been draped in black. Candles burned throughout the voyage.

Maximilian's brothers, Karl Ludwig and Ludwig Viktor, escorted the body on a special train through snow-covered mountains to Vienna. At eight o'clock in the evening on January 18, 1868, snow was falling as a team of torch-bearing Hussars carried the casket to the chapel of the Imperial Palace. The coffin was placed on a black-draped bier surrounded by two hundred candles in tall, silver candelabras.

So many representatives—from every nation in Europe—were on hand that not all of them could fit into the Church of the Capuchins. Many had to stand outside in the snow during the funeral on January 20. Finally, Maximilian was laid to rest in a crypt inside the imperial tomb of the Austrian dynasty.

Not everyone was quite as solemn or impressed as those in Vienna. Historian Ralph Roeder wrote that "for a month, for two months, Maximilian was all the rage in Paris. Then his death became [another] historical event. A few [would] seek the causes of his fall, but the majority [would] no longer think of him."

Perhaps the greatest insult came from Austrian Emperor Franz Joseph. He had invited his friend Prince Albert of Saxony to be his guest for the annual fall hunting party, an event in which the late Maximilian had often participated. Franz Joseph said the lovely scenery reminded him of his late brother, but, "All the same, though our party has lost one of its best members," wrote the Austrian emperor, "we may still look forward to good sport." Franz Joseph was not about to let Maximilian's demise stand in the way of his favorite recreation.[3]

Charlotte

Doctors withheld the news of Maximilian's execution from Charlotte when it reached Europe. That was not difficult, because by then she was in her own little world, almost never speaking of Maximilian. She was in good physical health, and her sister-in-law, Queen Marie Henriette, described her as "never so beautiful" as she was at that time. However, her mind was rapidly deteriorating. Moments of sanity were fewer and farther between, and her behavior had at times become violent. It was the summer of 1867, and Charlotte was only twenty-six years old.

At times she would be entirely silent; at others she would talk endlessly with imaginary people in any of five different languages. She was aware of her condition, sometimes referring to herself as "the mad woman." Life went on like that for Charlotte for another sixty years until—at the age of eighty-six—she died in 1927.

One might think that Charlotte was the longest-living survivor of this story, but the noted British biographer Jasper Ridley says that's not quite the case. "One of the young soldiers in the firing squad that had executed Maximilian," wrote Ridley, "was still living in 1952, at the age of one hundred and eleven."[4]

Benito Juárez

Juárez and William Seward patched up their differences, each one praising the other in speeches during Seward's tour of Mexico in 1869. Conveniently forgetting Seward's embargo on the shipment of arms to Mexico, Juárez praised the former secretary of state for all the help the United States had given Mexico during the French intervention and the Maximilian regime. Seward called Juárez "the greatest statesman" he had ever encountered.

General Porfirio Díaz opposed Juárez in the election of 1871, but lost. Díaz then mounted a revolution against Juárez, but it failed. Juárez lived until 1872, when he was struck by a heart attack while lifting a child who had fallen.

Juárez's return to Mexico City on July 19, 1867, began a new era for Mexico. As he said when the country was free of foreign control, "Let the people and the government respect the rights of all. Among individuals as among nations, respect for the rights of others means peace." To clarify the unsettled question of presidential tenure, Juárez called for a special election to be held in October of 1867. The winner would serve until November 30, 1871.[5]

Porfirio Díaz

Díaz saw an opportunity to challenge Benito Juárez for the presidency of Mexico, taking advantage of unrest in the military. The army had numbered ninety thousand when Díaz reclaimed the capital after the ten-week siege, but Juárez had laid off sixty thousand of them without pensions as the hostilities with the French and the Imperialistas faded into history. Díaz lost in October of 1867, but decided to run again in 1871, when the three-man race also included Sebastián Lerdo de Tejada. The three-way split gave none of the candidates a majority, so the Mexican Congress chose Juárez as the winner. Lerdo placed second and was named chief justice of the Mexican Supreme Court, a post like that of the vice president in the United States, which meant that he would be next in line for the presidency.

Díaz led a rebellion against Juárez and Lerdo, but it failed. After Juárez died of a heart attack in 1872, Lerdo became president. In 1876, Lerdo was reelected president, but Díaz won the position as head of the Supreme Court. Unpredictable and arrogant, Lerdo alienated his supporters. American businessmen were backing Díaz, because Lerdo had blocked them from extending their railroads into Mexico. Within months, Lerdo had resigned and left the country, and Díaz had arrived in the capital and proclaimed himself president.

The Díaz presidency turned into a severe dictatorship that lasted until 1910. By then, the pressure was building from revolutionary forces like those of Pancho Villa and Emiliano Zapata. The old, heavy, white-haired dictator knew his time was up. He fled to Veracruz and headed for Europe aboard a German steamer. Porfirio Díaz died as an exile in Paris in 1915.[6]

Agnes and Felix Salm-Salm

Agnes and her dog, Jimmy, followed Prince Felix Salm-Salm to Europe, where she and the dog met him in Paris. After leaving the ship at Brest, France, and boarding a train, Agnes had to disguise the dog as a baby to get him into the first class compartments. Felix, seeking military employment, hoped that Austrian emperor Franz Joseph would welcome him, but Franz Joseph—the one who would rather go hunting than worry about his deceased brother—was becoming bored with visitors who had any connection with Maximilian.

If Franz Joseph wasn't eager to welcome the prince, Felix's creditors were. He was arrested in Vienna and had to pay twenty-five hundred dollars just to be released. Felix and Agnes escaped to Switzerland and lived under the name of Von Stein. Finally, with the help of the former Prussian consul who had come to the aid of Felix and Maximilian in Querétaro, Felix became a major in the Fourth Regiment of the Prussian guards. Felix published a book, and immediately life began to brighten for the Salm-Salms, as they rubbed elbows with royalty and high society at balls and dinners.

In the summer of 1870, Felix's regiment marched off to the Franco-Prussian War. On August 21, 1870, Agnes learned that her prince had been killed in a battle three days earlier. For thirty years after that, Agnes wandered through Italy and Switzerland, dodging Felix's creditors, when—out of nowhere—a wealthy relative in the United States died and left her his fortune.

Finally, in April of 1899, Agnes returned to New York City to present the Civil War battle flag to the surviving veterans of the Union army's Eighth New York Regiment. Twenty-eight of them showed up and shook hands with the woman they had called their Soldier Princess. The event received widespread local press coverage. Returning to Europe, Agnes lived with the memories of three wars and all the adventures she had enjoyed with her prince. She died in 1911.[7]

General Jo Shelby

After the tragic destruction of the Carlota Colony, Shelby became active in another Confederate colony at Tuxpan. As Maximilian's empire evaporated with the emperor's execution at Querétaro and the Díaz takeover of Mexico City in the summer of 1867, Joseph Orville Shelby returned to his home in Missouri. President Grover Cleveland later appointed Shelby as United States marshal for Kansas City. He died in February, 1897 and was buried in Kansas City.[8]

Leonardo Márquez

After hiding in Havana for twenty-eight years, using a pawn shop as his cover but actually living in poverty, the "Tiger of Tacubaya" returned to Mexico City in 1895. He was seventy-five years old, and said that he felt that he had nothing to lose by coming back to face his old enemies. He was right. President Porfirio Díaz was too absorbed with the civil unrest occurring throughout the country to even bother with him, so Márquez lived peacefully in a Mexico City suburb, all but unnoticed, until he died in 1905. The general who had captured Maximilian—Escobedo—had died three years earlier.[9]

William Seward

Seward was more than satisfied with the way that Benito Juárez had resolved the situation with Maximilian, and he went out of his way to show appreciation. Through Matías Romero, Seward provided a ship for Juárez's wife and family to return to Mexico. Señora Juárez and her family of fifteen (including three servants) boarded the American vessel *Wilderness* at New Orleans for the trip to Veracruz on June 17, 1867, two days before Maximilian's execution. Despite his earlier differences with Matías Romero, Seward made amends by giving Romero the use of the same ship in October. The Mexican ambassador had a U.S. senator and a congressman as his guests when they sailed from Charleston, South Carolina, to Veracruz.

Many had predicted that the United States would acquire parts of Mexico, such as the states of Baja California, or Sonora, after the death of Maximilian. Seward insisted that he only wanted to see the Mexicans free from foreign intervention, and that the United States was not interested in the purchase or acquisition of any land. His statements and writings earned respect from European countries for the independent course established by the United States and for the patient arranging, through diplomatic and other non-military means, the American "Waterloo" of Napoleon III.[10]

Matías Romero

One of the last disagreements Romero had with William Seward before the seven-year intervention in Mexico finally ended was over a request for clemency. The U.S. State Department asked Juárez—through Romero—to treat Maximilian with leniency if he were to be taken prisoner. Juárez and his cabinet resented the request, and so did Romero, who pointed out that the United States had never asked the French to spare Juárez's life if he were to be caught first.

Beginning in 1859, Romero had been in Washington for the last two years of the Buchanan administration, all of Lincoln's time in office, and all that of Andrew Johnson, who succeeded Lincoln. Romero had seen crisis after crisis: from the Southern secession, to the Civil War and its reconstruction, to the entire French intervention in Mexico. He took a four-year break from 1878 to 1882, but then returned to represent Mexico in Washington until his death in 1898.

"We have obtained our victory," declared Romero after the demise of Maximilian, "by our own efforts without the aid of any foreign nation—in spite of the moral influence of all Europe and the continental powers. We have opposed this gigantic combination with nothing more than the suffering and patriotism of our people and the firm sympathy of the United States."[11]

Marshal Bazaine

Bazaine was called upon once more to lead French troops in the Franco-Prussian War. Prussia's Bismarck had been preparing for the confrontation for years while Napoleon III had his troops tied up in Mexico, so the French forces were ill prepared and vastly outnumbered. There was one defeat after another, until Napoleon III himself was taken prisoner at Sedan. Following a long siege at Metz. Bazaine was also finally forced to surrender.

The Germans laid siege to Paris, and the French Second Empire collapsed. A republic was named in its place, but it represented a much weaker France. The German Empire had come into being.

Bazaine was court-martialed and sentenced to prison, but the former señorita, whom he had married in Mexico City, arrived at the fortress prison off the coast of France with her cousin. The cousin managed to get a rope smuggled to Bazaine, who slid down the wall of the prison to the small boat where his wife waited. They rowed to a ship that was headed for Spain, where Bazaine lived out the rest of his life in Madrid. After his death, the former Señorita Peña returned to Mexico. She died there a few years later in a mental institution, lonely and forgotten.[12]

General Jesús González-Ortega

As a result of the dispute with Benito Juárez over succession to the presidency, Ortega remained in prison until August 2, 1868, well after the July elections that year. He was no longer considered a threat to Juárez, but his manifestos and proclamations issued from behind bars and some attention from the press caused increasing embarrassment to the Juárez administration.

While it can be said that Ortega's political life was curtailed by Juárez's actions, the reality facing Mexico at the time demanded the stability and continuity provided by Juárez's leadership. One dilemma that Ortega faced was that he had claimed the acting government of the country was illegal—including the Congress—but then he submitted a petition to that allegedly illegal Congress requesting an investigation of his charges.

Finally, on August 19, 1868, just over two weeks after his release from prison at Monterrey, Ortega had moved to Saltillo. At that time, he issued a manifesto to the country conceding all political support to Juárez. Since the public appeared to have accepted Juárez and the government seemed to be operating normally, Ortega acknowledged that he had little choice but to accept reality.

After losing an election in October 1868 for governor of Zacatecas, González-Ortega declared that he intended to retire from any participation in public affairs. There were moves by his supporters in 1869 to nominate him for the Zacatecas state legislature and for the Mexican national Congress, but he declined to come out of retirement. Others tried to use his name in an unsuccessful rebellion against Juárez, but Ortega declared that he was surprised that anyone would use him as their excuse to overthrow the government. The rebellion failed in January 1869.

In the presidential elections of 1871, Ortega was asked to declare his support for one of the three candidates: Juárez, Lerdo, or Díaz. He chose Juárez because of Juárez's ability to keep Mexico united during the previous fourteen years, in spite of formidable challenges. That was the last of his public statements. After the death of Juárez in July 1872, the Lerdo administration, and the rise to power of Porfirio Díaz, Ortega kept in contact only with his immediate family and dedicated himself to study and writing. He acquired one of the most extensive libraries in Mexico, a collection which now makes up a major portion of the public library of Zacatecas. He never discussed politics again, and he apparently did not keep up with current events in Mexico.

In January 1881, President Manuel González of Mexico restored Ortega to his rank as general of the Mexican Army, expressing "a debt of gratitude to the military leader of the Reform and to the heroic defender of his country's soil against the foreign invader." Ortega became ill a month later and died at his home in Saltillo on February 28, 1881. After a military funeral in Zacatecas, Jesús González-Ortega was buried alongside other national heroes at the Panteón de Dolores in Mexico City.[13]

Sara Yorke

The Yorkes gave up their property in Mexico City, and the family eventually moved to Brattleboro, Vermont. In 1870, Sara moved to Philadelphia, where she lived with two of her uncles before marrying a prominent socialite by the name of Cornelius Stevenson.

As Mrs. Sara Yorke Stevenson, she raised a son and became active in Philadelphia's musical and intellectual communities. She was among those who established a folklore society and the Free Museum of Science and Art at the University of Pennsylvania. She was the first woman to be a Harvard lecturer at the Peabody Museum, and the first woman to be awarded an honorary degree from the University of Pennsylvania. She was active in civic and academic organizations, especially in the field of archaeology; she visited Rome and toured Egypt on behalf of the archaeology department at the University of Pennsylvania.

In her sixties, she was still active as curator at the Pennsylvania Museum and as the literary editor of the *Public Ledger* in Philadelphia. In 1899, her book, *Maximilian in Mexico,* was published. It was dedicated to the memory of Matías Romero. Sara Yorke Stevenson died in 1921. The book was rereleased in 2004, and is available on both Amazon.com and Barnes&Noble.com.[14]

Distinguished Ex-Confederates

After Lee's surrender at Appomattox, Shelby's Confederate army corps and more than two thousand civilians migrated south of the border, hoping to build new homes and apply their Southern agricultural skills to Mexican soil.

Among the most prominent was Commodore Matthew Fontaine Maury, who a decade earlier had established the new United States Naval Observatory in Washington, D.C. Maury and Maximilian had been corresponding since 1855, when the archduke, as commander-in-chief of the Austrian navy, had sailed around the world on a scientific expedition. As soon as he showed up in Mexico City, Maury was not only appointed as the emperor's commissioner of colonization and immigration, but also was named director of Mexico City's Astronomical Observatory.

When he discovered that he could no longer work with Maximilian's various ministers, Maury requested a leave of absence to visit his family in London, where they had gone after the Civil War. While he was there, he got a letter from Maximilian saying that the Colonization Commission had been abolished because of budget considerations. Maury returned home to become a physics professor at Virginia Military Institute. He lived next door to an old friend, General Robert E. Lee. He spent much of his time traveling throughout the country, promoting a government agency that would do for farmer what his wind and current charts had done for sea captains. He is still known in Washington as the "Father of the Weather Bureau."

Other prominent Southerners who returned to the United States included General Shelby's adjutant, Major John Edwards, who had edited the *Mexican Times*. Like Shelby, he returned to Missouri, where he was one of the two men who founded the *Kansas City Times*.

Judge Alexander Watkins Terrell left Mexico to open a law office and become a state senator in Texas, where he sponsored the bill that created the University of Texas. He was known for many years as the "Father of the University." Later, President Grover Cleveland appointed him ambassador to Turkey.[15]

Sudanese Soldiers

French Colonel Henri Blanchot, who had harshly criticized the French army and Maximilian several years earlier in his letters home to Paris, had nothing but praise for the Egyptian and Sudanese who had also come to Mexico under the French flag:

Under the burning sun of the Tierra Caliente they had relieved the French troops who were being annihilated by the merciless climate...May I add a word of gratitude to these friends...who have generously rendered us so important a service. They were superb, those ebony sculptures draped in white cashmere, those descendants of the warriors of the ancient Pharoahs, who impressed the onlooker with their height, the pride in their posture and the dignity in their bearing. They exhibited a self-respect eager to win the admiration of French soldiers; their manner of saluting the officers and presenting arms were an eloquent characteristic deeply flattering to France.

The Egyptian and Sudanese troops had guarded the railway and the approaches to Veracruz until the last French soldier was safely aboard one of the ships leaving for Europe. Before they boarded their own vessel *La Seine,* the same ship that had brought them from Egypt in 1863, Bazaine reviewed them personally and thanked them for their service and devotion in the name of France and Emperor Napoleon III.

The Sudanese battalion did not leave much of a mark on the history of Mexico, but their four years of service alongside the French had made a great impression on them. Old soldiers in Africa handed down legends from the experience for several generations.[16]

The Gardener's Daughter

In 1917, a Mexican by the name of Sedano was charged with spying for the Germans during World War I. He was convicted and executed in Paris by a firing squad. Sedano turned out to be the son of the gardener's daughter from Cuernavaca, Mexico. His father had been Emperor Maximilian.[17]

Justo Sierra on Cinco de Mayo

The famed Mexican historian and philosopher Justo Sierra wrote eloquently about the significance of Cinco de Mayo, strongly suggesting that, in addition to Mexico, the United States may also have been at risk:

> The Fifth of May set back Napoleon's designs in regard to the United States a full year. At the very moment when Zaragoza was fighting the battle of Puebla, Robert E. Lee was winning battles for the south. It was a moment when the French Emperor, with an unarmed republic virtually at his mercy, might have joined forces with the southern rebels...

Sierra says that considering the number of combatants at Puebla on May 5, 1862, or the military result, which was an orderly French retreat to await reinforcements, the battle was not of the first or second rank. However, "its moral and political results were immeasurable. The entire nation was thrilled with enthusiasm. Surely no Mexican, whatever his party, was downcast by the victory. The remotest Indian village felt the electric current of patriotism that sped like lightning through the land, awakening many a sleeping conscience. The people were inspired to make a supreme effort."

As for Mexico's entire seven-year struggle to regain its sovereignty, Sierra wrote,

> Mexico lost on battlefields and in consequence of the war certainly more than 300,000 souls, but meanwhile acquired a soul of her own, a national unity. Destroying a throne, appealing constantly against force in behalf of law, mortally wounding the military power of France and the Empire of Napoleon III, incarnating in Juárez an adamant resistance against any foreign meddling in our sovereign affairs—neither European intervention nor American alliance—Mexico redeemed her independence, acquired through self-knowledge, and won for herself a secure place in history.[18]

Notes

Chapter One

1 Wyke called…"bare-faced robbery." Haslip 155.
2 "State of anarchy," "wretched country," "our interests." Roeder 386–389.
3 "an idiot and a rascal,"…"money nor ministers." Roeder 386–389.
4 For the first time…predators. Schoonover (*Dollars*) 55.
5 As Francisco…"…in Veracruz." Roeder 392.
6 Even President…to Spain. Roeder 391–393.

Chapter Two

1 he considered Zaragoza…of treason. Roeder 404–405.
2 Napoleon "wishes to…eyes of Europe." Ridley 79.
3 Saligny would not…power as "sick." Roeder 414.
4 "Mr. Juárez…but robbery." Ridley 83.

Chapter Three

1 This called for…was going on. Roeder 414.
2 Wyke had already…"the present century." Ridley 91.
3 Those foreigners who…"…condemned by God." Siemens 73.
4 The women of Veracruz…onto clothing as ornaments. Siemens 75–76.
5 "Mexicans! We have not…if they dare!" Ridley 96.
6 "The decency, the dignity…twenty thousand more men." Roeder 420–421.

Chapter Four

1 "What has happened"…asked Lorencez. Roeder 429.
2 "We are so superior…master of Mexico." Garfías 30–31.
3 Over the next…Lorencez had claimed. Palou 37.

4 Whenever one of the *indígenas* (Indians)...any Mexican forces. Roeder 442–443.

Chapter Five

1 General Arteaga had...artillery pieces, whatever. Garfías 34, 42.
2 As the recruitment...at least four men. Beezley 70.
3 "Very well...obliged to report it." Roeder 444.
4 The sermons...would be forbidden. Callcott 45.

Chapter Six

1 As Saligny was about...with twenty-five hundred men. Roeder 444.
2 "As soon as our troops...obliged to report it." Roeder 444.
3 The Mexicans turned...even get set up. Garfías 42–47.
4 Suddenly—*BAH-OOM!*...our approach," he said. Niles 46.
5 Then came something...to tell about it. Ridley 99.
6 "So much," said..."discipline and morality." Roeder 446–447.

Chapter Seven

1 "The national arms...on the enemy." Roeder 449.
2 "As for money...regrettable truth." Roeder 449.
3 "Soldiers and sailors!...of heroic courage." Roeder 447.
4 Not everyone..."not with flowers." Ridley 101.
5 "I have sufficient...the French nation." Roeder 449.
6 "An accident...Sara lay sleepless." Niles 67.
7 Although French Newspapers...home from Mexico. Ridley 102, Roeder 453
8 "Such are the fortunes...fatigues and privations." Roeder 453.

Chapter Eight

1 One such woman...have been there either. Salas 34–35.
2 Transportation and supply lines...at all costs. Siemens 78–79.
3 In Washington,...by the French. Callahan 285-291, Hanna and Hanna 70-76.
4 Seward told Dayton...the Mexican issue. Hanna and Hanna 121-125.
5 "When once the shades...carries a revolver." Niles 73–74.
6 "ever since the beginning...over Mexico today." Roeder 454.

7 Napoleon told Forey…wanted no more of them. Roeder 455-456.

Chapter Nine

1 On the morning…in charge all along. Roeder 452.

2 There was a lull…and so was his career. Roeder 454.

Chapter Ten

1 Pickett's instructions…or picking cotton. Hanna and Hanna 51-53 and Schoonover 93-99.

2 The newspaper *El Siglo*…stand still long enough. Schoonover 26–31.

3 Working closely…Rio Grande in retaliation. Schoonover 38.

4 Little boys in Orizaba…"…shoulders as guns." Read 304–305.

5 There were lots of good…worth the detour. Siemens 165–187.

6 "There is a deliberate…a single day of rest." Roeder 462–463.

7 After watching more reptiles…without a hitch. Ridley 109.

Chapter Eleven

1 If putting on plays…new dancing jobs. Ridley 109–110.

2 "I have lost all hope…march upon Monterrey." Schoonover (*Dollars*) 41.

Chapter Twelve

1 "The native alone…act of creation." Roeder 467-472.

2 General Forey's hesitation…by the French public. House of Representatives, 37th Congress, 2nd Session, Document #100 (*Present Condition of Mexico*), 532–536.

3 All of this…all but invincible. Cadenhead 70–71.

4 In Washington, D.C.,…as long as it takes. Ridley 120.

5 As Captain Henry Loizillon…"…of addressing us." Roeder 476.

6 "Perote was a sad little village…simply a sad little village." Roeder 477.

7 All the French got…later became Napoleon III. Ridley 143.

Chapter Thirteen

1 Captain Loizillon wrote…"desert or disband." Roeder 492.

2 One unlucky colonel…more proclamations. Roeder 493.

3 Almost nine months ago…be a terrible one! Roeder 494–495.

4 "During that day…that we were soldiers." Roeder 495.

5 "This first easy success…everyone's mouth water." Roeder 496.

6 Loizillon said…in five or six days. Roeder 494.

7 As Francois DuPin…by 5:00 AM. Ridley 124–125.

8 Just before General Forey's…to do their best. Scholes 91.

9 "The Emperor Napoleon III…humanity, and civilization." Ridley 126.

10 Trying to be helpful…"…prepared for him." Roeder 497.

11 Another woman was…house-to-house fighting. Ridley 126.

Chapter Fourteen

1 "When a council of war…as many others as possible." Roeder 500.

2 "There has been neither direction…what has happened." Roeder 501.

3 The little village of Camarón…worst defeat in legion history. Garfías 94–101.

Chapter Fifteen

1 Inside Puebla…seen fireworks. Niles 80–82.

2 The trap set…listed as missing. Roeder 503–504.

3 Colonel Francois DuPin…distance of each route. Ridley 123–126.

4 At the American Embassy…"…Thomas Corwin." Niles 83.

Chapter Sixteen

1 Just when everyone…General Achille Bazaine. Roeder 505–507.

2 At about the same time…personally with Forey. Cadenhead 73–74.

3 "Nothing has occurred…distance from Puebla." U.S. House of
   Representatives, 38th Congress, 3rd Session, Corwin to Seward, May 1, 1863.

4 Sara Yorke and…"next few days." Niles 74–77.

5 "The soldier,…"of General Forey." Roeder 507.

6 The perception of Bazaine…"skillfully toward his goal." Roeder 507.

Chapter Seventeen

1 On the morning…over open fires. Cadenhead 73.

2 Things got worse…on the way out. Cadenhead 75.

3 Captain Loizillon…"…will be the result." Roeder 511.

Chapter Eighteen

1 As the news…against the invaders. Cadenhead 75–76.
2 The news of the Puebla…"strange and weird sight." Niles 87–89.
3 Then, too, without…their own citizens. Ridley 133.
4 There was also trouble…on to Mexico City. Hill and Hogg 29–31.
5 Another factor was…"…of Mexico had been saved." Cadenhead 74–75.

Chapter Nineteen

1 As the delegation…entered Mexico City. Ridley 133.
2 In Washington, D.C.,…President Benito Juárez. Schoonover, ed. (*Mexican*) 28–29.

Chapter Twenty

1 "Old criollo fogies…watched from afar." Ruiz 247.
2 No one dared…and no one else. Roeder 512.
3 "The people were attracted…their true value." Roeder 513.
4 Among those "families…"…"…best of friends." Stevenson 94–96.
5 "We had no sooner…tapers in our hands." Roeder 519.
6 Meanwhile, General Jesús…problems later on. Cadenhead 76.
7 To the north…"…here only by force." Roeder 517–519.

Chapter Twenty-One

1 "The 10th of June…of the Clerical Party." Roeder 520.
2 The three regents…over the group. Roeder 523.
3 "The officers of…S'il Vous Plait." Niles 97–98.
4 "I am sorry to see…but simply religious." Corti, vol. 1, 387–388.
5 As a matter of fact…Captain Loizillon. Ridley 143.
6 Madame Cornu became…rest of the findings. Roeder 529-530.
7 Even before Bazaine…of his success. Hanna and Hanna 91, and Roeder 530-531.
8 What Forey didn't realize…at this time. Hanna and Hanna 91–92.
9 Maximilian was still…wasn't over yet. Ridley 138.

10 While her husband…play a waiting game. Niles 92–96.
11 Despite the success…"…within a week." Ridley 142.

Chapter Twenty-Two

1 Saligny and Forey…never received it. Hanna and Hanna 93.
2 "Unfortunately his ideas…in the New World." Roeder 541.
3 In Richmond, Virginia…might just be up for grabs. Hanna and Hanna 118.
4 Even though he…couldn't let go. Roeder 531.

Chapter Twenty-Three

1 General Forey, still trying…the country entirely. Hanna and Hanna 104–105.
2 "The Bear" finally…vanquished by Mexico. Roeder 533-534.
3 At about the same…"…a monkey" to gather them. Hanna and Hanna 109.
4 As if the internal…really paying attention. Schoonover (*Dollars*) 111–112.

Chapter Twenty-Four

1 Among the units…unscheduled stop. Niles 151–152.
2 At Miramar…visited her in Vienna. Haslip 197–202.
3 Matías Romero…"…the Foreign Department." Schoonover (*Dollars*) 117–118.
4 In Mexico City…his faithful spouse. Ridley 153.

Chapter Twenty-Five

1 "What man of any dignity…a cabbage head." Hanna and Hanna 127.
2 "A family quarrel…your exalted mission." Hanna and Hanna 128.
3 The cat-and-mouse game…released Pepita. Ridley 190–192.
4 While all of that…Request granted. Cadenhead 88.
5 In New York City…on their way to Mexico. Niles 105-110.

Chapter Twenty-Six

1 It was only about…very same day. Haslip 246.
2 They had hoped…Charlotte was crying. Haslip 246–247.
3 One thing the new…musicians from Cuba. Ridley 174 and Kendall 195–200.

4 As Maximilian would soon…an imperial Mexico. Hanna and Hanna 138–143.
5 Another problem…return to Mexico. Ridley 192–194.

Chapter Twenty-Seven

1 Among those up…would get his promotion. Niles 154.
2 Even with Colonel Gallifet…departed in silence. Ridley 195–200.
3 It was a quiet Sunday…a brief telegram.. Niles 156–160.
4 There was sensational…"General Felix Salm-Salm." Niles 161.
5 On June 26, 1865,…"…agrees with him." Haslip 318–320.
6 Confederate General Jo Shelby…going to reach Mexico. Davis 25–26.

Chapter Twenty-Eight

1 Agnes Salm-Salm…on Felix's behalf. Niles 160–162 and Ridley 242.
2 It was the Fourth of July…"…commence for Monterrey." Davis 64–68.
3 The French knew…they had ever been. Ridley 235–237.
4 In late 1864…City of the Saddle [Monterrey]. Davis 97–98.
5 The only major negative…returned to their lodging. Davis 103–104.

Chapter Twenty-Nine

1 General Jo Shelby…toward San Luis Potosí. Edwards 62.
2 In Paris, reality was…Webb's idea "an inspiration." Ridley 238–239.
3 "Pierron made Matehuala…the summer time." Edwards 68.
4 Bazaine's invasion…just the Port of Veracruz. Hill and Hogg 97–101.

Chapter Thirty

1 Autumn had arrived…entire French army. Ridley 228.
2 The horrible atrocity…"…kill or be killed." Roeder 606–607.
3 Bazaine didn't realize…eighteen months later. Hanna and Hanna 262.
4 Secretary of State…dinner was served. Hanna and Hanna 264–265.
5 Matías Romero was thrilled…"…quickly wiped out." Ridley 205.
6 It was just a few weeks…in October of 1867. Ridley 239.
7 On September 3, 1865…They were not wanted. Edwards 94.
8 Shelby told them…"Dinner not ready yet?" Davis 169.

Chapter Thirty-One

1 Napoleon III's letter…shared them with Charlotte. Haslip 372.
2 When Charlotte learned…for his new country. Haslip 376–377.
3 Back in the…United States Senate. Schoonover (*Dollars*) 226–227.
4 "The Emperor and…without a *sou*!" Davis 162.
5 "Do you know…Vienna Lunatic Asylum." Haslip 431.
6 Maximilian was wavering…"…councillors of state." Haslip 448.

Chapter Thirty-Two

1 Even Maximilian didn't…"At last we are free." Haslip 459.
2 For American newspaper…Life was good. Niles 180–181, 210–215.
3 That was in 1865…"…and the torches finished." Edwards 120.
4 Elsewhere throughout…rest of his life. Edwards 121.
5 Sara Yorke had been…final French withdrawal. Niles 242–255.
6 It was February 13…"It is a mouse-trap." Smith 248–254.

Chapter Thirty-Three

1 It was just over two weeks…executed on the spot. Smith 247.
2 Later, Díaz gathered…lesson of Puebla elsewhere. Ridley 260.
3 Roast mule was on the menu…dumping into the water. Smith 254.
4 Prince Salm-Salm…treating our soldiers humanely." Haslip 473.
5 One strange way…in clean uniforms. Smith 256.
6 By the second week…to have his revenge. Ridley 263.
7 It was the afternoon…Now, it was too late. Smith 260–261.
8 At four o'clock…granted the request. Davis 164.

Chapter Thirty-Four

1 General Escobedo was…what she was trying to do. Haslip 480–481.
2 As of May 25,…executed in the courtyard. Ridley 263–264.
3 It was very late…escorted out of town. Hyde 277–280.
4 The Iturbide Theater…June 13. Smith 271.
5 Generals Miramón and Mejía…death by firing squad. Hyde 282–285.
6 President Benito Juárez…"Please, please!" she groaned. Niles 263–267.
7 "Madam, I am grieved…"…Prince Salm-Salm's life. Hyde 286.

8 On a parade ground…sword slashed downward. Smith 279.

Chapter Thirty-Five

1 "I have undertaken…slightest disorder." Ridley 278.
2 Former British Captain…had also died. Kendall 319–331.
3 The Díaz strategy…but to no avail. Ridley 278–279.
4 It was six o'clock…for many years. Ridley 280.

Epilogue

1 Mexico's Isolation Ridley 284–286.
2 Napoleon III and Eugénie Ridley 282–283.
3 Maximilian's Corpse Hyde 297.
4 Charlotte Ridley 290.
5 Benito Juárez Sierra 341.
6 Porfirio Díaz Ridley 287–288.
7 Agnes and Felix Salm-Salm Niles 320–332.
8 General Jo Shelby Hanna and Hanna 227.
9 Gen. Leonardo Márquez Ridley 288.
10 William Seward Callahan 331.
11 Matías Romero Schoonover, ed. (*Mexican*) 167.
12 Marshal Bazaine Ridley 287.
13 Gen. González-Ortega Cadenhead 117–144.
14 Sara Yorke Niles 242–255.
15 Ex-Confederates Hanna and Hanna 224–235.
16 Sudanese Soldiers Hill and Hogg 110.
17 The Gardener's Daughter Ridley 288–289.
18 Justo Sierra on Mexico Sierra 312, 341.

Bibliography

Beezley, William H. *Judas at the Jockey Club (and Other Episodes of Porfirian Mexico)*. Lincoln: University of Nebraska Press, 1987.

Cadenhead, Ivie E., Jr. *Jesús González-Ortega and Mexican National Politics*. Fort Worth: Texas Christian University Press, 1972

Callahan, James Morton. *American Foreign Policy in Mexican Relations*. New York: MacMillan Company, 1932.

Callcott, Wilfrid Hardy. *Liberalism in Mexico 1857–1929*. Hamden, CT: Archon Books, 1965.

Corti, Count Egon Caesar. *Maximilian and Charlotte of Mexico*. Trans. Catherine Allison Phillips. New York: Alfred A. Knopf, 1928.

Dabbs, Jack Audrey. *The French Army in Mexico, 1861–1867*. The Hague: Mouton and Co., 1963.

Davis, Edwin Adams. *Fallen Guidon: The Saga of Confederate General Jo Shelby's March to Mexico*. College Station: Texas A&M University Press, 1995.

Edwards, John N. *Shelby's Expedition to Mexico: An Unwritten Leaf of the War*. Austin, TX: The Steck Co., 1964. (Facsimile reproduction of 1872 original by *Kansas City Times*, which Edwards cofounded.)

Garfías Magaña, Luis. *La Intervención Francesa en México: La Historia de la ExpediciónFrancesa Enviada Por Napoleón III Para Establecer el Segundo Imperio Mexicano*. Mexico City: Panorama Editorial, 1986.

Hanna, Alfred and Kathryn. *Napoleon III and Mexico: American Triumph Over Monarchy*. Chapel Hill: University of North Carolina Press, 1971.

Haslip, Joan. The Crown of Mexico: Maximilian and His Empress Carlota. New York: Holt, Rhinehart & Winston, 1971.

Hill, Richard, and Hogg, Peter. *A Black Corps d'Elite: An Egyptian Sudanese Conscript Battalion With the French Army in Mexico, and its Survivors in Subsequent African History, 1863–1867.* Michigan State University Press, 1995.

Hyde, H. Montgomery. *Mexican Empire: The History of Maximilian and Carlota of Mexico.* London: MacMillan & Co., Ltd., 1946.

Kendall, J. J. *Mexico Under Maximilian.* London: T. Cautley Newby, 1871.

Krauze, Enrique. *Mexico—Biography of Power: A History of Modern Mexico 1810–1996.* Trans. Hank Heifetz. New York: HarperCollins, 1997.

Krauze, Enrique, and Fausto Zerón Medina. *El Vuelo del Aguila.* Set of six DVDs on the life of Porfirio Díaz, in Spanish. Mexico City: Televisa, S.A. de C.V., 1996.

Menard, Valerie. *The Latino Holiday Book.* 2nd ed. New York: Marlowe & Co., 2004.

Meyer, Michael C., William L Sherman, and Susan M. Deeds. *The Course of Mexican History.* 6th ed. New York: Oxford University Press, 1999.

Meyer, Michael C., and William H. Beezley, eds. *The Oxford History of Mexico.* New York, Oxford University Press, 2000.

Monroy, Salazar. *Battle of May 5th, 1862.* Trans. David López Castillo. Mexico City: Secretaria de Educación Publica, 1950.

———. *Senda Sublime de Gloria: Centenario de la Batalla del 5 de Mayo.* Puebla, Mexico: Editorial Salazar Monroy, 1962.

Niles, Blair. *Passengers to Mexico: The Last Invasion of the Americas.* New York: Farrar & Rhinehart, 1943.

O'Connor, Richard. *The Cactus Throne: The Tragedy of Maximilian and Carlotta.* New York: G. P. Putnam's Sons, 1971.

O'Flaherty, Daniel. *General Jo Shelby: Undefeated Rebel.* Chapel Hill: University of North Carolina Press, 1954. (Reprinted, 2000.)

Olivera, Ruth R., and Liliane Crété. *Life in Mexico Under Santa Anna, 1822-1855*. Norman: University of Oklahoma Press, 1991

Payno, Manuel. *Los Bandidos de Río Frío*. 1891. Mexico City: Editorial Porrúa, 2001.

Palau, Pedro A. *Cinco de Mayo*. Puebla, Mexico: Gobierno del Estado de Puebla, 1976.

Pruneda, Pedro L. *Historia de la Guerra de México Desde 1861 a 1867*. 1867. Mexico City: Editorial del Valle de México, 1978.

Raat, W. Dirk, ed. *Mexico—From Independence to Revolution, 1810 to 1910*. Lincoln: University of Nebraska Press, 1982.

Read, John Lloyd. *The Mexican Historical Novel, 1826-1910*. San Marcos: Southwest Texas State Teachers' College, 1929.

Ridley, Jasper. *Maximilian and Juárez*. London: Phoenix Press, 1993. (References are from paperback edition, 2001.)

Roeder, Ralph. *Juárez and His Mexico*. 2 vols. New York: Viking Press, 1947.

Rolle, Andrew F. *The Lost Cause: The Confederate Exodus to Mexico*. Norman: University of Oklahoma Press, 1965.

Ruiz, Ramón Eduardo. *Triumphs and Tragedy: A History of the Mexican People*. New York: W. W. Norton & Co., 1992

Salas, Elizabeth. *Soldaderas in the Mexican Military: Myth and History*. Austin: University of Texas Press, 1990.

Scholes, Walter V. *Mexican Politics During the Juárez Regime, 1855–1872*. Columbia: University of Missouri–Columbia, 1957.

Schoonover, Thomas D. *Dollars Over Dominion: The Triumph of Liberalism in Mexican-U.S. Relationships, 1861–1867*. Baton Rouge: Louisiana State University Press, 1978.

Schoonover, Thomas, ed. *Mexican Lobby: Matías Romero in Washington, 1861-1867*. Lexington: The University Press of Kentucky, 1986.

SEP (Secretaria de Educacción Publica). *Zaragoza, Ignacio: Antología de la HistoriaMéxico, Parte Sobre la Batalla de 5 de Mayo, 1862.* (Zaragoza's letter of May 9 to War Minister.) Mexico City: Secretaría de Educacción Publica, 1993.

Shaara, Jeff. *Gone For Soldiers.* New York: Random House (Ballantine Books) 2000.

Siemens, Alfred H. *Between the Summit and the Sea: Central Veracruz in the 19th Century.* Vancouver: University of British Columbia Press, 1990.

Sierra, Justo. *The Political Evolution of the Mexican People.* 3 vols. Trans. Charles Ramsdell. Mexico City: J. Ballesch & Co., 1902.

Smith, Gene. *Maximilian and Carlota: A Tale of Romance and Tragedy.* New York: William Morrow and Co., 1973.

Stevenson, Sara Yorke. *Maximilian in Mexico: A Woman's Reminiscences of the French Intervention 1862–1867.* New York: Century, 1899.

U.S. House of Representatives:

37th Congress, 2nd Session (Vol. 8, Library of Congress), Document #100, *The Present Condition of Mexico: A Report From the Secretary of State Relative to Mexican Affairs, 1862.* Library of Congress, Serial 1136.

———, Document #120, 1862. Library of Congress, Serial 1137.

37th Congress, 3rd Session, Document #23, 1863. Vol. 5, Serial 1161.

———, Document #54, 1863. Vol. 6, Serial 1162.

38th Congress, 1st Session, Papers Relating to Foreign Affairs, 1864. Vol.1, Serial 1206.

39th Congress, 1st Session, Executive Document #13. *Slavery or Peonage in Mexico, 1865.*

———, Document #31, 1866.

———, Document #73, 1866. *Report From the Acting Secretary of State on the Condition of Affairs in Mexico, 1866.*

————, Document #93, 1866. *Report by the Secretary of State on the Evacuation by the French, 1866.*

39th Congress, 2nd Session, Document #1, 1867.

————, Document #17, 1867.

————, Document #76, 1867. *Report by the Secretary of State on the Present Condition of Mexico, 1867.*

————, Papers Relating to Foreign Affairs, 1867.

United States Senate:

40th Congress, 1st Session, Executive Document #20. *Correspondence Relating to Recent Events in Mexico, 1867.*

Index

978-0-595-84448-7
0-595-84448-0

Printed in the United States
104200LV00004B/296/A